FROM PSYCHIATRIC PATIENT TO CITIZEN REVISITED

FOUNDATIONS OF MENTAL HEALTH PRACTICE

The Foundations of Mental Health Practice series offers a fresh approach to the field of mental health by exploring key areas and issues in mental health from a social, psychological and a biological perspective. Taking a multidisciplinary approach, the series is aimed at students and practitioners across the people professions, including student nurses, social workers, occupational therapists, psychiatrists, counsellors and psychologists.

Series editors:

Thurstine Basset worked as a community worker and social worker before becoming involved in mental health training and education in the 1980s. He is Director of Basset Consultancy Ltd and has experience of working with a number of universities, statutory and voluntary mental health organisations, service user and carer groups. He has published widely across the fields of mental health training and education. In collaboration with Theo Stickley, he is a co-editor of *Learning about Mental Health Practice* (2008). He is also an editor of the *Journal of Mental Health Training, Education and Practice.*

Theo Stickley is Associate Professor of Mental Health Nursing at the University of Nottingham. He has authored and edited many books and journal articles about mental health. Each represents his interest in promoting a fair, just and genuinely caring way in which to think about and deliver mental health care. His area of research is promoting mental health through participatory arts and he advocates a creative approach to care delivery.

Available now:

Working with Dual Diagnosis: A Psychosocial Perspective by Darren Hill, William J. Penson and Divine Charura
From Psychiatric Patient to Citizen Revisited by Liz Sayce
Models of Mental Health by Gavin Davidson, Jim Campbell, Ciarán Shannon and Ciaran Mulholland
Values and Ethics in Mental Health: An Exploration for Practice by Alastair Morgan, Anne Felton, Bill Fulford, Jayasree Kalathil and Gemma Stacey

FROM PSYCHIATRIC PATIENT TO CITIZEN REVISITED

LIZ SAYCE

 palgrave

First published 2016 by
PALGRAVE

Palgrave in the UK is an imprint of Macmillan Publishers Limited, registered in England, company number 785998, of 4 Crinan Street, London, N1 9XW.

Palgrave Macmillan in the US is a division of St Martin's Press LLC, 175 Fifth Avenue, New York, NY 10010.

Palgrave is a global imprint of the above companies and is represented throughout the world.

Palgrave® and Macmillan® are registered trademarks in the United States, the United Kingdom, Europe and other countries.

ISBN 978–1–137–36041–0

This book is printed on paper suitable for recycling and made from fully managed and sustained forest sources. Logging, pulping and manufacturing processes are expected to conform to the environmental regulations of the country of origin.

A catalogue record for this book is available from the British Library.

A catalog record for this book is available from the Library of Congress.

Library of Congress Cataloging-in-Publication Data

Sayce, Liz.
   From psychiatric patient to citizen revisited / Liz Sayce.
       pages cm
   ISBN 978–1–137–36041–0 (paperback)
 1. Mental illness—Public opinion.   2. Discrimination against the mentally ill.   3. Stigma (Social
   psychology) 4. Mental health laws. I. Title.
   RC455.2.P85S292 2016
   362.19689—dc23

Printed in China

2015033227

My madness took me places I had never been. It showed me the universe without its clothes. It stripped my mind of all its chattels. It rubbed my nose in the divine. It turned the lights off all over the undulating continent of my brain. Many people pass through this territory at some time in their lives. Most manage to skirt their way around the edge of it and look on with dread at a distance. But those who are forced right into its belly come out with richer pictures of a being that has been lost and found again. (Mary O'Hagan 2014, p. 113)

Contents

List of Figures

Preface

The idea that one of the biggest priorities in mental health is overcoming discrimination and stigma has moved from an 'edgy' radical challenge in the 1990s to mainstream policy today, routinely included in policy documents. But the big question is how best to do it. What is the theory and evidence that should guide us – those of us living with mental health challenges, families, mental health staff, policy-makers and allies who want to support the endeavour?

The time is right for a re-think.

Major international authorities on discrimination have been calling for re-consideration of the approaches likely to be effective. Professor Bruce Link, in 2011, argued that the 'mental illness is an illness like any other' message had facilitated help-seeking but not changed core stereotypes underpinning discrimination (see Chapter 3). Professor Norman Sartorius gave a lecture in 2014 entitled 'Postulates of anti-stigma work re-examined', in which he put forward and demolished many of the basic tenets of anti-stigma campaigns so far (see Chapter 7).

People with lived experience have built social movements and peer support, and revalued difference:

> Don't make us normal, make us welcome (Mason 2011, p. 88)
> Madness is a profoundly disruptive and full human experience that deserves
> respect (O'Hagan 2014, p. 7).

It is 25 years since the first laws were passed to outlaw discrimination on mental health grounds – starting with the Americans with Disabilities Act in 1990. In that period there have been numerous anti-stigma and anti-discrimination initiatives. Many countries, including the UK (but not – at the time of writing – the US), have ratified the UN Convention on the Rights of Persons with Disabilities, which codifies rights of people with mental health issues to liberty, family life, employment, education and much more.

In that period there have been some ground-breaking initiatives, from campaigns to legal strategies, from opening up employment opportunities to outlawing discrimination in everything from education to jury service.

Yet still the rates of employment and social participation of people with mental health conditions remain shockingly low. Fear and prejudice persist. One problem is that people with mental health challenges have been caught up in the demonisation of benefits claimants in those countries pursuing rapid austerity measures. But when, for this book, I interviewed seven leaders in anti-discrimination work, they talked of wider challenges, of still working and waiting for the 'big breakthrough'.

This book is designed to illuminate what may help or hinder that breakthrough.

The vision is one of a shared, deep commitment to everyone's right to participate; where people living with mental health challenges are completely confident in their right to belong; and where our common humanity is assumed by all.

A note on language

This book focuses on achieving human rights. It draws on thinking about citizenship – made up of social, economic and political rights – but is wary of the risk of inadvertently excluding those whose 'citizenship' is contested by border controls.

Working for positive rights can galvanise more action than only combating the negatives of discrimination; this book focuses on that prize. In talking of unfair and unequal treatment, I prefer the term discrimination to 'stigma', for reasons analysed in Sayce (1998) and Sayce (2000). In brief, 'stigma' risks emphasising the 'marked' individual rather than the systemic processes that discriminate. By analogy we do not talk about black people experiencing the stigma of being black, or encourage people to break through racial stigma by talking about it. We put the onus of responsibility where it belongs, on the people and institutions practising racism, and work for material changes in people's lives, from employment to 'stop and search'. In response to this critique, Link and Phelan (2001) proposed a major reconceptualisation of stigma, as the whole process of categorising and discriminating against people deemed 'different'. I use 'stigma' only in this reconceptualised sense.

There is no consensus on preferred language of people living with mental health challenges. I choose not to deploy 'users of mental health services' as it seems bizarre to define your identity in relation to a service: there is more to life than the services you choose (or often do not choose) to use; and other groups do not use this narrow definition (there are no 'users of blindness services', for instance). Being a disabled person conveys the essential insight of the disability movement that we are 'disabled by society' – but with lay interpretations of disability cohering around wheelchair users and even being bedridden this does not seem an identity likely to catch on widely. I do not use the term 'mental illness' as it is positively counter-productive in work to change attitudes on mental health (see Chapter 3). Reclaiming the term 'madness' is powerful, and I use it, though it is no more universally accepted than the term 'queer' reclaimed by parts of the lesbian, gay, bisexual and transgender movements. I tend also to use more neutral terms such as living with mental health 'challenges' or sometimes 'conditions', as a 'condition' is essentially neither positive nor negative. I sometimes use living with mental health problems or difficulties, particularly when citing others' research – and also to acknowledge that the challenges can at times be hard, as can other people's attitudes. But I believe that overstating 'problems' and 'difficulties' entrenches the negative associations with madness that feed into discrimination. In the absence of agreed language a certain flexibility and neutrality of language is designed to be as inclusive as possible.

The scope of the book

This book focuses primarily on the UK, but draws learning from countries going through similar policy and/or economic developments including Australia, New Zealand, the US and Northern Europe. There is potential learning from other parts of the world – not least because recovery rates are higher in areas where there are fewer psychiatric services and greater expectations that people will retain their social and economic roles (Warner 2009); but the question of how to transfer this learning across hugely different contexts and cultures is beyond the scope of this particular book.

A personal note

As a young woman I had acute anxiety attacks and counted cornflakes as my weight dropped beyond the fashionably thin. Whilst writing this book I had another burst of madness, when train lines became very frightening. Madness and fear of madness have featured through my life. I also write from a position of sharing my life with someone with long-term fluctuating mental health difficulties, who has experienced discrimination at a number of levels.

Three years ago I was told by a consultant physician that my late mother, who had developed dementia, 'should go into a nursing home' – no mention of choice, or independent living, or how to sustain social networks and familiar places (she did not go into a nursing home – she stayed in her own home, in accordance with her wishes, where her friends and neighbours visited her regularly). And a younger person close to me, living with mental health challenges, was told there was no support with employment from mental health services in their borough.

Most people know something of the experience of exclusion through madness, or the fear of it – personally, from work colleagues, family or friends. People know it is hard to talk openly, without fear of being seen differently, treated less favourably.

It is in the interests of everyone to break through – to address and neutralise fear, deeply appreciate our common humanity, and ensure everyone can participate and belong. Without fear people are free to live fuller lives. Without fear wider contributions to communities increase.

In the 1990s I worked at Mind and with others helped change the focus from having a service to having a life. Since 2000 I have worked in wider disability rights and have often deliberately put the experience of mental health issues at the heart of disability initiatives – rather than adding it as an afterthought to discussions of physical access and adaptation. I have co-led formal investigations, using legal powers, and communications campaigns, and leadership programmes – all with engagement and leadership of people with mental health challenges working alongside people with other experiences of disability.

Achieving equality and full participation, whether through mental health or broader initiatives, is not straightforward. I hope this book helps people debate how best to frame the questions, consider the solutions and approach the task.

Acknowledgements

In 2000 I published a book, *From Psychiatric Patient to Citizen*, setting out the imperative to challenge discrimination on mental health grounds. A lot of people helped, five of whom have since died. I would like to honour their contributions: Judi Chamberlin, the pioneering mad activist, who read every word of that first draft book and deeply influenced my thinking on working with the wider disability movement; Caroline Gooding, who was a mentor and later colleague to me, and was personally responsible for ground-breaking improvements in UK anti-discrimination law; Paul Miller, who embraced the rights of people with psychiatric disabilities as Equal Employment Opportunity Commissioner responsible for disability under the Clinton administration; Jane Elliott, my oldest friend, who translated a Chinese disability law to aid my research, as well as supporting me in untold ways; and my mother, Olive Sayce, who offered meticulous proof-reading and occasional challenge coupled with constant support. Their influence lives on.

For this book I would like to thank all the activists who I have been lucky enough to meet and learn from: their ideas have added immeasurably to this book. I particularly thank the seven leaders in anti-discrimination work who shared their thinking with me – Peter Beresford, Mark Brown, Andy Imparato, Bruce Link, Lyn Mahboub, Mary O'Hagan and Graham Thornicroft. I am grateful to Emma Watson, Mark Hudson and Agnes Fletcher for their work on discrimination within mental health services. Others who have helped through everything from sourcing information to inspiring conversations include Sue Baker, Sue Bott, Jane Campbell, Neil Crowther, Claire Henderson, David Sparrow and all my colleagues at Disability Rights UK. Phil Friend as Chair was helpful through great discussions and supporting me to combine working, health, living and writing.

This book is written in a personal capacity.

Theo Stickley has been a pleasure to work with as editor, and Thurstine Bassett and all colleagues at Palgrave have made the whole process of producing the book smooth and effective.

Finally I thank my partner Rachel, who, when we moved into a house on the site of a former psychiatric hospital, oversaw building works while I typed, put up with my obsessive pursuit of the history of the people who had lived there, and offered support and inspiration.

1 | Competing Histories of Madness

Chapter Summary

- The continuing denial of full citizenship
- The recent arrival of civil rights
- Different versions of history: how society has behaved towards those they view as 'mad'
- Narratives: of professional progress; psycho-geography; containment of irrationality; oppression of people who are 'different'
- History in microcosm: one asylum
- The unheard voice of the 'mad' person

There are many historical narratives of 'madness' and society's response to it. They give us different versions of our history. This chapter threads through narratives and evidence, and explores the history of one asylum in London, to illustrate how the voices of people deemed 'mad' are largely absent from the formal record.

Partial citizens: The continuing history of discrimination

Rights to equal citizenship for those of us facing mental health challenges are recent and remain partial.

In 2000, I described the 'illusion of citizenship', documenting discrimination in areas from immigration to parenting: for instance, being asked, on entry to the United States on the visa waiver form, whether you had committed genocide, terrorism – or had a history of mental illness; and being subjected to a level of scrutiny of one's parenting skills that would never apply to (imperfect) parents with no diagnosis of mental illness (Sayce 2000).

Thornicroft (2006) documented international evidence of discrimination, in domains from friendship to employment, health to the media.

This book focuses on how to overcome discrimination – not on documenting it – but it is worth pulling out key themes to understand the terrain. Discussing the impact of discrimination does not imply that people should be viewed as victims – rather as people who can mobilise a range of peer, personal and institutional power (see Chapter 5).

Citizenship is a contested concept, at worst used to police people's rights at a nation's borders. Nonetheless the core definition of citizenship – the right to full and equal participation in society (Buckmaster and Thomas 2009) – is central to the experience of people living with mental health challenges. I use it for that purpose, analysed in terms of social, economic and political citizenship.

Social citizenship

Those of us with mental health challenges are less likely to participate in culture, leisure and sport than others (Office for Disability Issues (ODI) 2013). Rights to equal participation are very recent: the right not to face discrimination in services (from pubs to insurance) came in 1999, in school or college in 2001.

Many live isolated lives: ODI (2013) found that 26% of people with mental health problems reported having no, or only one or two, close contacts they could rely on, compared to 8% of non-disabled people (and 14% of people with any impairment). Asked about actual contacts in the previous week, 36% of people with mental health problems had seen no one or only one or two people, compared to 17% for non-disabled people (and 22% with any impairment). Restrictive factors included transport, money, other people being busy – and rejection.

The British Social Attitudes Survey 2009 found the public was much more comfortable interacting with people with some types of impairment than others: whilst 98% were comfortable with someone with a physical impairment moving in next door, only 67% felt the same about someone with a mental health condition. The closer the interaction became, the greater the discomfort: whereas 91% were happy for a family member or friend to marry someone with a physical impairment, only 54% felt the same about marriage to someone with a mental health condition (Staniland 2011).

Economic citizenship

Only at the very end of the 20th century did it first become illegal in Britain to turn someone down for a job on the grounds of a history of mental health problems (under the Disability Discrimination Act 1995, replaced by the Equality Act 2010). In 1978 Mind had sent a dossier of cases of employment discrimination to the Minister of Health in Callaghan's Labour Government. He replied saying he doubted there was sufficient discrimination of this kind to merit new law (cited in Bynoe et al 1991). In truth, discrimination and the fear of it were endemic. By 2001 a survey of employers found only 37% would be prepared to take on someone living with a mental illness, as compared to 62% who would take on physically disabled people, 78% long-term unemployed people and 88% lone parents (DWP 2001). Sayce (2010) found people with mental health conditions were four times as likely as those with physical health impairments to be open to no one at work, usually for fear they would be passed over for promotion or otherwise treated less favourably.

Shockingly, by 2012 only 14% of people experiencing 'mental illness, phobias, panic or nervous disorders' were employed – unchanged over a decade. Those with 'depression, bad nerves or anxiety' were doing slightly better, at 33%, up from around 20% in 2000, but still way below the rate for disabled people (46%) let alone non-disabled people (76%) (ODI 2013). Sayce (2010) found people with mental health conditions were less likely even than other disabled people to be in senior jobs.

The 2009 British Social Attitudes Survey found only 44% of respondents would be comfortable having someone with a mental health problem as their boss – compared to 92% with a boss who was physically disabled.

For reasons of under-employment and unemployment, the experience of mental health challenges leaves people more likely to live in poverty than others. Poverty, joblessness, and the reduced social networks they bring (Clark 2014) are 'vulnerability' factors in developing mental health conditions; and once you are diagnosed with a mental health condition, poverty and joblessness become more likely, in an endless vicious spiral. This restricts economic participation and impacts on whole families. Policies of 'austerity' can make the spiral deeper: there is further to fall. Clark (2014) found a quarter of all UK households had no or negative assets and predicted that by 2017 a million households would be spending half their income on servicing debt. Use of food banks was growing: they served 913,138 people in 2012–13 (Trussell Trust 2014). The 'fall' hit people living with mental health challenges particularly hard. As the largest single group of claimants of Employment and Support Allowance (ESA) (in younger age groups about half had a mental health problem as their primary impairment, and the proportion was growing, Banks et al 2015), many were required to participate in the Work Programme as a condition of benefit. The most common reason for sanctions, i.e. benefit reduction or withdrawal, was non-participation in this ineffective programme, which had a 94% failure rate with disabled people in year 1 (Crowther and Sayce 2013). The use of sanctions on ESA claimants grew threefold from June 2013 to June 2014 and 60% of those affected had mental health challenges (Mind 2014). Mind reported increasing numbers of calls relating to poverty, and a trend of people calling because of fear, particularly financial fear (O'Hara 2014).

Political citizenship

People with mental health challenges do not have the same legal rights as other citizens: in particular the UK's mental health laws permit compulsory treatment of people even when you have 'capacity', i.e. are able to understand and process information and make decisions yourself (see Chapter 4).

There are also barriers to engagement in political processes. The Speaker's Conference (2010) found that disabled people (including those with mental health challenges) experienced financial, practical and attitudinal barriers to standing for election – including 'referred prejudice'; that is, 'the tendency of political parties to assume that disabled people would find it difficult to get elected ... because there is perceived to be public reluctance to vote for them' – a justification that might be rephrased as 'of course we are not prejudiced but we are worried the voters will be'. And only in 2013 was legislation (the Mental Health (Discrimination) Act) finally passed to put an end to the discriminatory requirement that any MP sectioned for over six months had to stand down – a provision that did not apply, for instance, to being away for over six months for treatment for heart disease. Until very recently, unsurprisingly, MPs who did experience stigmatised conditions tended to keep quiet about them.

Former cabinet minister and peer Chris Smith 'came out' about his HIV status in 2005, inspired by Nelson Mandela; he was diagnosed in 1987 but remained silent for nearly 20 years. And only in 2013 did MPs begin to speak about their own mental health issues. John Woodcock MP stated he was in treatment for depression and hoped that his openness would help tackle stigma. He added that because Alistair Campbell (former prime ministerial communications advisor) and others in public life had started to open up, 'their decision made it easier for me'. The 2013 Act also removed the bar on serving on a jury for people receiving mental health treatment – almost a decade after the Government's Social Exclusion Unit had pointed to the absurdity of refusing someone jury service just because they were receiving counselling or anti-depressants.

Themes underpinning discrimination

In the middle of the 20th century (1955) about 150,000 people were living in long-stay mental hospitals in the UK. This is how one woman in Tooting Bec Hospital described day to day life:

> The day started at 5.30am when the lights were turned on in the dormitory
> which I shared with 31 other people ... All our hair was combed in the same style,
> parting on the right, and straight back. If we were lucky we got to put our own
> teeth in, which had been soaking in the pot with 31 other pairs of teeth overnight
> (Cited in Simmons 1995).

The old asylums may have gone but the history of segregation and indignity faced by people living with mental health conditions has not (Sayce 2000; Thornicroft 2006). For many, discrimination is multi-faceted: Rehman and Owen (2014) found that people from black and minority ethnic (BME) communities living with mental health challenges experienced racism in every sphere of life, including mental health services, and discrimination on mental health grounds in every sphere, including their own communities.

There are a number of narrative themes that have underpinned – and still underpin – exclusion.

The first is a pernicious refusal by powerful institutions to take the testimony of someone with a known mental health history seriously. This has generated a widespread denial of justice, as police and prosecutors have failed to act in the case of an 'unreliable witness'.

Quarmby (2011) describes how in 1830 the Superintendent of Bedlam, Dr Edward Wright, was found at night with unclothed women patients. He denied wrongdoing, arguing that the patients' testimony was 'unreliable', just as people are often deemed 'unreliable witnesses' today (see box below).

However, recent rights are beginning to create a commitment to change:

Using the law to tackle hate crime and discrimination

In 2003 'disability-related hate' was recognised as an aggravating factor in crimes under Section 146 of the Criminal Justice Act, following concerted lobbying by disability organisations. This meant a higher sentence could be imposed, in recognition of the motivator of hate or harassment. By 2013 the Equality and Human Rights Commission (EHRC) (2013) found that since the Act, reporting levels had been generally low. The reason for not reporting was – in two thirds of cases – believing the police would not be interested or would not do anything.

In 2009 the case of R(B) came before the High Court. R(B), who had a mental health condition, had had part of his ear bitten off. His original case was dropped just before the hearing – as he was not viewed as a reliable witness – despite the clear evidence of harm: he evidently did not bite off his own ear.

The High Court criticised the CPS (Crown Prosecution Service) for dropping the case. Keir Starmer, then Director of Public Prosecutions, addressed an EHRC conference with the words 'We got it wrong; we got it very wrong'. He issued a public apology in August 2009 and committed to ensuring that people with mental health problems could give evidence like other citizens, with support where needed. Thanks to R(B) taking this case through the courts, a systemic change began in the CPS.

Trust in the system nonetheless seemed to lag behind the apology: in 2012 Disability Rights UK asked disabled people (including people with mental health challenges) whether they would report a crime and encountered the following views:

'Experience tells me I will be treated as simply a nuisance or a moaner'

'I was frightened of comebacks, and more of the same. Who would believe me anyway?'

'Doesn't seem much point, no one is going to do anything about it and it will only make things worse if I do'

'They make excuses and make you feel worse about the situation. I have been made to feel it is our fault in the past'

Casting doubt on credibility can also lead to 'diagnostic overshadowing' in health settings: physical symptoms being put down to psychiatric ill-health and not investigated or treated. The Disability Rights Commission (DRC) found diagnostic overshadowing to be a factor in the early death of people living with schizophrenia and bipolar disorder. They experience a triple dose of inequality, being more likely to get the common killer diseases (heart disease, stroke, coronary obstructive pulmonary disorder, bowel cancer, some other cancers), less likely to get the recommended tests and treatments and, once diagnosed, likely to die faster than other citizens. The net result is death on average at least 15 years earlier than others, even after accounting for deaths from suicide (DRC 2006).

A second theme is a wider denial of competence – for instance, to work, raise children or live in ordinary housing. A stereotype of incompetence is evident in media stories of 'poor unfortunates', particularly prevalent from the 1980s, when journalist Marjorie Wallace wrote a series of *Times* articles on 'The Forgotten Illness' (schizophrenia), accompanied by black and white photographs of homeless mentally ill people on dark street corners. She alleged that de-institutionalisation was causing homelessness and desperation as the hospitals threw people out. The allegation was false: research consistently showed people had a higher quality of life after leaving hospital, with larger social networks; where they were dissatisfied it was most commonly because they wanted more independence – a flat of their own, rather than living in a group home (Leff et al 1996).

The theme of incompetence can also influence professional thinking and practice. Perkins (2001) describes the 'you'll nevers': you'll never have a job, you'll never be able to have children – a litany of negatives that people living with mental health issues hear from professionals, overtly or implicitly. The implicit version involves lowering someone's expectations, often under the guise of the need to be 'realistic' – in other words to adapt to the life of a mental patient. For instance:

> I wanted a job, I thought a first step might be washing dishes. My social worker
> said I needed to be realistic and that it might be best to start with a couple
> of hours of voluntary work a week. (Man aged 27, coming out of a period of
> psychosis. Personal communication 2013).

The problem is that rapid job entry with support is far more likely to lead to long-term employment than voluntary work (Sayce 2011); so expectations may be lowered permanently.

Similarly, a parent with a mental health condition can be faced with far more stringent criteria of good parenting than other parents and it can be exceptionally hard to demonstrate capability (Sayce 2009). For instance:

> When I had Tilly my mental health was bad; I split up temporarily from my husband; it was a hard time and I ended up in hospital. There was talk of taking Tilly into care. But I knew I wanted to bring her up. That motivated me. Pete and I got back together and we showed them we could do it. He has long-term mental health difficulties as well. But each time we met a new GP or a new social worker they took one look at our diagnoses and it triggered a new attention to 'risk' and more questions about whether we were capable of raising her – even though we were struggling no more than any family with a new baby. We did need support but there was absolutely no time that Tilly was at risk. Yet time and again we have had to prove we are better parents than anyone else. Tilly is 12 now and she's doing brilliantly at school – I'm really proud of her. But we had to assert our rights to achieve it. (Personal communication 2014)

A third and linked theme is the risk of violence: from incompetent judgement flows potential danger. The image of the 'mad killer' was particularly common in the 1990s after Christopher Clunis killed stranger Jonathan Zito in a London tube station. Killing strangers is extremely rare. Every homicide required a public inquiry, which always made front-page news. The stereotype of the 'big black and dangerous' psychiatric patient killing a stranger (Sainsbury Centre for Mental Health 2002) was repeated endlessly as every article referred back to pictures of (the black) Christopher Clunis.

In an era of strong safeguarding requirements and a near-obsession with risk management, professional fear of danger – and the career implications if anything goes wrong – leads to risk-averse practice. This means numerous restrictions on liberty and independence. Sayce (2009) argues that exaggerated notions of risk to self, risk to others and risk to staff have been used to deny disabled people everything from living independently to flying in aeroplanes (as when deaf people were asked to disembark because they would be a 'health and safety risk' in the case of evacuation). If the risk assessment on your notes includes even a hint of potential aggression – often minus the context, like being angry after being denied something important to you in hospital – then there is no right to challenge. The risk assessment follows you – like a 'ghost criminal record' as Abina Parshad Griffin put it (personal communication, 2008) – and erodes opportunities for independent housing, employment and more. Unlike a real criminal charge, there is no chance to contest it in court and prove your innocence.

A fourth theme is unreasonable, needy demand – evident in the image of the social security scrounger, the burden on society, draining us of resources. This media image, common in the 1980s (Golding and Middleton 1982), was revived in the 2010s, with particular reference to people who claimed to be 'disabled' but were playing golf, doing triathlons and the like. This is a slur particularly affecting people living through mental health challenges, which are by their nature less visible than quadriplegia or blindness, but no less 'real'.

Rather than write someone off as 'incompetent' or limit their activities because of 'risk' it is possible to support capability when people face challenges in (variously) giving evidence, explaining symptoms, or fulfilling roles like work or parenting; and to plan for difficult times, including through shared risk assessment, with the individual and service provider preparing together for future periods of distress or confusion. The Equality Act 2010 requires public bodies to take a positive and proactive approach to promoting equality and to make reasonable adjustments: thus the CPS should support people to give evidence, the GP should spend longer with someone who finds it hard to communicate needs. Both can reach out to people who may not be confident to report crimes or symptoms. These measures are designed to promote more equal outcomes, to avoid the double and triple jeopardies of having a mental health condition: not only the challenge of living with unusual experiences, but the consequence that someone can attack you with impunity because you are not a 'reliable' witness, that you will die young, that children may be received into care when you could – with a little support – care for them yourself.

Once certain citizens are believed to lack credibility and competence they can easily be denied voice, power and social roles. At the extreme, they may be completely excluded from society – institutionalised; or, under eugenics theories popular in the early 20th century, stopped from reproducing or viewed as 'useless eaters', as the Nazis put it when they began systematically killing people with mental or physical impairments before the Second World

War (see Sayce 2000). During the 20th century, people with mental health conditions were forcibly sterilised in numerous American states and European countries (including Sweden, Norway, Finland, Denmark, Estonia – and of course Germany). In Britain, proponents of compulsory sterilisation of 'mental patients' included Winston Churchill and Marie Stopes, and in 1931 a bill for compulsory sterilisation was introduced in Parliament by Labour MP A. G. Church. Although it was not passed, 89 MPs voted in favour. The present-day notion of the 'burden' of mental illness is not so far, conceptually, from the idea of 'useless eaters'.

It is small wonder that through history people have endeavoured to deny madness, to avoid its corrosive associations. For instance, William Blake saw visions, which deeply influenced his art; but he tried to distance himself from the taint of madness:

> Those who have been told that my Works are but an unscientific and irregular Eccentricity, a Madman's Scrawls, I demand of them to do me the justice to examine them before they decide (William Blake, cited in Ackroyd 1999, p. 300).

Narratives of 'mental health problems' are relentlessly negative. Other liberation movements have fundamentally re-valued their experience and identity: for instance, from being pathologically 'homosexual' to being out and proud. Increasingly people living with mental health challenges are replacing the narratives of burden, incompetence and danger with an exploration of the richness that madness can add to life (and see Chapter 5).

Reframing madness

I knew that in some respects my madness accelerated my maturity. It quickly taught me the grown-up virtues of resilience, acceptance and self-reliance while many of my friends were still living in youthful innocence ... Madness also gave me compassion where once I may have felt a range of pettier responses like fear, pity, impatience or indifference. Through the struggle to find dignity in my own suffering I learnt to encounter others who suffered as inhabitants in my world rather than aliens in someone else's. Compassion drove me further than an equal regard for individuals who suffered: it added clean energy to my sense of social justice (Mary O'Hagan 2014).

Increasingly people with lived experience are sharing stories – through websites, books, face-to-face peer support – thereby regaining control of the narrative; replacing hopeless accounts of unremitting illness, and cold scientific analysis, with the power of human storytelling: see, for example, www.scottishrecovery.net.

In 21st-century Britain there is both a continuing history of exclusion from citizenship on mental health grounds; and a very recent re-framing of madness and emergence of rights, used to challenge exclusion (as in the case of R(B) above). This dynamic offers a mix of progress and setbacks. In order to understand whether the position has changed for people viewed as 'mad' or 'mentally ill' it is useful to take a longer historical view.

Narratives of professional progress

One prominent historical narrative would have us believe in the value of unremitting scientific progress, whereby psychiatric and psychological treatments have incrementally improved, enabling people to shed symptoms, lead fuller lives and therefore become more accepted by the wider society (Fuller Torrey 2008).

A well-known example is the claim that the development of anti-psychotic medication in the 1950s facilitated the move from asylum to community care (Pazamanick et al 1967, p. 17). This became common currency: as one MP put it 'Tranquillizers have given infinitely more freedom to these patients' (Andrews et al 1997, p. 699).

This narrative has been challenged on both philosophical and empirical grounds.

The philosophical problem is the implication that people must become more 'normal' in order to be socially accepted: it seems to naturalise their exclusion unless and until they undergo the restorative powers of treatment. The counter-argument is that citizenship should be based on unconditional acceptance of difference: inclusion on the basis of common humanity, not contingent on a requirement to 'fit in' (Gowar 2014).

The empirical problem is there is no evidence whatever that treatments lead to greater citizen participation. Warner (2009) found through major international analysis that neither social recovery nor complete recovery (including symptom remission) improved with the advent of anti-psychotic medication in 1954; and in those parts of the world with the greatest access to psychiatric services, rates of recovery from schizophrenia were lower than in so-called developing countries with few services. In 'developing' countries, people with schizophrenia had higher rates of employment, were more likely to be married and had lower mortality rates: anyone able to work had to do so and social relations were less likely to be severed. The process of exclusion in the 'developed' world makes schizophrenia a more malign experience. In the UK, during the second half of the 20th century, when treatments and services proliferated (community mental health teams, day centres and the like), the employment rate of people with mental health conditions went down (Marwaha and Johnson 2004).

There were more complex factors at play than new medication in stimulating closure of the asylums.

> There they stand, isolated, majestic, imperious, brooded over by the gigantic
> water-tower and chimney combined, rising unmistakable and daunting out of the
> countryside – the asylums which our forefathers built with such immense solidity
> to express the notions of their day (Enoch Powell, Minister for Health, in a speech
> at a conference of the National Association for Mental Health (later Mind),
> Birmingham 1961).

Powell's landmark speech ushered in the period of de-institutionalisation, fuelled by a potent mix of resistance to institutions and raw economics.

The number of people in psychiatric institutions grew from a few thousand in 1800 to about 100,000 in 1900 and 150,000 in the 1950s. From 1955 the decline began.

From the late 1950s critiques of institutions by Goffmann and of psychiatry by Szasz, Laing and others began to throw doubt on the beneficence of psychiatric institutions. They argued that institutionalisation damaged rather than healed and that 'mental illness' was socially constructed – in some views, a sane response to an insane world. From the 1960s a series of inquiries into abuses in psychiatric hospitals brought the reality of confinement and coercion to public attention. Munson-Barkshire's book on scandals in 'chronic sector hospitals' lists 25 inquiries into abuses from 1968 to 1981.

From the 1970s survivor activism gave more systematic voice to people on the receiving end of treatments. The ground-breaking survivor text *On Our Own* by Judi Chamberlin argued for consumer-run alternatives; and UK groups like the Mental Patients' Union (in the 1970s), Campaign Against Psychiatric Oppression, Survivors Speak Out and UK Advocacy Network (in the 1980s), argued for legal rights, improved choices and survivor-run alternatives. In 1983 a new Mental Health Act required consideration of alternatives before compulsory detention.

Professionals developed new service models – group homes, then community mental health teams and housing with support.

Under Margaret Thatcher fiscal conservatives rode the wave for change and increased the momentum of de-institutionalisation. In 1981 Patrick Jenkin, Health Secretary, argued that 'care in the community must increasingly mean care by the community', revealing an economic sub-text of government rhetoric about improving people's lives.

Psychiatric medications and therapies may often be valued for reducing pain or managing symptoms. But there is no credible evidence that they have led specifically to improvements in the citizenship status or opportunities of people diagnosed with a mental illness.

This was not the first time that treatment was credited with improving the social position of people thought 'mad'. Scull (1993) argued that asylums were justified in the first place on the basis of scientific advance; and that it was ironic that supposedly more scientific, progressive approaches encouraged families and communities to stop bothering or coping with the troubled and the troublesome, thereby reducing opportunities for recovery. The asylum 'operated to reduce community and family tolerance' (Scull 1993, p. 373).

One learning point from this history is that it is useful to reflect on the unthinking assumption – still prevalent – that treatments *do* support social inclusion: witness the investment in IAPT (access to psychological therapies) on the argument that this will improve employment participation. Layard et al (2007) argued that the cost to government of investment in therapies would be fully covered by the savings in incapacity benefits and extra taxes that result from more people being able to work. In the event the savings did not materialise and there is no evidence that cognitive behavioural therapies improve employment outcomes specifically.

Nonetheless some anti-discrimination work relies on treatment as a core part of the strategy to reduce exclusion. Sartorius, for example, portrayed a cycle of stigma, which starts with the marker of difference, rooted in the 'occurrence of illness' and 'presence of abnormality', then goes on to stigmatisation, discrimination and life problems, which in turn create more impairment and disability, leading to further ill-health (Figure 1.1).

Sartorius argued that it is possible to break into this cycle at any point to reduce 'stigma'. The problem is that some parts of this cycle are essential to reducing stigma and discrimination effectively, while other parts are irrelevant. By intervening at the point of occurrence of illness – through treatment and reducing 'abnormal' symptoms – there is no necessary reduction in discrimination. Even with no symptoms, a psychiatric history is quite enough to get you turned down for a job, life insurance or running a company. The presence of abnormality is not the major driver of discrimination. Even if it were, where does that

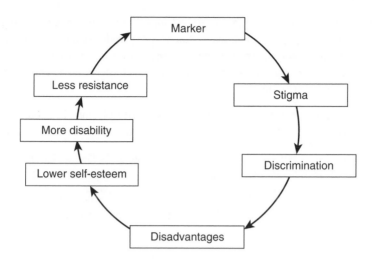

Figure 1.1 Breaking the cycle of stigma (from Sartorius 2000)

leave the person with life-altering psychotic or depressive experiences which stubbornly persist? Is the price of inclusion to diminish human differences? By analogy, we do not expect gay people to become straight or blind people to see, in order to free themselves of discrimination. In 2014 Sartorius adjusted this position, arguing the distinct point that when people 'get better' they 'go' from services and thus are not available as role models to counteract stigma.

Alongside the discourse that credits psychiatric treatment as the driver of liberty, there is another service-focused narrative: that community care was a failed policy, cynically promoted to save money, culminating in destitution and homicide. On this argument, professionals still hold the key – but through more traditional services, looking after 'vulnerable' people in 'asylums' (often with the epithet 'in the true sense of the word': places of respite). Frank Dobson, then Secretary of State for Health, famously stated in 1999 'Community care has failed'. The implication was that it was a cost-cutting plot of his political opponents. This was part of a long-running narrative of incompetence and danger.

Frank Dobson was incorrect. Research consistently showed that people preferred living outside the institutions, as mentioned above. The proportion of homicides committed by people with mental health problems went down not up during the period of de-institutionalisation; and homelessness was a product of housing policy, not hospital closure (Taylor and Gunn 1999; Sayce 2000).

The narrative painting community care purely as cost-cutting under-estimated the progressive drivers of the policy: to replace oppressive institutions with (somewhat) improved life opportunities. It was perhaps achieved through an 'unholy alliance' between fiscal conservatives and social radicals – but the role of the radicals in promoting freedom should not be downplayed.

The professional and political narratives opposing de-institutionalisation can be read as resistance: from individuals and families understandably fearing an uncertain future, from some staff and trade unions seeking to protect jobs, from professionals wanting to sustain control over 'their beds', from politicians tuning in to wider social anxieties and seeking to 'contain' madness, paternalistically wanting the state to 'look after' people rather than enable their social participation. All this resistance was anticipated by Enoch Powell, in the water-tower speech cited above:

> Do not for a moment underestimate their powers of resistance to our assault. Let me describe some of the defences which we have to storm.

First, he cited resistance to the idea of leaving the buildings derelict or demolished ('Wouldn't this one make a splendid geriatric unit, or that one a convalescent home?') His response:

> Well, let me here declare that if we err, it is our duty to err on the side of ruth-lessness. For the great majority of these establishments there is no appropriate future use.

Secondly:

> Hundreds of men and women, professional or voluntary, have given years, even lifetimes, to the service of a mental hospital ... They have laboured devotedly, through years of scarcity and neglect, to render the conditions in them more tolerable ... From such bodies it demands no mean moral effort to recognise that the institutions themselves are doomed. It would be more than flesh and blood to expect them to take the initiative in planning their own abolition, to be the first to set the torch to the funeral pyre.

And thirdly, a complete transformation of a whole branch of medicine, nursing and admin-istration was required. 'Let us admit that we all have a great deal of the conservative in our make-up, and find it easier to envisage things going on much as at present, or with small or gradual modifications, than deliberately to choose and favour the unaccustomed, the drastic.'

Powell concluded that it was his duty, and that of Mind, to lean with all their might in the direction of 'more drastic and fundamental change'.

Radical words indeed. Powell was proved right about the resistance. In 2013 the Kings Fund convened a group to reflect on the experience of hospital closures. Professionals closely involved described hostility and even personal attacks (for example, having their tyres slashed) when they led the changes. The resistance was managed and defused, and few today mourn the loss of the old asylums.

Narratives focusing on treatment and services offer little promise of progress towards full citizenship.

Wider historical narratives

Historians of madness and psychiatry use a wider lens, going beyond debates about science and treatment.

Ackroyd (2001) writes of continuities in particular places: for instance, whilst Clerkenwell has long been associated with political radicals (from Wat Tyler, who led the 1381 Peasants Revolt, to Lenin) London as a whole has been linked with madness. In the 17th century, London was the only place in England to have a madhouse – Bedlam. Bedlam became a symbol of the madness and multiple distractions of the city itself – an 'intensification of the worst aspects of London life', as Smollett put it: 'All is tumult and hurry; one would imagine they were impelled by some disorder of the brain...' (cited in Ackroyd 2001, p. 621).

Pure psycho-geography can be criticised for seeming to constrain opportunity for change (will London always confine its 'mad'?). Ackroyd and other historians of madness analyse wider social and economic forces.

Bedlam was the first asylum in Europe, dating from the 14th century, a time when most 'insane' people were at liberty, often begging on London's streets, sometimes taken into the asylum overnight. They were not necessarily happily integrated into society: as beggars they wore a specific tin badge to show their status, and several historians have challenged Foucault for apparently romanticising the era before the 'great containment' (Foucault 1967; Scull 1993).

Yet from the 18th century the sheer scale and state organisation of separation and incarceration was unprecedented. Several historians argue that as the Enlightenment and complexities of industrialisation developed, and after the chaos of the Great Fire and plague, the containment of madness became a growing political preoccupation. Reason must prevail – and be seen to prevail. This involved a huge level of public 'show': not only could people visit the 'inmates' for a penny a time to watch the 'ravening creatures that had to be manacled or tied', but even the façades of Bedlam were grand and grandiose – full of Ionic columns and porticos – hiding far more squalid conditions within 'as if ... the whole purpose of the building was a theatrical display designed to depict the triumph over lunacy'. 'Outside it seemed to be a palace; inside, it closely resembled a prison.' The authorities sought to show visibly that madness could be successfully contained, as Britain extended its rule across the globe and pursued industrialisation at home (Ackroyd 2001, p. 620).

From the mid-18th to the mid-19th centuries the number of asylums grew. Scull (1993) argues that a shift occurred at this time, from madness being primarily a family and community concern to being viewed for the first time as a separate category of deviance, with the 'mad' increasingly separated – physically and symbolically – from society. This was achieved through a state-supported asylum system, in which new 'mad-doctors' diagnosed different medical categories of madness.

At first private madhouses prevailed (English Heritage 2014) – and before long scandals arose. In 1763 the *Gentleman's Magazine* condemned the 'many unlawful arbitrary and cruel acts' which went on in madhouses; and in 1774 the Regulation of Madhouses Act introduced a licensing system, following public concern that some non-lunatics were being unlawfully detained at the whim of their spouses or families (a concern that re-emerged in the 20th century when some women were hospitalised for having a child out of wedlock or otherwise offending social norms). When a Quaker, Hannah Mills, died in squalid and inhumane conditions in the York Asylum, William Tuke, appalled, vowed that never again should any Quaker be forced to endure such treatment. He set up 'the Retreat' in York in 1796, which practised 'moral treatment'. The emphasis was on restorative surroundings and beneficial work (Tuke 1813). Even at Bedlam, inmates could earn a little reward through taking on tasks – like helping in the kitchens or 'helping to capture escapees' (Andrews et al, 1997).

But as the 19th century wore on, the emphasis was more and more on warehousing people in large institutions. By 1867 psychiatrist Henry Maudsley was writing that in the eyes of the public 'lunacy was something so horrible and dangerous that its victims must be pushed like the leper of old, beyond the gates of the city' (Scull 1993, p. 309). Psychiatric leader Sir John Charles Bucknill thought large numbers of people were unnecessarily detained. He tried to reduce the segregation of patients in Devon – but was met by public resistance (the 'reduced community and family tolerance' noted by Scull, above). There was also professional resistance. In 1890 a Dr Strahan argued that only containment would keep the mad from breeding and enable degeneracy to die out (Scull, 1993). As mentioned above, eugenic theories were commonly used in 19th and 20th century Britain to justify segregation and to promote compulsory sterilisation.

These histories suggest that forces influencing the way mad people were treated included the growing need to demonstrate the power of reason over superstition as empire and industrialisation grew, and the aspiration to improve the genetic stock in a competitive world. The policy results included not only institutionalisation but also codifying bans on people with mental health problems from serving as company directors, jurors and MPs.

History in microcosm: One asylum

The history of one asylum – Tooting Bec, open from 1903 to 1995 – illustrates how the voices of people who lived in large institutions are largely absent from the formal historical record. From minutes, inspection reports and hospital histories, we have to detect clues about what life may have been like from the accounts of others. For instance, the architects responsible for the site stated:

> Two of the single rooms in each block have been padded by Pocock Bros,

and:

> Next Tooting Common the land is enclosed by a wrought iron fence 8 feet 6
> inches high, supported by cast standards (Metropolitan Asylums Board 1903).

Clearly, escape would not be easy. In any event, until 1958 all wards at Tooting Bec were locked (Simmons 1995). And anyone becoming disturbed could be contained in padded rooms.

Tooting Bec opened with 1,000 beds, rising to 1,886 after some First World War delays. It was designed to take in 'such harmless persons of the chronic or imbecile class as could lawfully be detained in a workhouse. No dangerous or curable person such as would under statutes in that behalf require to be sent to a lunatic asylum shall be admitted' (Powell 1930). These patients in a sense exemplified the 'great confinement' – the growing numbers who before about 1867 would have been supported by their families or in workhouses, largely 'looked after by other patients'; but were now filling the expanding mental institutions.

The Metropolitan Asylum Board (MAB) took great pride in the development of these large institutions that met different needs:

> The mental defective, classified from the highest grade of improvable patient to
> the senile dements and the lowest grade of imbecile child, are housed and maintained according to their needs in training colonies and hospitals (Powell 1930).

Darenth Park took those who could be trained:

> In school or workshop the patients try to turn to account such powers as they
> are endowed with. They have their dances, concerts, fetes, parties and cinemato-
> graphic shows, for the furtherance of which they have a band, whose members
> are drawn from their own ranks.

For men at Darenth, there were many activities: 24 listed, from tinsmithery to roadmaking. For women there were just six: domestic and laundry work, needlework, rug making, sock and jersey making.

Tooting Bec Hospital took 'the unimprovable type' (Powell 1930). In addition to this specialisation, the individuals were further categorised on admission. The 'receiving and classification houses' at Tooting Bec had accommodation blocks for four specific groups: 'Imbeciles'; 'Ringworm'; 'Ophthalmia' and 'Isolation'.

Tooting Bec was, perhaps, a warehouse par excellence – a place without workshops or reha- bilitative efforts. And what of the experience of people who lived there? The regular reports of the Commissioners of Lunacy who visited from 1903 onwards virtually all comment on the food:

> Brawn and sausages were a welcome change to the diet of both patients and
> staff (1916).

> The meal was stewed rabbit and potatoes, which appeared to be greatly enjoyed
> (1917).

In 1919 the Commissioners noted that for tea, jam was given on one day, marmalade the next, and cake once a week. Several reports comment on decisions to dig up turf so that turnips and parsnips can be planted (1917) and to convert disused buildings to the task of keeping rabbits (1918).

Another regular preoccupation of the Commissioners was activity – or lack of it:

> There is nothing besides prayer books and hymn books (1905).

> It would at least be worth an effort to attempt to arouse their dormant faculties
> by a fairly liberal supply of simple table games (1909).

One report even suggested that women could be offered draughts, noting that they might enjoy it as much as the men. The concern about lack of activity recurred repeatedly – suggesting little was done to act on the previous recommendations.

In 1917 a patient, Sarah Smith, died after being driven in an open motor car from Stepney to Tooting Bec. The jury's verdict was that the patient's lungs should have been examined before permitting her to travel, and:

> We recommend that the bathroom at Tooting Bec Asylum, where patients are
> stripped and examined on admission, should be kept at a warmer temperature
> than 50 degrees.

There is no comment on the practice of stripping and examining people on admission per se. Critics of institutionalisation note that the point of admission often strips people of clothes and identity, in a process of de-individualisation (Goffmann 1963).

Of the experience of life, the feelings, of the people living in Tooting Bec, the reports give only glimpses:

> One woman made complaint of ill-usage, but quite without reason. She had no bruise or mark, and was evidently in excellent condition (1917).

> Most patients did not speak to us. Those who did speak generally appealed for their discharge, and we had no complaint that appeared to have a substantial foundation (1905).

> Their conduct was quiet and orderly and except for complaints of being deprived of their liberty they appeared to be contented with their lot (1914).

The impression is of people speaking to the outsiders coming in about their desire for liberty – but not being taken seriously (this not being a complaint with a 'substantial foundation'); of reporting ill-treatment that was not believed; and all within an inspection regime that implicitly viewed orderly good behaviour and tidiness as the barometer of good care. The 21st-century reader is left wanting to hear the accounts of the individuals themselves – but their voices are absent.

The reports also imply a major divide between staff and patients. The fact that staff and patients had different rations is mentioned in 1917; and at the outset the innovation of having one laundry (whereas most asylums had one for staff, one for patients) is mentioned by the architects – but with the 'reassurance' that the laundry receiving rooms and packing rooms are separate, suggesting a typical 'them and us' institutional culture.

From the 1960s Tooting Bec was influenced by a new spirit of scepticism about institutions. Simmons (1995) notes that as early as the 1960s a forward thinking nurse, Una Budge, advocated that the hospital should close and the patients be able to live in the community.

Tooting Bec had its share of inquiries: in 1974 into the death of Mr D Carey (SW Thames Regional Health Authority 1974) and in 1984 into the death of an elderly patient, followed by a critical report from the Health Advisory Service.

By the 1980s many patients from Tooting Bec had left; and in 1995 the hospital closed. Whilst the hospital created a memorial to those staff who died in the First World War, and in two cases in the line of duty, there was no memorial to the thousands of patients who lived and died in the asylum – not even gravestones to mark where their ashes may have been placed. There is no memorial to Sarah Smith, who died after her cold car drive from Stepney in 1917. Some lives, it seems, matter more than others.

The history of the Metropolitan Asylum Board (MAB) from 1867 to 1930 gives a glowing account of the scientific advances that the MAB made before it was suddenly abolished in 1930: it is a self-justifying account, with no corrective from the viewpoint of those affected by the policy of expansion of the asylums. The inspection reports note the cold temperature – and the much enjoyed rabbit and fish pie – but make nothing of patients' constant requests for their liberty. The later history by Simmons focuses mainly on the history for the staff: the segregation of male and female staff until the 1960s, the hours of work (long), the rates of pay (low), the memorials to staff. There is no analysis of the hours and years of compulsory detention of the people who lived in the asylum, the lack of choice of who they lived with, the experience of seclusion (solitary confinement), the lack of choice of activity, the lack of opportunity to be heard.

The asylum was demolished and replaced by a private housing estate in 1999. The site contains two small plaques dated 1897 on the perimeter wall marking the boundary of the land owned by the MAB. Otherwise estate residents could be forgiven for not knowing that an asylum stood here, with its padded rooms and mortuary: the street names and estate name airbrush out that piece of history (Figure 1.2).

Figure 1.2 Plaque on the perimeter wall of what was Tooting Bec Hospital

Simmons' history does include one woman's testimony of life on the ward – cited earlier in this chapter. She noted that in the day the patients were lined up in the day room where, if they became restless, they were placed in a special chair with a tray that screwed down over their legs. They could try to slide underneath the tray but staff would stop them. If they were lucky they might have visitors. If not they would be given the remains of what was in a brown paper bag each week, as a 'gift':

> I could never understand why I had to have a large tin of talc and a tin of salmon
> brought for me every week.

Ms X mentioned that she liked going to the bowling green in the hospital grounds – but 'of course' was not allowed to go on to it. After she moved out she said:

> Now I have my own room in a home, I could go for a walk, or go shopping, or stay
> in ... in my room full of holiday mementos.

Life and choices had expanded. The *Independent on Sunday* (1993) interviewed a small number of former Tooting Bec residents for a feature on community care. The interviewees said they would never want to go back, and described benefits of their new life from having sex to a sense of liberty.

CONCLUSION

People living with mental health challenges remain partial citizens, with severe constraints on social, economic and political participation. The behaviours of institutions from the criminal justice system to health services and the media exhibit continuing discriminatory themes: undermining credibility, denying competence, implying (without proving) violence and alleging 'burden'. Re-valuing the experience of madness and those living with it is central to overcoming discrimination.

Competing histories suggest that discrimination and exclusion are not changed through professional interventions. There is no evidence for reduced stigma through the march of scientific progress and treatments, no matter how well-intentioned. Narratives explaining the categorisation and exclusion of 'mad' people in terms of wider political, social and economic forces have far more explanatory power.

Histories of madness often omit the voice of the person living the experience: their experience is defined by others. Where those historic voices are revealed, many focus on their individual plight – and in the context of the great containment many call for liberty. Some, however, call for wider social change – and this is the subject of the next chapter.

Reflective exercise

What do you think is the impact on people living with mental health challenges of the core narratives about 'mad' people: that you have questionable and unreliable judgement and are viewed as incompetent, potentially dangerous, unreasonably demanding?

FURTHER READING AND RESEARCH

Testimony: Inside Stories of Mental Health Care. Oral histories, held in the British Library

- Mental Health Media created an archive of 50 life story video interviews with mental health survivors, with funding from the Department of Health. They were filmed in 1999–2000. Interviewers themselves had lived experience of mental health challenges. The interviews include both people who have lived in long-stay hospitals, giving a lot of information about life on the wards in the 20th century, and those more recently diagnosed. See http://cadensa.bl.uk/uhtbin/cgisirsi/x/0/0/5?searchdata1=CKEY55 42415&library=ALL

Warner, R. (2004). *Recovery from Schizophrenia: Psychiatry and Political Economy* Third Edition. New York: Routledge.

- Analyses the experience of people with a diagnosis of schizophrenia in different countries; draws evidence-based conclusions about the economic and social factors that make a difference to recovery; and challenges the common view that services and treatments are most significant to recovery

Sayce, L. (2000). *From Psychiatric Patient to Citizen.* Basingstoke: Palgrave Macmillan.

- Documents the discrimination and denial of citizenship experienced by people living with mental health problems; and sets out an agenda for change based on rights, joining forces with the wider disability movement and utilising law, communications and grassroots initiatives

Thornicroft, G. (2006). *Shunned.* Oxford: OUP.

- Pulls together academic evidence of discrimination and stigma in different life domains; and proposes a framework for how to reduce them

Scull, A. (1993). *The Most Solitary of Afflictions: Madness and Society in Britain 1700–1900.* Haven and London: Yale University Press.

- A historical sweep that documents the 'great containment' from the 18th century onwards, and analyses with reference to stories and academic data the drivers behind society's construction and treatment of madness

2 | Voices of Resistance and Social Change

Chapter Summary

- Voices of resistance
- Collective action
- Changes in attitudes
- Changes in behaviour and experience

This chapter draws on historical narratives (from Chapter 1) and voices of resistance to answer the questions 'have people deemed "mad" come to be fuller citizens, participating socially, economically and politically?' and 'has discrimination on mental health grounds declined?'

Voices of resistance

Across Britain and more widely histories, like that of Tooting Bec (see Chapter 1), are being uncovered after years of obscurity – and celebrated, sometimes with emblematic power. In the grounds of High Royds Hospital in Leeds (now closed), 2,681 former patients were buried in unmarked graves. The Friends of High Royds Memorial Garden sold shares in a memorial garden and gained public support to re-open the chapel. A local builder, Alan Storey, whose great grandmother was one of those buried there, restored the chapel with the help of about 30 apprentice carpenters from Leeds College of Building (*Telegraph and Argus*, 12 December 2009).

Chair of the Friends, Derek Hutchinson, who had been an in-patient in High Royds, praised the way the community had come together and concluded: 'These people that are in the ground have been forgotten about after all these years and now they will never be forgotten about.'

Some authors have worked to reveal the voices of people living with mental health challenges over history. As historian Roy Porter put it:

> the writings of these outcasts, the so-called mad or ex-mad people ... contain astonishing insights into their own disturbances and into the wider question of normality and abnormality, imagination and judgement, authenticity and personality, power and oppression, the divided self.

> (Porter 1991, p. xv)

The more common 'individual story' is the case study, which appears in psychiatric literature from Freud onwards. Bracken and Thomas (2005) argue the 'case study' controls and constrains understanding of experience; and Hornstein (2012, p. 164) that allowing others to define your experience is a 'narrative surrender'. O'Hagan was so alarmed at finding that her clinical notes did not speak of her suffering or strengths that she placed side-by-side her own diary entries and the notes:

> I dragged the box into the daylight, grabbed a pair of scissors and started to match my journal entries with the hospital notes by date. Over the next few hours I created a linear collage of my journals interspersed with their notes, lined up from one end of the room to the other.

> I was astonished at what I saw; two parallel accounts of my madness that could never meet, just like the sun and the moon can never shine brightly in the same sky. ... They [the staff] wrote about what they saw on the outside through the thick lens of psychopathology. I wrote about what I felt on the inside, unfiltered by professionalism or pretensions of objectivity.

> (O'Hagan 2010)

Whereas Mary wrote of despair and fear, typical staff comments included 'Flat, lacking motivation, sleep and appetite good. Discussed aetiology. Cont. Li Carb. 250 mg qd. Levels next time.'

It is possible to get past professional accounts and hear directly from people deemed mad at different points of history. Hornstein (2012) has assembled over 600 first person accounts of madness in English, dating from 1436 to the present. She recounts the sheer ingenuity of people in institutions in getting their stories read by the people they chose – and not seized by others. In 1919 the dancer Nijinsky wrote an account of his madness in Russian, so his Hungarian wife could not read it and destroy his words; in 1895 Agnes Richter sewed her story into her jacket, so it could not so easily be taken from her.

Hornstein emphasises the psychological meaning of experiences like hearing voices; and contrasts psychological and peer support with reductionist biological analyses and treatment. 'Being in a group with other people who've had similar experiences, who accept each other's realities, no matter how strange they are, and who listen to one another in an interested, accepting way can be a life-saver' (Hornstein, 2012, p. 18). Her primary aim is not to challenge social structures that keep discrimination in place but simply to encourage everyone to listen to the narratives of people in distress and 'help create better ways of responding to emotional problems' (Ibid., p. 282). Hornstein is unconvinced by the value of anti-discrimination law and does not specifically address how collective action might reduce discrimination.

She does however document powerful voices of resistance to the way mad people are treated.

In the 1860s, Elizabeth Packard sewed petitions for her release into underwear that she was permitted to sew for children, and smuggled them out of the asylum. She viewed herself as a political prisoner.

In 1957 two MPs, of different political parties, published accounts of people confined in mental institutions called 'The Plea for the Silent'. One woman had challenged the doctors: 'the doctor told me that the mere fact that I suffered from claustrophobia was sufficient to necessitate that I should be sent to a mental hospital. I replied that I doubted whether a fear of being shut up could rightly be treated by locking up the patient' (Hornstein, 2012, p.162).

Both Porter (2001) and Hornstein include numerous accounts of actual or attempted escapes from institutions. The poet John Clare, for instance, escaped from an asylum in Essex and walked 90 miles to his home village, with almost nothing to eat except grass from the roadside. Porter cites Nathaniel Lee's famous comment on the power of psychiatry to decide whose version of reality will hold:

> They called me mad, and I called them mad, and damn them they outvoted me.

> (Porter, 2001, p.1)

Porter cites testimonies of recovery, to which liberty is often the vital precursor. Individuals speak of how they only recovered at the point of returning to their community or family. They write of battling and pleading to be released, but not being heard:

> My dearest love, upon my word,
> Your conduct is at least absurd,
> Leaving your husband here so long
> Is hardly subject for a song.
> Now, why the devil don't you get
> Me out of this madhouse, my pet?.

> (Extract from 'An appeal from a husband in Morningside Asylum to his wife' 1887)

The cry from the individual can act as inspiration to others: the poem above was published in the *Morningside Mirror*.

Some took a further step – to collective understanding and social action to tackle discrimination.

From having a voice – to influencing change

As early as 1620, a group of Bedlam inmates wrote 'the petition of the poor distracted folk of Bedlam'; and in the 19th century the 'great containment' met some resistance. John Perceval, son of Prime Minister Spencer Perceval (who was famously shot dead in the lobby of the House of Commons), was incarcerated first in Brislington Asylum near Bristol and then in Ticehurst Asylum in Sussex. In Brislington he was tied up in bed or in a straitjacket for months. After his release he published 'A narrative of the treatment experienced by a Gentleman during a state of mental derangement designed to explain the causes and nature of insanity, and to expose the injudicious conduct pursued towards many unfortunate sufferers under that calamity' (published 1838). He went on to found with other ex-inmates and relatives the 'Alleged Lunatics' Friend Society' in 1845. They campaigned for better protection against wrongful confinement and cruel treatment, and supported individuals: one such was the German academic Edward Peithman, who had been locked up in Bethlem for 14 years after annoying Prince Albert. Perceval secured his release. They also campaigned for better opportunities to live and work outside the institutions – more than a 'milksop' existence, as Perceval put it.

Some linked this struggle to other social movements: in the US, feminist Charlotte Perkins Gilman (1892) wrote 'The Yellow Wallpaper', a story illuminating how suppression of women's autonomy led to mental distress.

The next major wave of collective activism came from the 1970s onwards. The Mental Patients' Union (MPU) (formed in 1972) and CAPO (Campaign Against Psychiatric Oppression, in the 1980s) brought activists together to critique the power of psychiatry. Andrew Roberts, a founding member of the MPU, recalls that it was rooted in Marxism: psychiatry was viewed as a form of social control of the working classes in a capitalist state; and just as workers formed trade unions, so mental patients needed a union to fight political oppression and control (Roberts 2008).

In the late 1980s less politically aligned groups emerged and were able to grow in numbers and influence and to ride the wave of consumerism ushered in by conservative governments. Survivors Speak Out and UKAN (the UK Advocacy Network) argued powerfully for the newly termed 'service users' and 'survivors' to have a voice. They promoted radically improved individual choice and collective 'involvement' to shape services (Beeforth et al. 1990). Local groups from Camden to Chesterfield and Nottingham were active and people came together at a major conference in 1987 at the Edale Youth Hostel in Derbyshire, to network and debate demands.

This led to a proliferation of 'user involvement' in services – being on committees and appointment panels, taking up roles as 'user involvement co-ordinators', engaging in consultations to feed in to service policies, and arguing for consumer benefits: better information on drugs and their adverse effects, more choice of services, alternative treatments, better access to advocacy.

It was not straightforward. As Peter Campbell (2006), founding member of Survivors Speak Out described that period:

> Basically we were nowhere. Silent, excluded, outside the room ... And I think it's important now that service user involvement is established and accepted and seen as being a good thing, just to remember that 20 years ago – there wasn't any ... This wasn't something that the service providers ... suddenly woke up to and said, 'oh yeah this is a good idea, let's do it' ... almost every time I remember going to any event, the first five minutes at least of anything I ever said, was basically establishing the case for 'Why listen to service users?' 'What are the reasons for doing that?' ... And there was a great deal of opposition.

To add strength, in the late 1980s some took a conscious decision to 'infiltrate' Mind – which set up a user network (Mindlink) and promoted community-based services in place of the old coercive institutions.

However, by the early 1990s the limits of consumerism were becoming apparent: a Mind survey found people did not just want better information on treatments or more choices of the same old services – they wanted a life, with relationships, friendships, housing and work; they wanted equality. Like the Alleged Lunatics' Friend Society before them, the 1980s and 90s activists turned their attention from just opposing the injustices of incarceration, to forging a positive agenda to improve social and citizenship opportunities. They wanted user-run alternative services, civil rights, and challenges to multiple oppressions. In the spirit of the new times, radicalism was linked more to identity – feminism, gay rights, anti-racism – than to the class struggles that had underpinned the MPU.

There were a number of radical developments during this period.

Firstly, the development of survivor-run alternative services. Judi Chamberlin's ground-breaking book *On Our Own* – first published in the USA in 1977, in the UK in 1988 – argued that rather than amend a system that was not fit for purpose, consumers could set up patient-controlled crisis and peer support. She criticised not only the old asylums but importantly the 'community' services that were replacing them: they were not part of communities, but just replicated the power imbalances of the hospital, were usually run by psychiatrists and part of state bureaucracies.

A vision of user-led services

Instead of creating clear and stigmatising distinctions between those who are competent to give help and those who are weak enough to need it, these [patient-controlled] alternatives are creating new communities of equals, countering the alienation and power-lessness most people rightly sense to be a prime cause of their unhappiness.

Only by developing true alternatives can we prove that we can care for one another far better than psychiatry has 'cared' for its patients who have suffered under its control for too long. (Chamberlin 1988)

Fellow American consumer advocate Patricia Deegan (Deegan 1994) described the personal journey of recovery: not being rehabilitated by others, but building the life you want, with support that you choose, to find meaning in a life that is no doubt changed from the one you expected (prior to mental health challenges), but is fulfilling.

UK activists put their energies into establishing Hearing Voices groups, crisis houses and peer support groups, often with fragile funding.

Secondly, there were strong challenges to mental health services for the ways they compounded different discriminations rather than offering a restorative opportunity to recover from them. In 2014 the Open University brought together women involved in women's mental health activism from the 1970s onwards. They recounted the liberation on discovering feminist accounts of madness from Phyllis Chesler (1972) and Elaine Showalter (1987); and the campaigns like Stress on Women (1992–94), which succeeded in changing policy to stop mixed-sex wards and re-traumatisation (although implementation of the policy was to take longer) and also fought for support for women to raise children rather than lose them into care. They described the battles by black women and men to counter 'big black and dangerous' stereotypes. They recalled the first known national conference on lesbian, gay and bisexual mental health, held in 1995 by Mind and Stonewall, at which a Conservative minister finally stated that 'sexual orientation is not, should not, and never again will be a mental health issue' – reflecting the final removal of homosexuality as a mental disorder from the Government's central computer system in 1993. The Minister said it was 'totally unjustified discrimination' for same sex partners not to be treated as next of kin; and ended by wishing everyone a happy Gay Pride (speech by John Bowis, Minister of State for Health, 1995). His full speech was published in the *Independent* and civil servants competed thereafter to claim credit for drafting this ground-breaking speech.

Thirdly, in the 1990s the focus of campaigns shifted from better services to a better life, in line with the priorities of people with lived experience. In 1992, Mind's legal director Ian Bynoe published a paper with disability academics Colin Barnes and Mike Oliver arguing for anti-discrimination law. From then on Mind pressed for social inclusion. It secured coverage of people with mental health problems in Britain's first disability discrimination law (the DDA 1995), including – against some opposition – people with personality disorder. The vision was to overcome discrimination right across society, in areas including employment and education. Mind influenced national bodies to pursue 'social inclusion', a term favoured in the late 1990s by the Labour Government. This led to the Social Exclusion Unit undertaking a major inquiry into social inclusion and mental health in 2004, and to successive governments changing mental health service outcome indicators to include greater equality in employment and physical health. It led to significant funding for the Time to Change campaign, designed to challenge stigma and discrimination. And in the 2000s the Labour Government progressively improved rights to participation (see Chapter 6).

In 2000, Peter Campbell (2000), of Survivors Speak Out, was arguing that whilst user involvement within services had improved, discrimination in the wider society 'had got worse'. A consensus was growing that change in the wider society was needed.

Survivors Speak Out declined by 2000. Other groups surfaced: Mad Pride, which started by celebrating madness – but by 2014 was dealing with a different emergency, protecting benefits in the face of significant cuts (with 'Hands Off Our Benefits' being a prominent call);

and the National Survivor User Network, which supported user-led organisations to have a voice and engage locally with service commissioners and providers.

Waves of activism have tuned into different wider trends, from Marxism to consumerism, anti-racism and (more recently) 'co-production' or involvement in policy on more equal terms. They have secured different achievements – from improving treatment information, to debarring mixed-sex wards, to making discrimination on mental health grounds illegal. Sometimes, over time, riding the wave of a 'wider trend' has boxed activists in – as when consumerism hit the limits of its usefulness in the late 1990s. Repeatedly through history activists have returned to fighting discrimination to achieve equality and participation (or ending the 'milksop existence').

Since the 1970s the voices of people with lived experience have become louder. Rose (2013) has argued they became increasingly important, firstly in anti-psychiatry groupings, then consumer organisations, then in civil rights and then in shaping research and recovery, through peer support workers and user-led research.

These 'stages' are not mutually exclusive and can be inter-dependent: for instance, Rose's final stage includes involvement in 'recovery'. 'Recovery' is rooted in 'hope, control and opportunity' (Repper and Perkins 2003): for opportunity to be real, there must be not just peer support or user-led research but actual opportunities for employment, family life, housing, routes out of poverty. All these require civil and human rights to be met (ideas developed in subsequent chapters). Together these developments can, at best, amplify influence.

The next sections examine whether discrimination and exclusion have declined since this activism took off from the 1970s.

Changes in attitudes

'Attitudes are the real disability': thus reads a 1990s disability movement slogan. Patronising or demonising attitudes are one of the major barriers to participation that people living with a mental health challenge or other disability identify – alongside behavioural, structural and environmental obstacles. If, for instance, an employer believes someone who has depression will not be able to cope with stress, she or he is less likely to promote them.

One measure of positive change therefore may lie in public attitudes. However, someone can have positive attitudes, but still not give the person experiencing depression the promotion, perhaps because they fear their boss will criticise their judgement – a case of structural discrimination. Someone else may report 'positive' attitudes to give the researcher what they think they want to hear (Sartorius 2014).

For these reasons some disabled people argue that they do not care about attitudes: what matters is behaviours and outcomes – whether more people with mental health challenges escape poverty, secure jobs and promotions, get access to justice and suchlike tangible results.

Attitude and behaviour are linked – both ways. Attitudes can inform behaviours. For instance, the public health message that smoking harms children living with a smoker has been found effective; it tapped into and strengthened a belief that children must be protected, which prompted changes in behaviour. Some people stopped smoking, at least in the same space as children. But equally, requiring changes in behaviour can lead to changed attitudes. If you believe women cannot be good managers, and then have several women managers who you are obliged to treat as 'the boss', you are faced with 'cognitive dissonance': your behaviour and your pre-existing attitude contradict each other. One way of resolving the 'dissonance' is to change the attitude that women cannot make good managers – which is exactly what often happens when people interact with people from an 'outsider' group, on at least equal terms: they change their attitude. Hewstone (2003) found that in the case of prejudice against 'outsider' groups in terms of religion, ethnicity, disability and more, contact on at least equal terms does change attitudes.

There is no need to change attitudes first, so behaviours will follow; it is at least as likely to work the other way round. Banning smoking in public spaces makes some people view smoking as less acceptable.

There has been increasing interest in market economies in 'policy marketing': as direct government control declines (in some policy domains), the state seeks to 'nudge' the population (or sub-sets of it) to behave in particular ways, often by intervening at the intersection of attitudes and behaviour. Offe (2014) argues that this may be done through 'legitimate coercion' (for instance, laws), or incentives and disincentives (for instance, conditional benefit regimes), or signs and words. The signs and words may be used positively: for instance, in Bogota when water was scarce, each district's figures for water consumption were publicised, thereby celebrating those with low consumption and shaming the others. The result was that consumption went down in both groups. Or it can be used for 'negative responsibilisation of victims', for instance, conveying the message that those who do not find work are failing in their duties (irrespective of the labour market, or the barriers they face), or that people who drink large quantities of alcohol have only themselves to blame (irrespective of the role of alcohol advertising, or social stressors linked to drinking).

There are two lessons from this discussion. First, if initiatives succeed in changing attitudes, it does not necessarily mean that citizenship outcomes will follow: therefore improved attitudes are not a proxy for improved outcomes. Secondly, requirements and nudges can improve outcomes; sometimes this involves simultaneous changes in behaviour and attitude; sometimes it involves changing behaviours which subsequently impact on attitudes. Behaviour and attitude are inter-related in complex ways.

With all these provisos, it is worth examining whether attitudes towards people with mental health conditions have or have not changed.

A regular survey of public attitudes towards people with mental health conditions in Britain has been conducted since 1994 (TNS BMRB 2015). It shows that on a number of measures of *fear* of people with mental illness, attitudes have improved, for instance:

- The percentage of the public agreeing that 'residents have nothing to fear from people coming into their neighbourhood to obtain mental health services' increased from 62% in 1994 to 70% in 2014
- The percentage agreeing that 'most women who were once patients in a mental hospital can be trusted as babysitters' increased from 21% in 1994 to 29% in 2014.

This still suggests that nearly three quarters do not think women ex-patients could be trusted as babysitters; the shift is statistically significant but modest.

On some measures of desire to exclude or deny opportunity, attitudes also improved, for instance:

- The percentage agreeing that 'People with mental illness should not be given any responsibility' decreased from 17% in 1994 to 11% in 2014
- The percentage agreeing that 'Anyone with a history of mental problems should be excluded from public office' decreased strongly, from 29% in 1994 to 13% in 2013, but rose again to 16% in 2014
- The percentage agreeing that 'No-one has the right to exclude people with mental illness from their neighbourhood' increased from 76% in 1994 to 83% in 2014
- The percentage agreeing that 'People with mental health problems should have the same rights to a job as anyone else' increased from 66% in 2003 (when this was first asked) to 80% in 2014.

These changes are incremental and mainly modest, but over two decades a trend of improvement can be detected, which suggests potential for further positive change.

Women were generally more accepting, with less fear or desire for social distance, than men.

Despite these positives:

- The percentage agreeing that 'mental hospitals are an outdated means of treating people with mental illness' went down – from 42% in 1994 to 35% in 2014 – and younger people (16–34) were least likely to agree with this statement (only 27% of this age group agreed).
- Only just over half (56%) of the younger group agreed that 'people with mental illness are far less of a danger than most people suppose' – compared with 70% of the over 55s
- Overall the middle aged group (aged 35-54) had the most positive attitude scores.

It may be that younger people have no memory of the old asylums or the reasons for replacing them and simply do not see this issue through a human rights lens.

The survey also asked which of several statements usually describe someone who is mentally ill. This revealed that:

- The proportion agreeing with 'Has to be kept in a psychiatric or mental hospital' went up – from 46% in 2003 to 60% in 2014
- The proportion agreeing with 'Is incapable of making simple decisions about his or her own life' went up from 32% in 2003 to 40% in 2014
- The proportion agreeing with 'is prone to violence' went up from 29% in 2003 to 39% in 2014
- The proportion agreeing with 'Cannot be held responsible for his or her own actions' went up from 45% in 2003 to 48% in 2014
- The proportion saying they would feel uncomfortable talking to an employer about their mental health fluctuated: from 50% in 2010, to 43% in February 2011, to 48% in December 2011, 55% in 2012 and back to 48% in 2014. This finding may be linked to the recession and increasing anxiety about losing employment after 2008.

These findings suggest contradictory strands of thought. Whilst the public seems generally to be becoming somewhat more positive about the idea of people with 'mental illness' taking some responsibility, and especially taking public office, significant (and growing) proportions still agree that people with mental illness cannot make simple decisions about their life; have to be kept in a hospital; and are prone to violence. It seems the deep stereotypes of incompetence and violence still co-exist with more progressive outlooks. Half of those responding would not be comfortable talking to an employer about a mental health issue, which is perhaps unsurprising given the deep association in their minds between mental illness and incompetence.

Evans-Lacko et al. (2014) analysed the significance of these trends and found a positive, moderate, impact of the Time to Change campaign (2007–present) on attitudes relating to prejudice and exclusion – but not in relation to tolerance or support for community care. They suggest this campaign may have been strongest in disconfirming negative ideas on exclusion, rather than enhancing positive attitudes (for instance, about support to live a full life in the community).

One other measure that has changed from 1994 to 2013 is the proportion of the public who believe that 'mental illness is an illness like any other': this rose from 71% in 1994 to 78% in 2014. The reports view this as a sign of increased acceptance and positive attitudes; it is cited repeatedly as a positive, including in online factsheets on stigma and discrimination. In reality, viewing mental health challenges as a biological illness makes people more, not less, likely to view people as incapable of taking responsibility (see Chapter 3). This measure is very ill-chosen.

It seems the British public is becoming more likely to see mentally ill people as medically 'ill' and more likely to see them as needing to be in hospital (over half agreed with this statement), with young people in particular not seeing psychiatric hospital as an outdated treatment option. Whilst the public seems to see the point of opportunities to work and take up public office, this view is offset, and potentially undermined, by a view that 'ill' people cannot be expected to do very much at all: nearly half agreed with the statement that someone with mental illness cannot be held responsible for his or her actions.

This suggests a continuing oppressive form of benevolence. The intentions may be good and kind – the poor people, after all, cannot help their illness – but its implications are potentially devastating: being viewed as incapable of making decisions, thereby justifying others making decisions on your behalf.

It is particularly concerning that young people seem more likely to think people with mental illness need to be hospitalised. Younger people were also significantly less likely than middle aged people to agree that virtually anybody can become mentally ill; that residents have nothing to fear from people coming into their neighbourhood to obtain mental health services; that people with mental illness are less of a danger than most people suppose; and that people with mental illness have for too long been the subject of ridicule. On many measures they hold less inclusive attitudes than the generation before them.

This contrasts starkly with attitudes to other issues of equality. Ipsos Mori (2013) note that generation Y (born 1980 onwards) and generation X (born 1966–79) are:

- much less likely than older groups to believe a husband's job is to earn money whilst a wife's job is to look after the home and family
- far less likely to believe that homosexual relationships are always wrong
- much less likely to mind if a suitably qualified black person was appointed as their boss.

In all these cases, attitudes amongst all age cohorts have been changing over time – all ages have become more accepting of black bosses, gay relationships and non-rigid roles for husbands and wives – but in addition, young people are significantly more likely to hold these more accepting views than the older cohorts. Young people exemplify a new commitment to equality – but seemingly not in mental health, where younger people appear to demonstrate a degree of 'oppressive benevolence' – a commitment to people with 'mental illness' needing to be hospitalised, a greater tendency to go along with residents' fears when people with mental health conditions come into their neighbourhood to obtain services. This contrasts with a core thread of commitment to equality and justice in young people's attitudes to race, gender and sexual orientation.

Moreover, public attitudes towards people with mental health challenges lag far behind attitudes towards people with physical or sensory impairments and somewhat behind people with learning difficulties. The British Social Attitudes Survey (Staniland 2011) asked a public sample whether they would feel comfortable interacting with someone with these different impairments in specific situations: if the person attended a quiz team or club of which they were a member; or moved in next door; or was in a class at school with a family member, assuming necessary support was in place; or married a close family member or friend; or was appointed their boss; or became their local MP.

On every question, levels of comfort were significantly lower for people with mental health conditions:

- On attending a quiz team or club 97% were comfortable with the person with the physical impairment, 96% with sensory impairment, 88% with learning disabilities and 79% with the person with a mental health condition
- On moving in next door, the figures for comfort were 98% (physical impairment), 98% (sensory impairment), 90% (learning disability) and 67% (mental health condition)
- On being in a class at school, the figures for comfort were 97% (physical impairment), 96% (sensory impairment), 82% (learning disability) and 65% (mental health condition)
- On marrying a family member, the figures for comfort were 91% (physical impairment), 92% (sensory impairment), 66% (learning disability), 54% (mental health condition)
- On being appointed as your boss, the figures for comfort were 92% (physical impairment), 89% (sensory impairment), 52% (learning disability), 44% (mental health condition)
- On being elected as your local MP the figures for comfort were 95% (physical impairment), 92% (sensory impairment), 35% (learning disability), 35% (mental health condition).

The figures become more negative the closer the person becomes (from merely attending a quiz to marrying a family member); and the more responsibility the person has (as boss, or MP). This suggests that although there have been incremental improvements since 2009 (see above) the old stereotypes of incompetence and danger are still endemic.

Attitudes towards people with physical impairments pose significant barriers, but have generally improved over the last 30 years; attitudes towards people with mental health challenges have also improved on some indicators but have shown more variable and contradictory change.

In the 2010s a compounding factor has emerged: discriminatory attitudes towards people claiming benefits. Over the last 30 years, the public has become significantly less likely to feel proud of the welfare state and to support spending on benefits for people who are unemployed (British Social Attitudes 2013). 'In much popular discourse, the welfare state – once a towering achievement of the post-war Beveridge generation – has become a byword for social breakdown, irresponsibility and mistrust within communities', as the British Social Attitudes Survey puts it. The public increasingly believes that benefits are being claimed by people who do not 'deserve' them; and adherence to the belief that 'most unemployed people could find a job if they wanted one' has increased substantially over the past three decades. Around a third of the public expressed this view in the early 1990s; more than two-thirds by the mid-2000s. By 2012 there was a small change back towards supporting spending on welfare benefits: but there was no further growth by 2014 (British Social Attitudes 2015).

The public makes a distinction between older people (viewed as a high priority for social security funding), disabled people (the second priority) – and people who are unemployed who, many believe, 'could get a job if they tried'. Van Oorschot (2006) examined European public perceptions of the relative 'deservingness' of four groups, using the 1999/2000 European Values Study survey. Elderly people were consistently seen as the most deserving, closely followed by sick and disabled people; unemployed people are seen as less deserving still and immigrants least deserving of all.

The question for people with mental health challenges of working age is whether they are seen as 'disabled' – or as unemployed (and in some cases additionally as 'immigrants'). Disability activists campaigned throughout the 1990s and 2000s to widen the definition of disability, to ensure everyone who might be subject to discrimination was covered by equality legislation: thus in 2006, people with depression, multiple sclerosis and cancer secured better coverage under 'disability' discrimination law. Much government policy has gone the other way: trying to reduce the number of people eligible for 'disability' benefits, reassessing people on 'incapacity' benefits and moving people from these disability-specific benefits to Job Seekers Allowance. Since the largest, and growing, proportion of people on out of work disability benefits have a mental health problem as their primary impairment (Banks et al 2015), they are centrally caught up in this re-definition of who is 'disabled' enough to get disability benefits. In response, many people with mental health conditions are arguing that they are 'sick': see Chapter 4 for discussion of the objectives and risks of this strategy. The impact on long-term attitudes of re-drawing the lines between 'disabled' and 'non-disabled' people – between the 'deserving' and 'non-deserving' – needs careful tracking and debate.

Britain is not alone in finding persistent negative attitudes towards people with mental health conditions, with patterns of modest gains and some backsliding. Link (2011) notes that in the USA the public's desire for social distance from people who are 'mentally ill' has not improved and on some measures attitudes have worsened. In New Zealand, where a public education campaign 'Like Minds Like Mine' made gains – for instance more recognition that people with mental health problems are able to take responsibility – evaluation in 2004 found the public were willing to have increasing contact with people with a mental illness at decreasing levels of intimacy – i.e., most willing to mingle at a social event, least likely to want someone with a mental health problem to care for your children or live in your house (Ministry of Health 2005).

Later chapters will explore the effectiveness of different attempts to influence these entrenched attitudes.

Overall, there have been incremental positive attitudinal shifts in Britain and elsewhere; but a significant attitudinal challenge remains.

Changes in behaviour and experience

Behaviours and actual experiences of discrimination arguably matter more than attitudes.

Between 2008 and 2012 there was a 5.5% decrease in the median overall experience of discrimination across a number of life domains (friends, family, social life, physical health, dating, etc.): initially the reduction was greater (11.5%) but some gains were lost after 2011. There was no change in the proportion of people reporting *no* discrimination: in 2008 91% of people with mental health conditions surveyed reported at least one discrimination experience; by 2011 this had gone down to 88%; but by 2012 the rate had returned to 91%. There was no significant change from 2008–12 in reports of discrimination in any single specific life domain (friends, family, etc.) (Henderson et al. 2014); but there was an overall reduction of 5.5% across domains.

This suggests a varying picture, with both glimmers of potential longer-term improvement and persistent challenges.

Confidence to challenge discrimination went down slightly over the same period, from 61.2% to 57.8% (Dept. of Health 2013); and the proportion of people reporting that they concealed their mental health experiences went up, from 73% to 77% (Henderson et al. 2014).

TNS BMRB (2015) found an improvement in public 'intended behaviour' towards people with mental health problems – for instance, the proportion of respondents who said they would be willing to continue a relationship with a friend with a mental health problem rose from 82% in 2009 to 89% in 2014; those willing to work with someone with a mental health problem rose from 69% to 76%; and to live with someone from 57% to 66%.There was also an increase from 2009-14 in the proportion of the public reporting they had lived with, had a close friend with or worked with someone with a mental health problem.

However, Evans-Lacko et al. (2013) found no improvement in actual (as opposed to intended) reported behaviour by the public.

Again, younger people had lower scores on positive intended behaviour than the middle aged.

Specific types of exclusion or discrimination on which we have longitudinal data include use of compulsory detention and treatment; and employment rates.

On compulsion, there has been a significant increase in use of compulsory powers to detain and treat in England – both in hospital and in the community. When the Government introduced community treatment orders (CTOs) in 2008, the theory was that by requiring some people (a few hundred a year) to accept treatment in the community, fewer would need to be compulsorily detained in hospital, which would give people greater liberty, living in their own homes. The reality has been that since 2008 the numbers of compulsory detentions in hospital, far from declining, has risen inexorably; and in addition the number of CTOs has increased, leading to a significant net increase in compulsion. At the end of 2013–14 there were a total of 23,531 people subject to the Mental Health Act in England: 18,166 detained on longer-term hospital orders and 5,365 on CTOs. This is 6% (1,324) more than at the end of the previous year, and 32% greater than at the end of 2008–09, the year CTOs were introduced (Health and Social Care Information Centre 2014). The Act was used over 53,000 times to detain people in hospital in 2013–14, compared to just over 44,000 in 2007–8.

Moreover, in 2013 the initial proponent of CTOs, Professor Tom Burns, published an evaluation of CTOs and had the courage publicly to conclude they had had no positive benefits but had posed a threat to human rights. In 2014 the Office of the UN High Commissioner for Human Rights issued a statement saying that deprivation of liberty on grounds that included disability contravened the UN Convention on the Rights of Persons with Disabilities (see Chapter 4). Article 14 appears clearly breached by the UK's mental health acts and by the rising, ineffective use of compulsion. In a context when the rhetoric of choice and control has been ubiquitous, and when even the greatest proponent of CTOs sees them as a human rights risk, it is notable that coercion has continued to rise.

On employment, in the first decade of the 21st century the gap between the employment rate of disabled people (generally) and non-disabled people closed by around 10%. The gap stood at 30% in 2013 (Office for Disability Issues 2013).

In the case of people with mental health conditions, progress was more limited. People classified as having 'mental illness, phobia or panic' saw no improvement during this period. Their employment rate remained stubbornly below 20%. For people classified as having 'depression, bad nerves or anxiety' there was some improvement – from just under 20% to around 30% (ODI 2013). The Department of Health's dashboard shows that in the one year following this data, the employment rate of people with mental health conditions actually declined – from 29.5% to 27.7%; and for people with 'serious mental illness' from 8.8% to 7.9% (Dept. of Health 2013).

Taking a longer view, Marwaha and Johnson (2004) found that the UK employment rate in people with schizophrenia appeared to have declined over the previous 50 years. Barriers to employment included discrimination, fear of loss of benefits and a lack of appropriate professional support.

Perkins and Rinaldi (2002) found that unemployment among people with long-term mental health conditions increased in one London Borough from 80% in 1990 to 92% in 1999, and amongst those with a diagnosis of schizophrenia from 88% to 96%. More positively, Rinaldi et al. (2011) found this trend reversed after introducing individual placement with support (IPS) in a local service: employment rates improved, even when local employment rates generally were declining. This suggests that practical interventions to improve outcomes can reap results.

In a noticeable parallel with the pattern with public attitudes, there is clear evidence that people with mental health conditions are experiencing a particular intensity of discrimination and in some cases lagging behind other disabled people (although exclusion across the disability spectrum is severe). To give just a few examples:

- The EHRC's inquiry into disability-related harassment and hate crime drew on evidence that 'within the disabled population … those with learning disabilities and/or mental health conditions are particularly at risk and suffer higher levels of actual victimisation' (Chi Hoong Sin et al. 2009). A Mind survey found that 71% of people with mental health issues had been a victim of crime in the past two years, 22% had experienced physical assault, 41% ongoing bullying and 27% sexual harassment. Only 19% felt safe at all times in their own home (Mind, 2007). Chih Hoong Sin and colleagues argue that the dominant narrative on this issue needs to change from protection to justice, to accord disabled people more power to seek redress.

- EHRC-commissioned research into harassment at work found those most likely to face harassment were disabled people; and amongst disabled people, those with mental health conditions or learning disabilities (Fevre et al. 2008).

Multiple discrimination and exclusion are powerful: for instance, amongst the growing number of people subject to community treatment orders (CTOs), no less than 18% are people from black and minority ethnic communities .The problem of disproportionate levels of compulsion used with black people (especially men), with longer sections, has been known for 30 years, but Count Me In data still shows a continuing pattern, despite efforts of the Delivering Race Equality Strategy.

If these indicators are relatively unpromising, it is worth noting pockets of positive development. Time to Change evaluation shows that people in employment or who had retired reported significantly lower levels of discrimination compared to people who were unemployed or currently studying or volunteering (Hamilton et al. 2015). Evidence-based IPS programmes (see above) are enabling people in some areas to secure employment, skills and education, in significant numbers, which has the potential to reduce experiences of discrimination (Rinaldi et al. 2010). In some companies, people with mental health challenges are genuinely feeling more confident to be open about their experiences and 2013 legislation is sweeping away outdated laws to stop people with mental health conditions serving as company directors, jurors and MPs.

Peer support has been demonstrated to be effective in recovery (Repper and Carter 2011) and the employment of peer support workers in statutory and voluntary services has increased, with some NHS Trusts aiming for a critical mass of peer support workers. Peer-led alternatives to mainstream mental health services have been formed, albeit with fragile funding.

Yet something more is needed to scale this good practice up: to achieve a step change beyond single localities and organisations.

CONCLUSION

There have been voices of resistance to discrimination and exclusion throughout history – and some have gone beyond the individual voice, to forge collective action, from the Alleged Lunatics' Friend Society to the Mental Patients' Union, Survivors Speak Out and the National Survivor User Network. This has generated goals of inclusion, a successful fight for civil rights law, a re-framed purpose of services to support the life you choose, and examples of policies and practices that enable more people to pursue our own chosen journeys and 'belong' in society. Some things have changed as a result – laws on the statute book that protect (some) rights and freedoms, lives changed in particular areas through survivor-led services and employment support, more people involved in research and recovery and some people liberated to speak openly about our lives.

But the stark truth is that on some major measures of participation – like employment rates, and freedom from coercion – there are no signs of improvement in the last 20 years. There have been some important positive shifts in public attitude; but even here 'oppressive benevolence' towards 'ill' people co-exists with rejecting exclusion. These contradictory strands fall short of a strong new common belief in the justice of full participation. It is worrying that young people seem to have less inclusive and rights-based attitudes than the middle aged – in contrast to young people's attitudes on gender, race and sexual orientation.

And if it is lived experience that matters most, the reported experience of discrimination has shown a small welcome decline – but not a consistent one. Intended behaviour by the public has improved, but actual reported behaviour less clearly; employment rates remain stubbornly low; and some things, especially coercion, have got much worse.

Changes in attitudes – even if they are unequivocally positive – do not lead in a simple causal line to changes in behaviour. The relationship is complex. Evidence that being in employment or retired is protective against discrimination (Hamilton et al 2015) suggests that achieving economic participation may change the behaviour of other people towards you – and reduce the experience of discrimination.

There is no evidence that mental health professionals' 'interventions' or scientific progress have overcome exclusion. Change seems to have come through the collective voice and power of people with lived experience, and allies, who address wider social, economic and cultural forces. The brief history in chapters 1 and 2 note changes when movements of 'mad' people rode the wave of the moment – de-institutionalisation from the 1960s onwards and consumerism in the 1980s/90s. In both cases improvements flowed: people who left the institutions were consistently more satisfied with their lives after they left; and consumerism brought a measure of involvement and control which, as activist Peter Campbell notes, did make a difference to people's experience. This 'riding the waves' creates ethical dilemmas: for a movement to turn an opportunity to its own ends risks linking a progressive goal to completely different agendas held by other players; but it can pay dividends. It must serve the long-term agenda of people with lived experience, who repeatedly, historically, have come back to an ambition: not just better services, but a life of equality and full participation. There may be opportunities stemming from the high policy priority accorded to mental health by UK governments, particularly from 2014 onwards.

After a wave of activism it is easy to think a battle has been won. From the 1990s to the 2010s activists secured civil rights, a measure of voice and involvement and incremental reductions in discriminatory attitudes through campaigns like Time to Change. Yet history tells us that after Apartheid fell, de facto segregation and poverty of black people persisted; after the LGB movement in Britain gained an equal age of consent and equal marriage, homophobic bullying in schools persisted. In mental health, discriminatory legislation remains on the statute book (see Chapter 4); and the evidence that discrimination and exclusion persist is overwhelming. New waves of activism, with clear strategies and alliances, are both likely and needed.

Reflective Exercises

People with lived experience of mental health challenges have voiced concerns through history and at times come together to press strongly for greater citizenship opportunities. Can you identify learning from other groups of excluded or disenfranchised people that might be helpful to this endeavour? And is there a role for mental health services in enabling people to have a voice?

What do you think are the most important measures of progress: how do we know if citizenship opportunities are improving, and if discrimination is going down?

FURTHER RESEARCH AND READING

Survivors History website at http://studymore.org.uk/mpu.htm

- Includes a timeline, key figures and documents from the survivor movement in the UK, with links to other countries

Judi Chamberlin (1977). *On Our Own* (published by Mind 1988)

- Ground-breaking work from a survivor perspective, advocating consumer-run alternatives to psychiatric services. Influenced later survivor writers and activists

Pat Deegan at https://www.patdeegan.com/

- Has written powerful articles and blogs from a survivor perspective, including on recovery, independent living and links with the wider disability movement

Gail Hornstein (2012). *Agnes's Jacket.* PCCS Books. And website at http://www.madnessandliterature.org/Resources/bibliography-of-first-person-narratives-of-madness-5th-edition.pdf

- The book documents accounts by people of their experience of madness/mental illness – and seeks psychological explanations of the experience

- The website contains references to hundreds of first person narratives of madness – published, in autobiographies, websites and more

O'Hagan (2014) *Madness Made Me: A Memoir.* Openbox.

- A powerful memoir of madness, that replaces the language of psycho-pathology with the radical idea that there may be value in madness

Time to Change campaign at http://www.time-to-change.org.uk/

- Includes evidence from evaluations on how far attitudes and behaviours have changed towards people with mental health problems

- Includes links to anti-stigma campaigns in different countries at http://www.time-to-change.org.uk/news/global-meeting-anti-stigma-programme-london

3

Understanding the Problem, Understanding the Solution: Professional Models of Anti-Stigma Work

Chapter Summary

- The four drivers of stigma and discrimination
- The central role of power
- The hazards of the 'brain disease' model
- The risks of the individual growth model
- The importance of connecting, through common humanity

Introduction

> Depression isn't an emotion, it's a malfunction in the brain, as physical a reality as any other disease. You wouldn't tell someone with diabetes to stop taking the insulin. (Ruby Wax 2013).

It may seem intuitively plausible that comparing a mental to a physical illness will reduce the sting of stigma. Surely this comparison will mean those of us living with mental health challenges can acquire some of the relative positivity of arthritis or diabetes and benefit from greater parity between mental and physical ill-health.

It is plausible – but it is wrong.

> Biogenetic causal beliefs and diagnostic labelling as 'illness' are both positively related to perceptions of dangerousness and unpredictability, and to fear and desire for social distance. (Read et al. 2006).

A growing body of research finds that biological explanations of mental illness make the public more – not less – likely to experience fear, prejudice and desire for social distance.

To reduce discrimination requires more than good intentions or plausibility. It requires clarity about the conceptual models that best capture the causes and potential solutions to discrimination, and understandings from research and practice about 'what works'.

Ruby Wax herself has used her public position in ways that *are* likely to tackle discrimination effectively: setting up online peer support and speaking directly with large numbers of people in theatres across the land about her own experience, a type of 'contact on equal terms' which research shows does change attitudes (Hewstone 2003). But when she speaks in her comic repertoire of her genetic inheritance of depression from her mother, or presses for greater investment in brain research (see 'Ruby Wax tackles the black dog' – at http://www.mumsnet.com/bloggers/guest-blog-ruby-wax), she risks pulling people away from their (relatively benign) psycho-social explanations to biogenetic understandings which could entrench prejudice. The world is littered with examples like this of anti-stigma initiatives based on good intentions that have not – or not fully – met expectations (for example see Friedrich et al. 2013). What is needed is a clear understanding of what generates discrimination and how to break the cycle.

Understanding the drivers of stigma and discrimination

A seminal article by Link and Phelan (2001) proposed a major reconceptualisation of stigma. The term 'stigma' had been roundly criticised for focusing on the marked individual rather than the perpetrators of discrimination: by analogy we do not talk about the stigma of being black, or encourage people to break through stigma by talking about it; we discuss racism and how to make material change in people's lives, from employment to 'stop and search' (Sayce 1998; Sayce 2000). In response, Link and Phelan reconceptualised 'stigma' as the whole process of categorising and discriminating against people deemed 'different'. I use 'stigma' in this re-conceptualised sense.

Link and Phelan argue that stigma has four components:

1. Distinguishing between and labelling human difference
2. Linking the labelled person to undesirable characteristics
3. Separating 'them' (the labelled persons) from 'us', culminating in
4. Status loss and discrimination that lead to unequal outcomes or life chances.

The whole process is driven by power: 'Stigma is entirely dependent on social, economic and political power' (Link and Phelan 2001, p. 375). It is not enough, they argue, to label and disparage another group for them to become stigmatised: psychiatric service users may label some clinicians 'pill pushers', see them as cold, paternalistic and arrogant, and treat them differently from other clinicians. This does not make the clinicians a stigmatised group, because the patients 'simply do not possess the social, cultural, economic and political power to make their cognitions about staff have serious discriminatory consequences' (Ibid., p. 376). This analysis moves beyond the micro questions of cognitive processes to a much wider study of the social forces underpinning stigmatising attitudes and behaviours.

The vital question is what this means for selecting the most effective approaches to reverse the process.

Firstly, it is extremely unlikely that an approach will succeed without use of power. Not only would the patients in the example above be unable to stigmatise the clinicians: they would find it difficult in the extreme to resist being stigmatised by employers, the media, mental health services – unless they could mobilise power. In the 1990s the disability movement fought hard to replace a soft educational National Disability Council with a Disability Rights Commission (DRC) with legal powers – and won.

> The opening of the DRC is a truly historic day. Disabled people have waited a long time for this and finally have an independent and strong voice working on their behalf ... The government is delivering on its commitment to comprehensive and enforceable civil rights for disabled people and now the DRC will make sure that everyone else plays their part too. (David Blunkett, Secretary of State for Education and Employment, speech welcoming the opening of the Disability Rights Commission 19 August 2000. http://www.lgcplus.com/historic-day-as-disability-rights-commission-meets-to-prepare-for-launch/1382599.article).

The result was systemic changes stimulating equality – brought about by a judicious mix of legal powers and persuasion (see Chapter 6).

Power may derive from a social movement (witness the achievements of the environmental movement in shifting priorities of business and governments), law (think of the importance of American civil rights law in ending segregation in schools, universities, buses, lunch counters and so on), policy levers or financial incentives.

Power can be exercised by the state, through direct coercion, or a variety of behavioural 'nudges' (see Chapter 2). Citizens can assert power by lobbying government to change laws and policies or taking power into their own hands and demonstrating that different approaches work. They can exercise collective consumer power to influence business (witness boycotts of baby milk companies) or media: for instance, bombarding *The Sun* newspaper with complaints which led them to cut their 'Bonkers Bruno' headline part way through the day and replace it in the second edition by 'Sad Bruno in mental home' (Figure 3.1).

Figure 3.1 *The Sun*, 23 September 2003

A first task when planning anti-discrimination work is to decide the source of power and the target. The next question is which of the four components to disrupt. The first two components concern attitudes; the second two, behaviours. There is no need to work through them in sequence. Changed behaviour can lead to changed attitudes at least as much as vice versa (see Chapter 2).

It may be possible to go straight to component 4, omitting the first three altogether: for instance, a specific legislative change – such as removing the bar on people who have been sectioned being MPs – might be achievable without a widespread shift in societal attitudes.

To judge whether an initiative to overcome discrimination is likely to achieve its ends it is important to understand:

- Does it mobilise power?
- Does it reflect some or all of Link and Phelan's four components?
- Most importantly, does it disrupt unequal life chances and discrimination? (component 4). This must be the acid test of an anti-discrimination strategy: that it opens up participation opportunities that people can seize. In this sense I propose weighting the components: component four is most significant, but one to three may be important to disrupting it.

Successful movements for social change tend to combine use of overt power – for instance litigation, new legal rights – with cultural re-framing to achieve lasting changes in attitude and behaviour. In Martin Luther King's 'I Have a Dream' speech the positive image of black and white children being judged 'by the content of their character not the colour of their skin' drew support through its connotations of innocent harmony and justice. This discourse helped build the wider support necessary both to secure civil rights law and ensure its implementation. More recently the UK's LGB community campaigned successfully for civil partnership through high-profile advocates (such as Elton John and partner David Furnish) and a targeted legislative campaign. Once secured, every civil partnership became an opportunity to invite people to share the celebration – of the couple's commitment and often also the overthrow of injustice. This so reinforced the positivity of change that by 2013 a Conservative prime minister was able to drive through gay marriage – not just civil partnership – by framing it in terms of support for 'commitment, in society'.

Movement leaders focused both their legislative campaigns and shift of discourse with enormous care. During the first decade of the 21st century, public attitudes towards gay equality changed significantly. Legislative change – civil partnerships, an equal age of consent, gay marriage – was backed by communications strategies that 'framed' the change in terms that resonated with the public: commitment, contribution and freedom from bullying. Such significant change would not have occurred with only a communications campaign, or only legislative strategy.

To overcome discrimination often requires an iron fist in a velvet glove, deployed in differing balance depending on the change targeted. It also requires careful attention to Link and Phelan's components of stigma.

In 2000, I identified four common models of anti-stigma work: the brain disease, individual growth, libertarian and disability inclusion models (Sayce 2000). These models are all still used and evolving. In addition a fifth model has emerged, in the context of policies to address 'austerity': social security protection. This chapter and the next two discuss these models and how they are used, and assess how well they use power and address the drivers of discrimination in ways likely to reduce unequal life chances.

The brain disease model

From the 1970s onwards, biological explanations of mental illness overtook psychoanalytic models in professional discourse and training (Burns 2013). By the 1990s biology became for the first time a powerful underpinning of anti-stigma work:

> Open Your Minds: Mental Illnesses are Brain Diseases.

Thus ran a prominent 1990s American campaign led by the National Alliance for the Mentally Ill, the main American relatives' organisation. At the core of their anti-stigma message was the notion that a brain disease is 'no fault': not a moral weakness, not the fault of the parents, not caused by the environment. Instead it can be understood at the level of physiology: it is morally neutral. This brought relief to parents who in some cases had felt professionally blamed, the implication being that faulty parenting had generated madness.

> I tell my wife it's a brain disease. It's nobody's fault. You're a good woman.
> (National Alliance for the Mentally Ill video 1993).

People with lived experience may also appreciate the removal of moral taint. At a 2013 Royal College of Psychiatrists conference, a London consultant described successfully countering a local view that mental illness meant possession by djin, or evil spirits, through the argument that 'this is a chemical imbalance, something that happens, like diabetes'.

The brain disease anti-stigma message has continued unabated since the 1990s. Sometimes there is an explicit or implicit statement that the 'solution' to stigma is to seek biological treatment. For instance:

So before I start, I would like to thank the makers of Lamotrigine, Sertraline, and Reboxetine, because without those few simple chemicals, I would not be vertical today. (Ruby Wax 2012).

The Australian Beyond Blue anti-stigma campaign, now operating in several countries including the UK, promotes the message that depression is more than just a low mood – it's a serious illness, linked to many factors including genes (see www.beyondblue.org.au).

Undoubtedly for some people biological explanations satisfy a need to understand difficult experience. They 'fit' – or come to fit – with pre-existing world views. For others the message may be an imposition of a less welcome conceptual model.

Author Will Self describes being prescribed selective serotonin re-uptake inhibitors (SSRIs), accompanied by the reassuring message from a trusted GP that 'they worked'. He later read the evidence that SSRIs for many depressed people work no better than placebo and address a supposed chemical imbalance for which there is no evidence:

> it's essentially bunk: no fixed correlation has been established, despite intensive study, between levels of serotonin in the brain and depression. (Self 2013).

He critiques the over-use of anti-depressants – 46.7 million prescriptions in the UK by 2011 – and the role of pharmaceutical companies that fund the research into their own products, promote recognition in diagnostic manuals of a growing number of mental illnesses requiring treatment (from ADHD to oppositional defiance disorder), and expand the numbers of people affected under each category. Goldacre (2012) analyses how pharmaceutical companies selectively promote findings to demonstrate treatment effectiveness, using methods like suppression of negative studies, multiple publication of positive studies and hiding unhelpful data. Self continues:

> What has made it possible for someone recently bereaved or unemployed to have a prescription written by their doctor to alleviate their 'depression' is, I would argue, very much to do with psychiatry's search for new worlds to conquer, an expedition that has been financed at every step by big pharma.

He argues that as psychiatrists found themselves unable to identify medical 'cures' for severe mental health conditions they turned their attention to ever-increasing numbers of people with lesser levels of distress. Self asks: 'What, in essence, do psychiatrists specialise in, if not mind-altering drugs?'

What has this development got to do with combating stigma and discrimination?

The NAMI Open Our Minds campaign was funded by the Eli Lilly marketing department. There is money and power behind the message that mental illnesses are biological phenomena, requiring a 'solution' of medication (perhaps combined with other therapies). As the President of the American Psychiatric Association put it:

> As we address these Big Pharma issues, we must examine the fact that as a profession, we have allowed the bio-psycho-social model to become the bio-bio-bio model. (cited in Read et al. 2006).

A related message is that stigma must be overcome – so people are not deterred from seeking help. The focus may not be quite so explicitly biological, but is still narrowly set on help or treatment. For example, Cole-King (2013) wrote 'stigma kills' – because it stops people seeking help when they may be suicidal: 'We want to tackle stigma so people feel free to access the support'. She talks of 'confronting an epidemic of depression' (Cole-King 2013a) and has developed resources for people who feel suicidal that include messages such as '[health services] can offer you any medical treatment you might need' (Cole-King 2013b).

The aim of enabling people to talk about feeling suicidal is unarguably positive. However, as an approach to combating stigma or even reducing suicide it is decidedly narrow. Repeated studies show that people with mental health challenges experience stigma as worse than the original problem not primarily because they cannot seek help – often they are in touch with mental health services – but because of the exclusion they experience once diagnosed, including rejections by family and friends, loss of employment, loss of social status and discrimination by the mental health services themselves (Social Exclusion Unit 2004; Henderson and Thornicroft 2013). Moreover, these consequences of discrimination – being out of work and isolated – are significant risk factors for suicide (Blakeley et al. 2003; Mental Health Foundation 2010). An evidence-based suicide prevention strategy would seek to reduce stigma so people with mental health problems can build positive, participative, connected lives, not just 'seek help'.

There is a strong paradigm in anti-stigma work that says mental illness is an illness, the answer is treatment and we must break down stigma so that people avail themselves of the help. The English Time to Change campaign influenced an increase in media articles about mental health promotion – including the message that people can seek help – but no increase in articles about justice or injustice. The narrative about help-seeking has become so well established that it is 'easy' for journalists and anti-stigma campaigners alike.

It could be argued that this well-worn narrative hardly matters, if it contributes some drops to an anti-discrimination stream. However, recent evidence shows that the 'mental illness is an illness like any other' message is actively damaging to the anti-discrimination cause, in several ways.

Firstly, it is somewhat naive to think that physical health problems attract no discrimination and that greater parity would in itself solve the problem. From leprosy to cancer and HIV, stigma has attached itself to physical health problems through the ages. In 2005 after much lobbying the UK Government strengthened anti-discrimination protections for people with cancer and MS from the point of diagnosis, through the Disability Discrimination Act 2005 – because of evidence of discrimination these groups experienced in areas from employment to insurance. In 2010 the Government accepted there should be no pre-job offer health questions, following joint lobbying by Macmillan Cancer Care, National Aids Trust, Radar and Rethink. A physical illness or impairment is no protection against discrimination.

Secondly, the association between a mental health condition and biological illness tends to entrench stigma and discrimination. A disease of the brain – in particular – implies people are unable to take responsibility.

Read et al. (2006) reviewed peer-reviewed literature on biogenetic explanations of schizophrenia. They found biogenetic beliefs make the public more – not less – likely to believe the person is unpredictable and dangerous; more likely to experience prejudice and fear; more likely to desire social distance from the person affected; and more likely to behave in a harsh or punitive way towards them. Perhaps encouragingly, the public internationally still tended to prefer psychosocial explanations; and to believe that the behaviours of schizophrenia had some meaning that could not be reduced to symptoms of illness alone. However, agreement with biogenetic explanations was rising. Clinicians were more likely to believe the 'illness' paradigm than the public.

This may suggest that anti-stigma campaigns using the illness paradigm are an attempt by clinicians to persuade the public to adopt their interpretation; and that they are in part succeeding.

Both Read et al. (2006) and Sayce (2000) note that many anti-stigma initiatives use attitude measures that include endorsement of the 'illness' or 'disease' model as a supposed positive. In England, public belief in the 'illness' paradigm has been taking increasing hold (see Chapter 2). In reality this is likely to suggest an increase in damaging attitudes. A disease of the brain may suggest to others an impairment in judgement, autonomy, ability to control feelings and behaviours – with the potential result that those affected are more likely to be avoided, to be seen as completely 'other' and given fewer opportunities and responsibilities.

It is particularly concerning that the illness message increases the desire for social distance. Social distance is at the heart of discrimination (Thornicroft 2006) – by distancing, you make people 'other' and exclude them. Conversely, social proximity – for instance, engaging together on common goals – has positive effects in reducing prejudice (Hewstone 2003). The illness message risks reducing the very thing known to overcome discrimination – contact.

These risks were noted as long ago as 1981:

> The notion that psychological problems are similar to physical ailments creates the image of some phenomenon over which afflicted individuals have no control and thereby renders their behaviour apparently unpredictable. Such a viewpoint makes the 'mentally ill' seem just as alien to today's normal populace as the witches seemed to fifteenth century Europeans. (Bale 1981 – cited in Read et al. 2006).

Further studies have reinforced Read et al.'s (2006) concerns in relation to people with a range of psychiatric diagnoses, including depression and bipolar disorder.

Phelan (2005) found a belief in genetic explanations of schizophrenia or depression was associated in the public with more recommendations for hospitalisation and prescribed medication – but not seeing a therapist, psychiatrist or GP – and more pessimism about outcomes of treatment. There was a sense that the illness was serious, persistent, needed the most extreme or biological forms of treatment – but even with such treatment, success was unlikely. This suggests that if these beliefs took further hold there could be an increased expectation that people who are genetically different should be separated from the community and hospitalised; and a wider sense that there is little to be done.

Link (2011) found that the American public has become increasingly likely to believe that mental health problems are biological illnesses and that those affected should take prescribed medication: 92% thought people with schizophrenia should take medication in 2006, up from 83% in 1996; 65% thought this of people who are troubled in 2006, up from 53% in 1996. This suggests 'a broad sweeping change in public attitudes in the United States'. This could potentially drive an increased public appetite for psychiatrists to require people to take their medication; and there is indeed a trend towards increases in compulsory treatment in some countries (see Chapter 2).

During the same period Link found a small increase in the proportion of Americans thinking people with schizophrenia are violent (from 61% to 63%) and a decrease in those believing people with schizophrenia are able to decide about managing their money (from 30% to 27%). The change in core beliefs about the nature and causes of mental illness from 1996 to 2006 had facilitated help-seeking. Yet there had been no changes in negative stereotypes about violence; and beliefs in incompetence had become stronger. He concludes:

> We cannot address these problems through the message we have already delivered ... that mental illnesses are illnesses with biological and genetic causes that can be treated ... such messages do not solve the problems of stereotyping and discrimination. ... A strong and effective response to the stigma and discrimination associated with mental illness lies before us. (Link 2011).

Phelan (2005) found that genetic explanations increased the public's view not only that the problem (of depression or schizophrenia) was serious, but also that siblings would be affected. The transmissibility to siblings meant increased social distance from the (unaffected) sibling, especially with respect to intimate relationships: dating, marriage and having children. Siblings could be affected by taint and rejection even if they never experienced any mental health problem.

Although there was some evidence of reduced blame towards the individual directly affected, Phelan found little evidence that genetic explanations would reduce stigma:

> The most prominent expectation about the consequences of geneticisation is that it will reduce stigma, and public education campaigns and direct-to-consumer advertising currently promote the idea that mental illnesses are biologically based. The present findings do not confirm these positive expectations, and enthusiasm for this idea and practices based upon it should be re-evaluated.

Pescosolido et al. (2010) found that biological explanations increased public support for treatment but also increased stigma and community rejection.

The overall message from research is that the prominent biological narrative seems to support help-seeking – but intensifies stigma and discrimination. Whilst biological and genetic explanations may have had certain very modest benefits – possibly a reduction in blame (although this is not a consistent finding) – this is hugely outweighed by the damage these messages create. It may be no coincidence that anti-stigma campaigns led by clinicians and sometimes funded by pharmaceutical interests have focused primarily on reducing stigma to increase help-seeking. This has worked – but at the expense of backsliding in terms of social distance and exclusion.

The individual growth model

This model, far from emphasising biogenetic difference, tears down or minimises disease categories in favour of a continuum between mental health and distress. Most if not all of us experience distress, it argues, and can grow through it, to maximise our well-being. Stigma will be overcome as the population becomes more emotionally literate, more able to grow emotionally and spiritually, and stops seeing 'mental illness' as a problem experienced by other people. As the Time to Change campaign puts it (Figure 3.2):

Figure 3.2 Encouraging open conversation

Time to Change also emphasises the commonness of distress:

> One in five people have dandruff, one in four people have a mental health problem. I've had both.

The risks of a focus on 'individual growth'

From an anti-discrimination perspective there can be difficulties with the pure 'continuum', from mental health problems at one end to positive health at the other.

Firstly, it may entrench the very idea of polarity between positive health and intractable negatives of ill-health that the model supposedly disrupts. If one finds oneself at the 'lack of health' end of the continuum it is unclear why one would derive value simply from being 'on the continuum', any more than the pupil with the lowest marks in a class that values high marks would feel valued because she is 'in the class'.

The continuum model suggests that if you have a significant mental health condition you lack well-being, or quality of life; you would need to move 'up' the continuum to achieve them. This is the kind of assumption that leads to placing lesser value on the life of someone with, say, schizophrenia than other citizens. NICE (National Institute for Health and Clinical Excellence) measures the benefit of particular treatments in terms of the 'quality adjusted life years' (QALYs) likely to ensue post-treatment. Each year lived with perfect health is assigned the value of one. If the person has weaker health the value of each year lived drops, down to a minimum of zero for the person who is dead. If the extra years would not be lived in full health – for example, if the patient would lose a limb, or have a major mental health problem – then the extra life-years are given a value between zero and one – or in some cases, below zero (i.e. the life is viewed as being of less value than being dead). If some citizens' lives are defined as lower quality, then – put bluntly – it may be considered less worthwhile to treat them. At the extreme this attitude has underpinned the practice of placing 'do not resuscitate' notices on the notes of people with Down's syndrome or schizophrenia (DRC 2006).

Thus this version of a 'continuum' can lead to blatant discrimination.

People with physical impairments have argued vehemently against the assumption that impairment entails a lesser quality of life:

> I do not accept imagery, and heroic stories, that suggest my life is worth living only if I 'walk again'; I want to be accepted as I am. (Wheelchair user, cited in Sayce 2000).

Baroness Jane Campbell, who has a significant physical impairment and uses a ventilator, encountered an assumption from doctors – as though it was utterly obvious – that she would not want to be resuscitated if she stopped breathing. She describes trying to stay awake in hospital to keep safe; her husband was so concerned he put a picture of Jane receiving her degree above her bed, to demonstrate to staff the true nature of her life. Later, in an interview in the *Guardian* she described squashing an amendment in the House of Lords that would have made it easier to support disabled people to die:

> Some of the debaters talked about how terrible it must be to have someone else
> take you to the toilet. That's my life, mate! And I hate the term 'vulnerable people'.
> It sets the image up before they find out what you're really like. Really I'm bossy,
> I'm ambitious and have ants in my pants, and am excited about things and people.
> I love ideas. I love life. (Baroness Jane Campbell, *Guardian*, 11 July 2009).

It is eminently possible to have a significant impairment and very positive quality of life. The mental health 'recovery' movement emphasises the value of life WITH a mental health challenge – rather than assuming that life becomes more valuable the more the mental health problem is reduced.

> Recovery in mental health is not about waiting for the storm to be over. It is
> about learning to dance in the rain. (Peer recovery trainer, Central and North West
> London Recovery College, cited by Perkins 2014).

This particular set of problems with the 'continuum' model can be addressed by ditching the single continuum in favour of two cross-cutting axes (see Figure 3.3):

- from no impairment to a significant impairment/health condition and
- from positive to negative well-being.

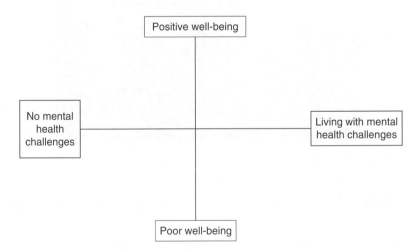

Figure 3.3 Analysing well-being and mental health challenges

On this model, a single individual can have both a significant impairment AND very positive well-being, or indeed no impairment and terrible well-being (Downie et al. 1990).

The second drawback with the individual growth approach is that whilst the notion that we all experience distress may be true, it is a statement so general and woolly as to mask highly significant differences that are crucial in anti-discrimination work. Some anti-stigma campaigns have focused so powerfully on common experiences (like understandable 'depression') that these are de-stigmatised at the expense of people who do have frightening experiences of madness. At worst such campaigns give airtime only to people who are 'normal-acting' – who seem 'just like you and me' but have had a bit of a bad time – and not to the person with a diagnosis of schizophrenia or personality disorder.

The first stage of the New Zealand Like Minds Like Mine Campaign deliberately aimed to de-stigmatise depression, drawing on the personal testimony of national rugby hero John Kirwan. Kirwan later wrote a powerful account of his own depression (Kirwan 2010). The result of this first stage was improved attitudes towards people diagnosed with depression – but not schizophrenia. Between 1999 and 2004 the New Zealand public became significantly more likely to view depression as a mental illness than schizophrenia (Fearn and Wyllie 2005).

In effect, mental health problems are de-stigmatised by steering public attention away from the more frightening diagnoses like schizophrenia towards the more understandable experience of depression.

One problem with this is the public often does not extend its acceptance of depression to madness. A very early anti-stigma campaign using the continuum model was rejected out of hand by the local community because they simply did not believe that normal and abnormal behaviour fell within a continuum (Cumming and Cumming 1957). When campaigns de-stigmatise 'ordinary' mental distress they can inadvertently reinforce the 'otherness' of the 'really mad'.

Like Minds later addressed this weakness by focusing specifically on busting myths about schizophrenia, including through a competition for advertisers. The winning entry is below, shown on billboards and websites in late 2013 (Figure 3.4):

Figure 3.4 Empathy with the experience of schizophrenia
Source: James Allan, 'reTHiNK', 'Mind and Body' and 'Like Minds, Like Mine'

The percentage of the public willing to accept someone with schizophrenia rose between 2000 and 2011:

- as a workmate, from 55% to 66%
- as a local half-way house resident from 51% to 60% and
- as a babysitter, from 11% to 23%.

(Wyllie and Lauder 2012).

It seems likely that this positive change reflects a deliberate move away from the 'mental illness is common' message, with its overwhelming emphasis on depression, to a more inclusive message that tackles more severe aspects of discrimination.

John Kirwan himself has taken care to be inclusive – by moving away from the safe language of ordinary distress:

> I've been loopy. I'm not frightened of being loopy ... I'm gloriously imbalanced. (Hewiston 2013).

A third problem with the 'individual growth' model is that it can imply that it is individuals and families who hold responsibility for change. We can all, it is argued, improve our own health. The corollary unfortunately can be blaming people for their cancer, diabetes – or depression, in a 'negative responsibilisation of health' (see Chapter 2).

Wide inequalities impact severely on mental health. Wilkinson's cross-national analysis of large datasets shows the powerful impact of high inequality on health – often via the intermediate variable of mental stress or distress. Once you use mental health services, inequality grows. You have a one in three chance of losing contact with friends; only about a 15% chance of being in employment; and are likely to die younger. Holt-Lunstad et al. (2010) found that people with adequate social relationships have a 50% higher chance of survival than people with poor social relationships: this effect on mortality is comparable to quitting smoking and exceeds many well-known risk factors such as physical inactivity and obesity.

It is dangerous to imply that individuals facing this type of exclusion can simply 'grow' their way to health in the face of such macro-factors.

Since Rosalind Coward (1989) wrote a searing critique of the alternative health movement and its potential to generate blame of the unwell, people with problems from cancer to schizophrenia have spoken out on the pain caused by this blame game. They have to use precious energy disputing the idea that they have somehow brought the ill-health on themselves through a combination of repressed emotion, poor lifestyle or inharmonious relationships.

There has been a growth of evidence and policy on 'well-being', with Health and Well-being Boards established across England and repeat surveys of the reported well-being of the population. Popularly known as the 'happiness index', this showed in 2013 that well-being had risen slightly in the UK since 2011–12. However, a generalised improvement masked major differentials. The areas with lowest levels of well-being included the North East, Stoke on Trent and Blackburn with Darwen – in all cases areas of high unemployment. Areas with high well-being – like Dorset, Bath and NE Somerset – all had low unemployment (ONS 2013). Critics have therefore argued that measuring well-being is no substitute for measuring inequality. Objective measures – for instance, inequality of life expectancy – are at least as important as how people 'feel'. Indeed, the fact that some people living impoverished lives have come to accept their lot does not mean society should sit back complacently. And even in an area like Dorset, inequalities in income and power will impact negatively on health; but may be missed in the generality. Overall, the focus on well-being may mask structural inequalities and their impact.

Fourthly, the individual growth model is often promoted by people seeking to purvey a plethora of psychological and spiritual treatments to ever larger numbers of people. Recent examples include baking therapy (provided via special health bakeries to help people with problems like depression, *Independent on Sunday*, 27 October 2013) and ecotherapy (a blend of psychotherapy and contact with nature, promoted by Mind in 2013). The survivor movement has long objected to turning ordinary activities into therapies with psychological experts to lead them: it is possible to bake bread, derive strength from nature or create art without a 'therapist'. Indeed, when art becomes therapy, it can disempower. One talented artist working in a special hospital was told she could not sell her work because, as art therapy, it was part of her medical notes and belonged to the hospital. Turning activities into therapies changes the power relationship.

Promoting therapies is not so very different from promoting medication in terms of how far it addresses discrimination: neither tackles the structural sources of discrimination; both focus narrowly on 'treatment' to 'improve' your health, rather than changing the world around you; and both risk de-powering you. The growth message may persuade more and more people to seek help; but once they have sought help they are still subject to exclusion by friends, employers and health staff.

The potential – and risks – of ditching identity politics

Despite these significant objections, since 2000 certain developments may hint that we should not completely discard the aim of challenging the very notion of the difference of madness.

Identity politics may be on the decline – replaced by a more dynamic understanding of 'superdiversity'.

There is growing evidence that disability and health conditions are dynamic: there is not one group of people who are 'disabled', another 'non-disabled'. In 2013 the UK Government published a compendium of evidence which found that 19% of the population was covered by the Equality Act definition of disability and most went in and out of the experience: only 2% were born with their impairment. Identity is fluid: only 24% of 'disabled people' consider themselves 'disabled'. Increasingly people experience more than one impairment: indeed the number of people with three or more impairments was set to rise by a third by 2018. So there is not a group of 'blind' people, another of 'people with mental health problems': multiple experiences overlap. Families are increasingly multiply affected: for instance, nearly half of disabled children live with a disabled parent (ODI 2013).

This picture is echoed in relation to other aspects of identity; and the trend to more fluid and less categorised identity just might give grounds to hope that old categories could shift. Fanshawe and Sriskandarajah (2010) argue that Britain is becoming super-diverse: not only more diverse than ever before, but diversity itself is also growing more diverse. Ever-growing numbers of people live in families of mixed racial, cultural and religious heritage: for instance, one in eight couples have different religious affiliations. They often feel 'boxed in' by the census categories that give no space for (for instance) people of Southeast Asian and African descent, or Muslim and Catholic parents. With increasing mobility – for instance, Polish people went from the 13th most common foreign-born group in the UK to the most common in just four years (2004–8) – our understanding of the make-up of the country is undergoing rapid change. The old identities simply do not hold. Many young people – and more people overall – have both same-sex and opposite-sex relationships but may not feel a need to identify neatly as gay, straight or even bisexual. Identities are shifting, with more fluid interests and allegiances.

If recognition grows that our categories 'do not hold', there may be an opportunity to open discussion of a plethora of different mental health experiences, rather than a sharp divide between the ill and the well; or a linear 'continuum'. Rather than talk of schizophrenia and depression, perhaps we could seriously explore our wide spectrum of specific experiences – from hearing voices to unusual fears, from feeling blank to feeling euphoric.

Just as ethnic super-diversity might take us away from believing there is one central 'majority' group surrounded by several 'minorities', like satellites, perhaps we could think not of 'normal' thoughts and feelings at the centre and different forms of 'madness' at the edges – but rather of multiple different cognitive and emotional experiences, with no central 'norm'. We might focus on the fluidity of the experience – the fact that, as for 'disability' overall, people go in and out of different experiences, we are not 'mad' or 'sane' or even on a continuum between the two.

In 2012 Andrew McDonald, a senior civil servant, spoke about an experience that convinced him we should abandon the overly sharp distinction between disabled and non-disabled people. Sitting in a New York bar, he noticed his hand was not quite working. He thought nothing of it. His life remained unchanged until he was eventually diagnosed with parkinsonism. He felt a wall come down between his past life and his (non) future. As with the experience of receiving a psychiatric diagnosis he felt his life was over. He concluded that 'our land is your land'; we should abandon overly sharp distinctions, understand how many of us go in and out of different experiences, and view disability as part of human life – not a life apart.

On this argument we could endeavour to replace a polarity *or* a continuum (between sanity and madness) with a scattering or spectrum of different experiences, all interesting and part of human life.

> Eventually the folly of all this will dawn on people and we shall all joyously realise that we are all abnormal, disabled, impaired, deformed and functionally limited, because, truth be told, that is what it means to be a human being. (Bickenbach 1999).

We might see that a norm of perfection is an illusion – and that so-called imperfections are what makes us strong as a community.

In principle this trend could be reinforced by the passage in Britain of the Human Rights Act 1998 and Equality Act 2010: no longer do we have numerous pieces of separate legislation reinforcing the politics of different identities (gender, race, disability), but the beginning of an approach based on human rights and equality for all. 'Beginning' is the word, as the Equality Act still requires you to demonstrate that you fit the 'disabled' category to qualify for protection from disability discrimination.

Whilst this emphasis on common humanity has attractions, it is set against the persistent human tendency to make sense of the world by categorising. This enables people to think quickly – by placing a new person or experience into a category (McGarty et al. 2002). In this sense the tendency to stereotype is hard-wired. Identity may be shifting – but that may just mean we have new categories rather than the old ones. Public beliefs about the category of people needing help with mental health challenges has changed: it has grown larger, and is understood more in biological terms. A change in how particular identities are boundaried and understood still persistently leaves out-groups.

The well-being agenda (see above) may have potential to mitigate discrimination, if – and only if – it addresses structural inequality and power. A renewed policy emphasis on public health from 2012 placed some emphasis on 'jobs, decent homes and companionship' – alongside individuals' own lifestyle choices (Duncan Selbie Friday Message 25 October 2013). It remains to be seen in a time of growing inequality whether this will result in substantive change in employment and housing. In mental health services, the growth of recovery-focused practice has brought an increasing emphasis on living well WITH a mental health problem (rather than assuming the only hope available is to get rid of the symptoms).

> Recovery is ... a personal journey of discovery: making sense of, and finding meaning in, what has happened; discovering your own resources, resourcefulness and possibilities; building a new sense of self, meaning and purpose in life; growing within and beyond what has happened to you; and pursuing your dreams and ambitions. The challenge for services is to assist people in their journey. (Perkins 2012).

Some companies have used well-being strategies as a way to arm both managers and employees – with or without mental health conditions – with useful tools. BT, for instance, introduced its policies on mental health by talking about stress, to emphasise the relevance to everyone; but the tools themselves placed responsibilities on managers, enabling them to understand the workplace adjustments that could – and legally should – be made for people with the whole gamut of mental health issues. Noticeably the use of power in this case relied on 'disability' legislation as well as organisational power: which suggests at this point in history the category of disability is needed in addition to appeals to shared experiences of 'stress'.

All these developments suggest there may be mileage for anti-discrimination work in drawing people in to understand our super-diverse humanity, and the wide range of experiences it contains – 'forget your perfect offering, there is a crack in everything', as Leonard Cohen put it in 'Anthem'.

If we stressed both our common humanity and our real differences and fluidity of experience, that could be profound.

In relation to Link and Phelan's components of stigma, the individual growth model attempts something very challenging – to overcome the very first component, 'distinguishing between and labelling human difference'. It is challenging because the way that human beings make sense of the world is by categorising; and changing our categories of identity is likely still to leave out-groups.

It may therefore be easier to revalue difference (to address component 2, to say madness is interesting or that people with mental health challenges make great contributions) rather than to assert that there is no such thing as 'normal', with no more difference between 'mad' and 'sane' behaviour than between all our other differences and fluctuations. This latter narrative is attractive – but history tells us madness tends to be categorised; the narrative may not be readily adopted. It is not easy to imagine public recognition of mad behaviour as just another different human experience, with no norm to compare it to.

There is no evidence as yet that this approach has actually reduced the stigma attached to people undergoing extremes of experience, or with diagnoses like schizophrenia or personality disorder; or any evidence such categories are being seriously re-cast (despite academic attempts: see, for instance, the work of Richard Bentall, who has long argued that schizophrenia is a construct without validity, based on a fairly arbitrary clustering of experiences or 'symptoms'). The endeavour of replacing differences of identity (mad or sane; service users or professionals) with differences of experience is vitally worth exploring. It could enable a much deeper appreciation of common humanity, with ever-changing and varied experiences. And moving away from the inexact categorisation of diagnosis would help.

Nonetheless, given the persistent human tendency to categorise, and the relative lack of power behind the super-diversity narrative, it would be highly risky to rely on super-diversity as a sufficient strategy to reduce discrimination.

CONCLUSION

The 'brain disease' model does not match the requirements of Link and Phelan's model for reversing the cycle of stigma and discrimination. It uncritically distinguishes between and labels human difference (component 1), and goes on (component 2) to link the labelled person to supposedly more desirable characteristics (they are just 'ill'). However, it is clear from research that the brain disease conception is NOT more desirable than other conceptions – it is fraught with difficulty, it increases the desire for social distance and a belief in incapacity. The model does nothing to overcome separation between 'them' and 'us' – in fact it may make it worse – and nothing to stop status loss and unequal life chances. It does of course mobilise power – the fifth requirement. But it is the power of vested interests, the financial and political power of large pharmaceutical and clinical interests to set a new narrative that is likely to increase use of their services and products, but not enable people facing discrimination to improve life chances. In effect it uses power to questionable ends.

The growing hold of the 'brain disease' model in the public's mind has been associated with an increase in help-seeking, but at the expense of entrenching discrimination.

The brain disease model and its variants – any that assume a biological explanation will reduce discrimination – should not be used as a message in anti-discrimination work. This is not to argue that we should suppress evidence of the biological aspects of our being, or airbrush genetics out of our discourse – but that we should resist the blandishments that these messages are a panacea for stigma. They are not. They do more harm than good.

The 'individual growth' model attempts to disrupt the very first of Link and Phelan's components – differentiating between different human experiences. It has a number of significant drawbacks. Using a simple 'continuum' model of distress risks de-valuing people at its less 'healthy' end and de-stigmatising some experiences of mental health challenges at the expense of others. The model risks blaming people for their own experiences and missing the structural determinants of discrimination. There are particular risks in downplaying difference: for instance, suggesting we all experience distress on a continuum is likely to be interpreted in terms of 'us' (the people we identify with – perhaps slightly expanded), in contrast to the 'really mad' people.

Some of these risks can be mitigated; and there is new potential in the erosion of 'identity politics', in favour of a deep acceptance of both common humanity and multiple differences of experience. However, with categorisation hard-wired into human thinking, it would be unwise to rely on super-diversity of experience as the one way to reduce discrimination: it would require people not just to re-draw boundaries around 'mad' experiences but actually to get rid of the whole concept of a norm from which madness can be judged.

There is one further weakness in this approach. It mobilises little power; and where it does, it is partly the power of psychological treatment providers (as opposed to the pharmaceutical and medical interests behind the brain disease model). Serious attempts to reduce discrimination should not be co-opted by interests purely trying to peddle one type of therapy or another.

Other models, with more rights behind them, must also be considered, and these are the subject of the following chapters.

Reflective Exercises

Do you think biological explanations or human growth explanations will be more acceptable to some communities in Britain than others? What implications might that have for anti-discrimination work?

Have a look at the messages of anti-stigma campaigns like Beyond Blue and Time to Change. Do you think they are likely to reduce discrimination, and if so, why?

FURTHER READING AND RESEARCH

Link, B. G. and Phelan, J. C. (2001) 'On the Nature and Consequences of Stigma', *Annual Review of Sociology*, 27, pp. 363–385.

- An overarching analysis of the drivers of stigma and discrimination and the power underpinning it

Read, J., Haslam, N., Davies, E. and Sayce, L. (2006) 'Prejudice and Schizophrenia: A Review of the "mental illness is an illness like any other" Approach', *Acta Psychiatr Scand.* November 114, 5, pp. 303–318.

- A review of international literature finding that the 'mental illness' message has counter-productive effects

Sayce, L. (2003) 'Beyond Good Intentions: Making Anti-discrimination Strategies Work', *Disability and Society.* 18, 5, pp. 625–642.

- A discussion of effective and less effective strategies to tackle discrimination and exclusion

Not Dead Yet at http://www.notdeadyetuk.org/

- The UK campaign by disabled people against devaluing disabled people's lives and against assisted suicide

Repper, J. and Perkins, R. (2003) *Social Inclusion and Recovery: A Model for Mental Health Practice.* Edinburgh: Bailliere Tindall

- A book that links 'recovery' to the goal of social inclusion and rights

Like Minds Like Mine – New Zealand anti-stigma campaign. At http://www.likeminds.org.nz/

4 | Activists' Models of Anti-Discrimination Work

Chapter Summary

- The libertarian model
- The growing use of coercive powers
- The discriminatory use of risk assessments
- Libertarian analysis and campaigns
- New social security campaigns
- Risks of paternalism and 'writing people off'
- The need for a longer-term vision of participation, with bridge building between activists

The libertarian model

People with a diagnosis of mental illness, unlike other citizens, are in the extraordinary position that they can be forced to accept medication against their will – even when they have the capacity to decide for themselves; and can be deprived of their liberty on the grounds of putative future violence, rather than crimes actually committed. In the case of people with mental health conditions, the diagnosis itself brings a different set of rules, thresholds of risk and permitted actions, which can lead to outright coercion. The presence of these different rules is itself discriminatory. As psychiatrist Tony Zigmund put it:

> Suppose I have two patients, one with schizophrenia and one with cancer. Both patients recognise that they are ill, that their illnesses can be treated and that there would be consequences to not receiving treatment. They both have the same understanding of their illness and the proposed treatment – in legal terms they are both capable. The patient with cancer may refuse my treatment and if I go ahead with it I will be committing an assault. But I will have a legal duty to impose treatment on the patient with schizophrenia ... If my patient has both conditions he will be able to refuse treatment for the cancer but not for the schizophrenia. This is unfair, absurd and makes the mentally ill lesser citizens.
> (Dr Tony Zigmund, writing in the *Independent* 30 June 2002).

The essence of the libertarian position is that people with mental health challenges should not be deprived of liberty or the right to accept or refuse treatment on grounds that include presence of mental disorder. They should experience such deprivation only on an equal basis with other citizens – and extremely rarely. For instance, if other citizens can be medically treated without consent only when they are unable to understand information, make and assert choices, and only if every effort has been made to enable them to have a voice (advocacy, advanced decision-making) – then the same should apply to people with mental health conditions. It should make no legal difference whether the difficulty in making decisions derives from delirium, drunkenness, unconsciousness or psychosis: the same framework for decision-making should apply. Otherwise, as the Disability Rights Commission put it, laws permitting discriminatory decision-making render one group of people (those with psychiatric impairments) 'lesser citizens' (DRC 2002).

In 2014, this argument was endorsed in a statement from the UN High Commission on Human Rights, which said 'liberty and security of the person is one of the most precious rights to which everyone is entitled' and explained 'the absolute prohibition of detention on the basis of disability'. Some states, they noted, had mental health laws that used actual or perceived disability (including mental illness) as one of the grounds for detention; but 'this practice is incompatible with article 14 as interpreted by the jurisprudence of the Convention on the Rights of Persons with Disabilities committee' (article 14 of the UN Convention requires non-discrimination).

On this analysis the UK's mental health laws are in breach of the Convention and there is no place for distinct mental health law – it is discriminatory per se, as it allows and even requires state intervention for reasons that include the presence of mental illness.

Psychiatrist George Szmukler argues that mental health laws governing involuntary treatment fail to respect the autonomy of people with a mental illness (in contrast to people with a physical illness); and allow a form of preventive detention on the basis of 'risk', without any offence having been committed. These laws thus exemplify assumptions that people with mental disorders are not fully self-determining and are inherently dangerous, the very assumptions underpinning discrimination through history (see Chapter 1). He argues instead for a law based on capacity, whatever the cause (Szmukler 2010).

This argument is given particular salience by the growing use of coercion under mental health law, especially in England. The Care Quality Commission (2015) found the Mental Health Act was used 53,176 times to detain people compulsorily in 2013–14 for over 72 hours, 30% more frequently than in 2003–04. Community treatment orders (CTOs) were introduced in 2008 on the theory that they would enable liberty: numbers compulsorily detained in hospital would fall, and the people under CTOs would number 400–600 each year. The reality proved very different (see Chapter 2): CTOs are roughly ten times the numbers projected, with disproportionate use on black British people; numbers detained in hospital against their will have also steadily increased; and overall, compulsory powers are used over 50,000 times a year in England, and rising.

The backdrop to the introduction of CTOs was a few isolated and massively publicised homicides and incidents (like Ben Silcott climbing into a lion's den), to which Government responded in 1998 with a National Service Framework for mental health: its Foreword from Frank Dobson described some patients as 'a nuisance and a danger'. Burns (2013), once a leading advocate of CTOs (see Chapter 2), concluded that public safety fears had led to the adoption of measures that seriously curtailed patients' freedoms.

It appears that politicians succumbed to public fears (hugely exaggerated – see Chapter 1); and once CTOs were in place, the pressure on psychiatry to stop every tragedy meant clinicians seized on the new power to try to contain risk. In the 2010s, as in the 1990s, psychiatrists were under public pressure to stop homicides (and suicides), the supposed crisis whipped up by parts of the media (Figure 4.1).

Article 14 of the UN Convention implies that preventive detention on grounds of possible future crime should be decided no differently for people with mental health conditions than anyone else. If that were enshrined in domestic law, the expectation that psychiatry should 'lock up' potentially dangerous people might be subject to greater debate: would all citizens wish to be judged on the basis of crimes not yet committed?

It is not only people subject to mental health legislation who experience high levels of coercion. Another type of institution full of disabled people is prisons. The Prison Reform Trust says 20–30% of prisoners have a learning disability, the Centre for Mental Health that 70% have a psychosis, neurosis, personality disorder or other mental health problem. And the numbers in prison keep growing: doubling from 42,000 in 1993 to 85,000 in 2011 in England and Wales. And as the overall number rises, so does the number of people with mental health challenges.

Of course, there are gangsters and crooks who have mental health conditions. The argument that just because someone has a mental health problem they should be 'diverted' from custody veers immediately into paternalism, suggesting they cannot take responsibility and should be treated rather than punished. This runs counter to principles of equality. People in distress are almost always able to make choices about their actions – albeit that there can be strong mitigating circumstances (such as poverty in the case of theft). Denying any responsibility is patronising (Sayce 2000). In any event many people would prefer a finite

Figure 4.1 Amplifying public fear. *The Sun*, October 7, 2013

prison sentence to the uncertain hospital incarceration where liberty is dependent on nebulous risk assessment.

But the prisons are full of people who get poor educational qualifications, are excluded from school, develop mental health challenges, become NEET (not in education, employment or training), have no hope – and end up in jail. There is a pressing need to improve opportunities at an earlier stage to make this life story less common.

Another group subject to loss of liberty are those not compulsorily detained, but nonetheless placed without consent in institutions. When Steven Neary went into a care home for respite for a few days – Steven had autism and a learning disability and lived with his father – he was kept in for a whole year. The case went to the Court of Protection which found that the London Borough of Hillingdon had breached Steven's human rights. As the Equality and Human Rights Commission put it 'Steven, like everyone else, has a right to personal freedom and a family life and the state should not take away this without good reason' (Press release, June 2011).

This is an example of the inadequacy of deprivation of liberty safeguards, under the Mental Capacity Act 2005 and Mental Health Act 2007 (Series 2012). In 2013, the House of Commons Health Committee described this situation as 'profoundly depressing and complacent' and gave the Government a year to conduct a review and come up with an action plan (Health Committee 2013).

Shami Chakrabarti (2014), Director of Liberty, stated 'there are many prisoners in the UK who are not in prisons' – those in residential care who want to live in their own homes, those in institutions against their will.

Risk and rights

The libertarian position is supported by a narrative of human rights – the right to liberty, autonomy and equal treatment – and a challenge to how risk analysis is applied to different citizens. Sayce (2009) documents how risk is applied in ways that directly lead to discriminatory treatment of disabled people. This applies to risks to self, staff, service users, the wider public – and even cats. A woman was turned down by the Cats Protection League because she was deaf – there might (allegedly) be a risk to the cat and 'the cat comes first', as a spokesperson put it. On 'risk to self', Mr Paul applied for two jobs – as handyman and supervisor. He was accepted for the first, but turned down for the second – as there was (allegedly) a risk the job would be too stressful for him, given his bipolar disorder. Under the guise of benevolence, he was refused a job – quite unfairly, as the Tribunal in this instance ruled. And then there is the 'risk to others'. Deprivation of liberty under mental health law occurs on the grounds you might commit a crime in future – an accusation from which it is very hard to defend yourself.

The aversion to risk is fuelled by an unbalanced public expectation of risk management, whereby psychiatrists can be publicly pilloried for one decision followed by a suicide or homicide; but there is no criticism whatever for the thousands of decisions that result in compulsory detention and treatment of people who would never have harmed themselves or anyone else.

Crawford (2000) used homicide data to conclude that to prevent one person with a diagnosis of schizophrenia from committing homicide you would need to detain approximately 5,000 people with the same diagnosis who would commit no crime. The ethical implications of this are profound but little addressed.

Having a 'risk assessment' on your health notes (described by Parshad-Griffin as a 'ghost criminal record') can restrict housing and service choices with no chance to challenge its conclusions (see Chapter 1).

Libertarian campaigns

In the 1980s and 1990s a significant focus of user-survivor activism was rooted in a libertarian push to get the state off our backs: to stop or limit compulsory treatment and detention. In the USA street protests to 'stop forced electro-shock' and stop CTOs were commonplace (Sayce 2000). In Britain, Mind had high-profile legal directors in the 1980s (Larry Gostin, who brought American civil rights conceptions to the British mental health debate) and 1990s (Ian Bynoe) who led reforms to mental health law and legal challenges to assert rights to liberty and privacy, particularly in secure hospitals. Through the 1990s the Conservative Government's attempts to introduce compulsory community treatment were thwarted by survivor organisations, like Survivors Speak Out, working with Mind and legal leaders. This was against a backdrop of constant front-page headlines about homicides and madness, with images of 'black killers' threatening the British (often blond) family (see Chapter 1). Even so, the push for compulsory treatment was prevented.

The survivor movement's focus on liberty went together with a push for better choice of services, particularly access to talking therapies rather than drugs alone: libertarianism was interwoven with demands for state action and investment.

In the early 2000s the Mental Health Alliance was created to counter the Labour Government plan for CTOs, bringing together an impressive diversity of organisations – from survivor organisations to the Royal College of Psychiatrists and even SANE (headed by Marjorie Wallace, who had previously promoted images of people with mental health problems as helpless and potentially dangerous to increase attention to mental health). It mobilised intellectual power, with propositions for capacity-based legislation, together with parliamentary lobbying and street protests. Nonetheless, the campaign was unsuccessful.

As a result of both this campaign failure, and the financial crisis of 2008, the focus of protest changed. Libertarianism moved firmly off the agenda. At a time when the state was shrinking in the name of responding to austerity, the emphasis turned to preserving services and social security benefits (see next section). Many campaigners turned to fighting to preserve services and benefits that – just a few years earlier – they wanted to radically overturn. For instance, day centres ten years earlier had a reputation for being ghettoised services, at worst offering basket weaving or yoga in segregated surroundings, with little or no help to access real opportunities from employment to friendships. By 2013 some national activists were speaking publicly about the need to save day centres from cuts.

In this context mental health organisations sometimes campaigned against civil liberties positions. In 2012 the Supreme Court heard the case of Rabone v Pennine Care NHS Trust. The case was brought by the mother of a woman who, following discharge from hospital when a voluntary patient, had taken her own life. Mind intervened to establish the principle that NHS Trusts should have a duty to protect people from suicide at discharge, even if they are not under any form of compulsion. The Supreme Court ruled unanimously that the hospital did have this duty. From a civil liberties position, this was a major setback – likely to compound risk aversion and mean even people in hospital voluntarily would be denied choice about discharge. They would be more likely to be sectioned when seeking to leave, for fear the hospital might be liable or a consultant lambasted.

To many policy experts and activists working for liberty, it seemed ironic that Mind had intervened to incentivise psychiatrists to be even more risk averse, with the likely result that they would use compulsion more. This seemed a classic example of the discrimination of benevolence – stopping people making choices, because they might (might) be a risk to themselves. Perhaps strangely, the leaders in policy work to promote liberty recently have been not so much voluntary sector campaigners, but progressive psychiatrists – like George Szmukler – and survivors and lawyers working with them. In the 1990s, survivor activists and Mind campaigned for rights to liberty against overly coercive psychiatrists: there was at least one demonstration outside the heavy doors of the Royal College in Berkeley Square. By 2013 these rifts had been largely healed, not least through the collaborative Mental Health Alliance; but now progressive psychiatrists were in effect campaigning against a protective model of care promoted by (amongst others) voluntary sector organisations. Some viewed this as a curious reversal. It was perhaps also ironic that there was little campaigning on coercion when it was on the rise.

The introduction of CTOs, despite united opposition from the mental health sector, can perhaps be understood in terms of wider developments in risk containment and pre-emptive legal powers.

Rose notes that some commentators believe we have lived for some time in a 'risk society', no longer structured by belief in progress and distribution of goods, like wealth, health or life chances; but rather saturated by fear and foreboding, structured by the distribution of 'bads' or dangers (Rose 1998).

Pre-emptive legal powers are increasing. Nicola Lacey argues that criminal offences in general have increased significantly: for the 637 years from 1351 to 1988, the main Halsbury Laws of England contains 1,382 pages to cover all criminal laws. For the next 19 years, up to 2008, it contains 3,746 pages. In just 13 years up to 2010 over 3000 new criminal offences were added to the statute book. (Lacey 2014). Lacey argues that a hybrid of criminal and civil law has developed – for instance, anti-social behaviour orders – which criminalise an increasing number of behaviours, with mandatory interventions to prevent crime, like stopping people drinking in public spaces or curtailing migrant rights. These hybrid powers are likely to impact on some groups more than others, creating an inequality in the distribution of freedoms. It may be that the introduction of CTOs against opposition took place through a wider political commitment to compulsory requirements and sanctions to prevent crime or social disorder, which impacted on people with low social power, including those with mental health conditions.

International pressures for change

It remains my view that the right to legal capacity is one of the most invisible human rights issues in Europe today and is also one of the most important. Too many people with disabilities are denied the right to make choices in their lives ... And too many countries are not doing enough to remedy the situation. (Thomas Hammarberg, former Commissioner for Human Rights at Council of Europe, cited in Mdac 2013, p. 1).

Mdac (2013) documents deprivation of liberty across Europe, finding that through inadequate approaches to legal and mental capacity people were denied even the most basic rights – where to live, when to get up, what to eat; as well as being stripped of the right to enter into contracts, vote, marry, consent or otherwise to sex, become a juror. In effect the policies were incapacitating people – with a label of incompetence becoming a self-fulfilling prophecy: if a person does not have the chance to exercise independent decisions, he or she can never learn to do so (Mdac 2013, p. 7). Most citizens are permitted to make foolish decisions, but 'the freedom to make poor choices is a privilege that is denied to the person who is labelled mentally ill' (Ronald Bassmann, cited in Mdac 2013, p. 10).

Mdac (the Mental Disability Advocacy Center) are especially critical of guardianship – which they found led to 'catch 22' scenarios, such as a desire to leave a particular place of residence being interpreted as a symptom of mental illness; often without redress.

While many of Mdac's examples come from former Soviet bloc countries, complacency in the UK would be unwise in the extreme. The Committee on the Rights of Persons with Disabilities (CRPD) makes clear that Article 12 of the UNCRPD requires governments to replace impermissible *substitute* decision-making with *supported* decision-making. Impermissible approaches include decisions based on the objective 'best interests' of the individual – rather than respecting the individual's own preferences. 'Best interests' lie at the heart of the English Mental Capacity Act, which suggests it is non-compliant. States are expected to ensure all citizens have legal capacity – which is distinct from mental capacity. Laws that deprive a person of a range of rights once deemed 'mentally incapacitated' – whether in consumer rights, contracts, employment or voting – need to be changed. States have to ensure every effort is made to enable individuals to make decisions, through (for instance) circles of friends.

In England, the case of Connor Sparrowhawk (known as Laughing Boy), a young man with learning difficulties, autism and epilepsy who died in a specialist assessment unit, brought attention to the large numbers of people warehoused in institutions, receiving assessments that missed the point and support that depowered them. An online campaign, 'Justice for LB' raised profound questions about rights and freedoms (see https://107daysofaction.wordpress. com/tag/connor-sparrowhawk/).

The Mental Capacity Act (MCA) 2005 and the Mental Health Act (MHA) 2007 are key pieces of legislation in England and Wales that allow for the deprivation of legal capacity. The MHA allows for forced detention and psychiatric treatment and the appointment of guardians. The MCA allows for deputies to be appointed for welfare and/or property matters, and in respect of detention in hospitals or care homes, under a section entitled 'deprivation of liberty safeguards' (Mdac 2013, p. 52).

As the UN Committee on the CRPD visits the UK to investigate progress in 2016–17 there is an opportunity to review and strengthen UK laws (the legislative frameworks differ across England and devolved nations). This has profound implications for the future of mental health and mental capacity law.

The core argument of Szmukler and colleagues has been there should be no separate mental health law – but rather one fair mental capacity law, applying to all citizens. In effect the two laws should fuse. In Northern Ireland legislation was under development in 2015 that would do just this. However, the analysis above shows that it is not enough to slot the rights of people with mental health challenges into existing mental capacity law. The MCA in England and Wales is also non-compliant with human rights principles. What is needed is a completely fresh legal framework, based on a presumption of legal capacity, with strong requirements to enable citizens to make decisions, and only a residual provision for the very rare situations where someone is unable to express preferences (Mdac 2013).

The Northern Ireland development is one of the first in the world to attempt this. It will be vital to share international developments, including from Canada. In Ontario, a person who is detained under Mental Health law can only be treated against their will in an emergency, or to enable them to be fit for trial, or if they are not deemed 'capable' and their substitute decision-maker has given consent (Davidson 2011). Whilst substitute decision-making is unlikely to comply with the UN Convention (supported decision-making being the goal), the general ban on treating someone against their will except in an emergency is a major step. The goal for the UK and elsewhere needs to be legal frameworks that include no separate mental health law – no power for the state to restrict the freedoms of people with mental health conditions on different grounds from other citizens – and one fair framework to cover legal capacity, ending the denial of liberty under inadequate deprivation of liberty safeguards. This would be revolutionary.

With the exception of Northern Ireland, there are few organisations promoting these rights in Britain today. Despite the UN position, despite robust academic evidence that CTOs do not work, the people campaigning for a fresh approach tend to be academics (like Lucy Series), lawyers and clinicians.

There are also a few individual campaigners taking a more libertarian than state protectionist campaigning position. Simon Stevens, a significantly disabled man who says 'I'm big, I'm ballsy. I am the rebel with cerebral palsy' (http://www.simonstevens.com/), argues that disabled people should take responsibility and stop demanding endless services and protections. His is a relatively lone and contested voice.

There has been one significant campaign win in the UK from a broadly libertarian position:

The campaign to ditch exclusion from being an MP, company director or juror

In 2004, after lobbying from mental health activists, the government's Social Exclusion Unit recommended that the bar on people in receipt of psychiatric treatment from serving on juries should be scrapped. As Rachel Perkins put it 'As an NHS Director living with bi-polar disorder, I am trusted with a budget of £5 million – but not with serving on a jury'. The Government accepted the recommendation – but over the next eight years failed to implement it. It seemed this was because of a variety of operational concerns – will judges have to test people's mental capacity instead? How will they know if people are able to serve?

Following the 2010 election, at a time of major austerity measures, mental health organisations realised that a campaign to persuade government to remove egregious discrimination without spending requirements would have more chance of success than major spending demands. They started with an emblematic example of discrimination: the fact that MPs who were sectioned under mental health law for over six months were required to stand down. If they were (say) in hospital with heart disease, the response would be an assumption that they could return once well. Why the difference for someone with a mental health condition? This caught the imagination of politicians, including Conservative Minister Mark Harper, who strongly supported a new Mental Health (Discrimination) Bill. He stated:

> The main purpose of the Bill is to send a very clear message that having a
> mental health condition is nothing to be ashamed of or to be kept secret ...
> The Bill aims to put an end to cases whereby a mother taking medication for
> post-natal depression is unable to perform jury service, or where an MP who is
> sectioned under the Mental Health Act for more than six months is forced to
> resign while an MP who suffered a serious physical illness would not have to.
> Removing the provision whereby directors of public or private companies can
> be removed 'by reason of their mental health' would also help end the stigma
> attached to mental illness. (http://www.markharper.org/archives/673).

The Mental Health (Discrimination) Act became law in 2013, thanks to smart campaigning to remove state restrictions in a time of cost constraint, achieving cross-party support.

The social security protection model

In the 2010s a division of view emerged in the disability movement. It mirrored a 1970s split between campaigners promoting disability benefits (who formed the Disability Income Group (DIG)) and those in UPIAS (Union of Physically Impaired People Against Segregation) who wanted – not social protection – but rights and equality. Whereas DIG's top priority was the relief of poverty, for UPIAS a paternalistic provision of benefits and segregated services was no win at all: only full inclusion and equality was worth the fight.

In the 2010s, as government embarked on the biggest reduction in social security spending since the foundation of the welfare state, this split re-emerged with renewed force. Newer campaigners like We Are Spartacus and blogs like 'Diary of a Benefit Scrounger' reprised and developed the arguments of DIG, arguing for safeguarding social security, with a particular focus on the battle-ground of assessments like the hated Work Capability Assessment (WCA) – where reduced entitlements were felt the hardest. Meanwhile others – more in the tradition of UPIAS – argued that an economic downturn was an opportunity to use public resources better, replacing segregated special schools, residential homes and separate workplaces with inclusive practices and support that put choice and control in the hands of disabled people. To them, arguing to keep social security benefits as they are was unthinkable.

One of the sharpest differences was over Remploy factories, set up after the Second World War to provide experience to returning disabled soldiers as a route to open employment. By the 2000s, however, it was clear progression into open employment was a rarity and many of the factories were struggling to be viable. Both Labour and Coalition governments instigated closure programmes. Disabled people's organisations working with employees coming out of the factories found many very able to work in mainstream employment (but convinced otherwise by years in more sheltered employment) and some leading very institutionalised lives, with no choice or control over simple things like relationships or going shopping. Others found securing work much harder. Remploy factories had a poor record of employing people with mental health conditions so this debate was less relevant in mental health; but the dynamic was one in which some anti-cuts campaigners suddenly fought to protect factories – which others in the movement had long seen as segregated – allying themselves with trade unions rightly fighting to protect the interests of their members.

There were parallels in the mental health campaigning world. In the 1970s anti-psychiatry groups like CAPO (Campaign Against Psychiatric Oppression) fought against the National Schizophrenia Fellowship because it campaigned to slow hospital closures and create more services; CAPO wanted an end to all coercive services.

By the 2010s new voices in mental health were fighting for social security protection, poverty their greatest concern. In 2010 a group of incapacity benefit recipients formed the Mental Health Resistance Network (MHRN), who in 2013 took legal action against the Government, arguing that the WCA discriminated against some groups of disabled people, including those with mental health problems or autism. In May 2013 three upper tribunal judges ruled that the WCA did indeed put these groups at a substantial disadvantage, because many have problems filling in forms, seeking evidence and answering questions. MHRN argued many of their members had experienced relapses, self-harm and suicide attempts as a result of the WCA, and needed higher levels of medication and even hospitalisation in the lead-up to reassessments. Some were unable to cope with an appeal.

This type of campaigning is relevant to anti-discrimination for two reasons.

Firstly, disabled people – generally – have been 'hardest hit' by reductions in benefits and services. National and local governments have a duty to promote equality, under the Equality Act 2010, and to ensure no disproportionate negative effect on disabled people. Demos (2013), with Scope, found disabled people were set to lose £28.3 billion in benefits and services by 2018. 26,600 people would experience the 'triple whammy' of having their Employment and Support Allowance (ESA) uprating capped at 1%, then losing it (through time limits), then losing Disability Living Allowance (DLA) (through Personal Independence Payment reform). This loss would be worth from £3,400 to £4,600 a year. An estimated 3,000 people would be hit by six different cuts, each household losing £23,000 over five years. Demos commented: 'Our research reveals that disabled people are bearing the brunt of the austerity measures'. Just Fair (2014) documented breaches of the UN Convention on the Rights of Persons with Disabilities and recommended re-consideration of the 'bedroom tax' and fundamental reform of ESA and the WCA, to ensure an adequate standard of living for disabled people.

Secondly, poverty impacts on people with mental health conditions even more acutely than other disabled people: for instance, one in four people with mental health problems face problems of debt (ODI 2013).

The 'Hardest Hit' campaign brought together disabled people's organisations and mental health charities like Mind and Rethink. They identified overwhelming fear of cuts: a 2012 survey found 85% of respondents thought losing their DLA would drive them into isolation, and 95% that it would be detrimental to their health (Hardest Hit 2012).

Disabled People Against the Cuts (DPAC) is a more overtly political group, formed to fight government cuts: its website includes a song headlined 'another Tory organised scam'. It brings together activists of the left, trade unionists and some disabled people's groups. DPAC pursues direct action including demonstrations against the companies carrying out the WCA.

Campaigns against policies that impact disproportionately on people with mental health challenges could play a significant role in anti-discrimination work. However, some activists have framed these campaigns with the argument that many people in receipt of out-of-work benefits are too 'sick' to work; and need to be 'looked after'. DPAC's website includes the following quote:

> The moral test of government is how that government treats those who are in the
> dawn of life, the children; those who are in the twilight of life, the elderly; and
> those who are in the shadows of life, the sick, the needy and the handicapped.
> (Hubert H. Humphrey . Former US Vice President).

Many disabled people, including those with significant impairments, would reject utterly the notion of living 'in the shadows of life' or being 'needy' and 'handicapped'. They would argue like Jane Campbell (see Chapter 3) that they simply want the right to participate as full (not shadow) citizens, able to contribute once barriers are removed and support available on their own terms.

Where the previous generation of disability rights campaigners argued for change – the right to work, to ever-increasing participation – the social security campaigners took up a different fight, to preserve out-of-work benefits, even if that risked sustaining a paternalistic system. There were two powerful drivers.

Firstly, campaigners with lived experience fought to preserve benefits and resist sanctions in the face of potential destitution. Sanctions against people on ESA rose three-fold from 2013–14 (see Chapter 1) and many moved from benefits to nothing (rather than to work). Discussion of disabled people's employment was in effect hijacked by government's focus on *requiring* people to move towards work – so campaigners responded with resistance.

Arguably the baby of the right to work was thrown out with the bathwater of compulsion. As one young disabled person put it in 2013 'I wanted employment advice. I want to get out of volunteering and into paid work. All they offered me was benefits advice. I didn't want benefits.' In 2015 Jane Young argued at Disability Rights UK's AGM that it was important to argue for the right to work *and* to campaign against sanctions, and not to confuse the two.

Secondly, social security campaigners believed disability rights campaigners had completely under-played the impact of long-term illness, presuming that – for all 'sick and disabled people' – once barriers were removed, participation would flow. This might work for someone with a stable physical impairment, who just needed an accessible environment – but was totally inadequate for someone living with severe pain, fatigue or confusion. On this argument, drawing everyone into the term 'disabled people' (as defined by the Equality Act) has masked the real experience of ill-health: even after barriers have been removed, they argue, the effects of illness remain and prevent many from working.

As early as the 1990s Jenny Morris (1996) argued against a version of the social model of disability that entailed a macho disregard for the pain of impairment. In mental health, Sayce (2000, 2003) argued for radical extension of understandings of adjustments and support needed, from 'ramps and lifts' to completely flexible education and work schedules, off-line support and changed management practices. The Disability Rights Commission adopted a policy of listing 'obvious', tangible adjustments *last* – after the subtler adjustments to the social environment – to foster changed perceptions of what 'disability equality' meant.

Creating an inclusive approach to disability equality is work in progress. Many employers still go no further than 'once and for all' physical adjustments. It is understandable that campaigners living with long-term health conditions despair of an 'equality' that seems to exclude them.

But is the answer to describe one's experience as 'sickness'?

Some people in some situations must voice the intensity of their pain and fatigue – against an assessment system that often fails to understand it. But one impact of the social protection campaigns has been that Ministers have talked proudly of increasing the number of people in the 'support group', those not expected to undertake any work-related activity. Cook (2014) notes that the proportion of people placed in the 'support group' at the end of their WCA rose from 12% in the last quarter of 2008 to 51% in the second quarter of 2013 (see Department for Work and Pensions 2014). Often a diagnosis of schizophrenia seemed enough to get someone in. This suggests that the social security campaigns may have achieved some social protection gains – but perhaps at the risk of 'writing people off'. Those in the support group, whilst in theory able to avail themselves of employment support, are of no interest to employment support providers given incentivisation payments. The risk is that the growing support group is becoming a new version of incapacity benefit, on which 2.7 million people were placed with no effective employment support to secure routes out of poverty.

There is, generally, an overwhelming 'illness/sickness' narrative applied to people with mental health challenges, which defines the problem as the illness, the answer as treatment (see Chapter 3). This narrow discourse omits the potential to live a full life WITH the mental health condition. It suggests you should be relieved of roles like employee or parent until you are 'better' (Sayce and Boardman 2008). This may be helpful at times of acute crisis – but for most people it is deeply disempowering as a long-term proposition. It is likely to lead directly to withdrawal of opportunities: if you are considered 'sick' you are highly unlikely to be offered jobs, promotions, educational or community opportunities.

An anti-discrimination position would rather argue for re-imagining the world of work: for instance, if you have a fluctuating condition, some jobs suit annualised hours, so you can work when well (or when less unwell – some fluctuating conditions do not include symptom-free periods); or an employer might commission work from pools of workers, who can cover for each other. It would argue for levers and incentives to strip away discriminatory employer beliefs and behaviours (Work Foundation 2015). It would argue for choice and control over truly individualised employment support (Crowther and Sayce 2013).

Whilst fear of destitution is one emergency, there is another: the fact that 14% of people with long-term mental health conditions are in work, when research tells us at least 60% could be, with effective support (see Chapter 2). If more and more identify as 'sick', there is a major risk of entrenching sky-high unemployment.

The 'sickness' paradigm in effect relieves society of the responsibility to enable participation for large numbers of people living with health conditions. For those of us with mental health challenges, the rhetoric is all about being unable to deal with the stress of assessments, being unable to fill in forms or answer questions, being – in effect – incapable; the very stereotype that all anti-discrimination work tries to destroy.

Social security campaigners have emphasised 'sickness' to swing the pendulum away from a 'disability' model. But when disability rights campaigners secured better anti-discrimination coverage for people with depression, MS and cancer in 2005, the purpose was to secure rights (to non-discrimination – from services to insurance – and adjustments at work and college). Separating 'sick' from disabled people risks withholding those rights: employers will think only of getting people treatment, not freedom from bullying or workplace adjustments. And in mental health, it would be extremely easy for vast numbers to come to see themselves as 'sick' – a conceptualisation that the mental health movement has fought against for good reason for decades, objecting to narrow biological explanations and a disproportionate emphasis on pharmaceutical treatments (see Chapter 3).

There are other ways of pushing the disability rights agenda to be more inclusive.

DWP (2013) found that 19% of the UK population would be covered by the Equality Act definition of disability at any time (though many go in and out of the experience). Three quarters do not identify as disabled people: rather they view themselves as having cancer, arthritis, depression or bipolar disorder.

The Disability Rights Commission researched the views of disabled people who did not so identify, and devised communications to convey their rights both to them and to those with duties towards them. Disability Rights UK developed this work by deliberately talking of 'people living with disability or long-term health conditions' both to reach out to a wide group to let them know their rights; and to ensure the voice of this large population is fully heard in campaigns to promote rights and freedoms. The last thing this pan-impairment organisation wanted was a return to the days when 'disability rights' was understood in terms only of wheelchair users (and often white male wheelchair users at that). Those rights apply to people living with HIV, cancer and mental health challenges, from all communities. It is critical to communicate this coverage – not least because some of the most serious discrimination is experienced by these groups. When the Equality Bill was going through parliament in 2010, organisations representing people with HIV, cancer and mental health challenges joined forces and successfully outlawed the hated pre-employment health questions that discriminate against people with non-visible, stigmatised conditions. To say that these groups are 'sick' and (by implication) cannot work would be to turn the clock back on significant campaigning and bridge-building between people with different experiences. We need links between long-term health conditions and impairments – not a radical divide.

It is important conceptually to:

- Distinguish between 'sickness' (or 'illness') (with all its unfortunate lay associations with denial of social roles) and 'living with a long-term health condition' (where all the accent is on 'living with' – living to the full, within constraints of pain, fatigue and other aspects of the condition) and
- Link 'living with a long-term health condition' to long-term impairment – because in both cases disabling barriers prevent full participation in society. This moves the debate away from the narrow illness/treatment model towards realising rights and freedoms, changing society so that people living with long term health conditions can participate fully.

We need to hear a range of voices. This may be the subversive voice of the person who has tactically hidden a mental health condition:

> I applied for a job as HR Director. I took up post and received, in my new role, a letter from occupational health about myself. It said do not employ this person; she has bi-polar disorder. I filed the letter away carefully and worked for some time in the role. (contributor to Radiate event 2011).

Or it may be the person who has thrown off the burden of the 'secret', found being open to be liberating, a boost to energy and productivity, and started a ripple effect enabling others to be open. Or the individual challenging discrimination where they find it, setting legal precedent and sharing learning. Or the employer who has re-structured a working life so someone with significant mental health difficulties can work when well.

Campaigns against the WCA are important, because of the discriminatory nature of its design and the fundamental fact that it has no validity. There is no evidence to support a correlation between the particular functional abilities assessed (like walking up three steps, placing your mobile phone in your pocket, or even concentrating) and the likelihood of securing work within a particular timeframe: the factors associated with getting into employment are nothing to do with diagnosis, or symptoms, or functioning, and everything to do with motivation, choice of job to go for, and truly individualised support. The WCA is a massive waste of money and human distress. But that does not mean it should be challenged through arguing that people with mental health challenges are 'sick' and often 'cannot work'.

This debate poses a huge dilemma for campaigners. In the immediate term, when large numbers of people are terrified of being driven into ever greater poverty, or forced to take part in completely ineffective work programmes, there is intense need and pressure to protest against unfair cuts and sanctions. However, if this is done by extending the numbers viewed as sick and unable to work, then the medium-term aim of full participation, including in employment, is undermined.

It is at least arguable that using the 'sickness' argument is not an effective medium-term strategy even to reduce poverty. For people with mental health conditions, who have far lower employment rates (under 20%) than other disabled people (almost 50%), and lower skills levels, poverty would be reduced most effectively through the blend of skills and support to get decent jobs; and benefits support for those in and out of work, recommended by the Joseph Rowntree Foundation's anti-poverty strategy (Schmueker 2014).

There is another problem with the social security protection argument. It is unconvincing to the British public. Crowther (2013) has noted that the majority of the public feel the benefits system breaks codes of fairness by providing rewards without commensurate effort. They believe the State should impose conditions and sanctions, cap the amount people can receive and make sure no one can have a 'free ride' courtesy of the taxpayer. Messages that address these feelings win the most votes. The political emphasis on an active welfare state, a 'hand up not a hand-out', predated the 2010 election and by the middle of the decade there was a clear cross-party consensus that benefit spending must be reduced, with high expectations that people would provide for themselves. British attitudes to poverty and benefits have changed: in the 1980s, whilst Americans thought the poor were to blame for their poverty and could escape it if they really tried, Europeans (including the British) were far more likely to view the reasons as structural (for instance, not enough jobs) (Julius Wilson 1997). Throughout the 1990s and 2000s British attitudes converged with American: the public wanted benefits spending reduced (British Social Attitudes 30 2013). Only in 2013 was there a slight dip back towards support for benefit spending, but by 2015 there was no further rise (British Social Attitudes 32 2015). Politicians from both sides of the main political spectrum continued to compete to demonstrate how tough they were on 'welfare' (although the new leadership of the Labour Party in 2015 showed an appetite for rejecting policies of austerity).

CONCLUSIONS

Libertarian model

Overall libertarian campaigning has declined, at a time when coercion has increased. Campaigners have been more focused on protecting services (see next section). In an earlier era, survivor activists like Judi Chamberlin were highly critical of campaigns to protect existing services, when what was needed was real alternatives, run by patients, based on a completely different balance of power (Chamberlin 1977).

In terms of anti-discrimination work how much does this decline in libertarian campaigns matter? In relation to Link and Phelan's (2001) components of stigma, a challenge to coercion represents a direct attack on the practice of being treated differently (component 4) and it uses power: the power of legislative change and litigation to achieve its ends. However, libertarian campaigns are based on 'negative freedoms' – freedom *from* coercion rather than freedom *to* thrive and participate fully in society. This can limit their effectiveness: because they do not actively revalue madness or the contribution of 'mad' people, they can meet resistance from a wider public, who do not understand why this (devalued) group should be freed. By analogy, Nelson Mandela (1994) argued that prison reform to improve the lives of black prisoners in Apartheid South Africa could not succeed on its own: behaviour towards people in prison would only change once black people's position in the whole society had changed. As long as the public wants black activists in prison – or people with mental health problems safely detained and compelled to 'take the meds' – then a libertarian argument will not convince them otherwise. What may convince them is to see what equal black people contribute, or what free people with mental health challenges contribute to society – which then stimulates questions as to why so many are incarcerated. As Tom Burns noted above, it was to placate public anxiety about safety that CTOs were introduced. Without addressing those fears, resistance to freedoms may be hard to overcome.

Finally libertarian campaigns of course risk playing into the hands of governments intent on reducing services: if campaigners succeed in 'getting the state off our back', we may find the state has shrunk away and withdrawn all support (the very reason why libertarian campaigns have been on the decline). And libertarian arguments are unlikely to be sufficient to create a sea change in attitudes and behaviours across society. Nonetheless, libertarian campaigns are important – perhaps more important now than at other times in history – and there are significant opportunities, particularly driven by international human rights conventions and investigations.

Libertarian campaigns should be part of the mix, but they need to be combined with other models.

Social security protection model

From the standpoint of Link and Phelan's components of stigma, social security campaigners are intervening directly to ameliorate unequal life chances (component 4). They use social media and public protest in an attempt to exercise power; however, given public opinion and considerable political consensus the power to preserve benefits spending and ameliorate poverty via social security is constrained. The campaigns have been vital in highlighting the harsh impact of benefit sanctions, in terms of both poverty and fear of poverty, which deters people from seeking employment. Whilst the campaigns may have contributed to higher numbers in the support group, they have not stemmed the flow of disabled people on to Jobseeker's Allowance, or the reduction in benefit spending overall. The threats of destitution and punitive sanctions may have pushed campaigners paradoxically to be co-opted into the Government's discourse – you can or you cannot work – and helped get more people into the 'cannot work' category; but this risked diverting attention from pressing for support and social security that enable full participation, including the right to work. Campaigners have focused on protection at the expense of the skills and employment support that are at least as necessary to reducing poverty and inequality. In this sense this model does not address the second of Link and Phelan's components of stigma: it risks entrenching, rather than disrupting, the negative association of 'disability' with incompetence.

Writers including Jenny Morris, Neil Crowther and Jane Young have endeavoured to build bridges between the social security campaigners and wider disability rights campaigners. A social security system that enables participation and reduces inequality is essential to equal lives. But it is not enough. There is a need to hear the voices both of people who are acutely unwell and unable to work in our workplaces – at least as they are currently configured; and those who want employment, skills and full participation, even if it takes re-imagining the world of work and support systems to achieve it.

Reaching consensus sometimes requires rising above the immediate terrain of the disagreement, and appealing to higher purpose. In this instance, the UN Convention on the Rights of Persons with Disabilities offers a framework, with its balanced emphasis on the right to an adequate standard of living and social protection (Article 28), on the right to work (Article 27) and on the right to live independently and be included in the community (Article 19).

Talking of 'people living with disability or long-term health conditions' has more promise than dividing people into 'disabled' or 'sick'. If there is no such bridge-building there is a risk that the 'sickness' model could grow, fuelled by both anti-stigma campaigners deploying the (counter-productive) message that mental illness is an illness like any other (see Chapter 3); and the social security campaigners, fighting against benefit cuts and sanctions by reference to 'sickness'. This could jeopardise the longer-term aim of equality and active citizenship. When people are in debt and relying on food banks, they fight primarily for immediate income. But we need to fight for both – income and full citizen rights.

True dialogue rooted in the UN Convention on the Rights of Persons with Disabilities could provide the grounds to move forward together.

Reflective Exercises

If a mental health worker enables people using their service to navigate the social security system and end up in the group not expected to seek employment (called the 'support group' in 2015), what might be the consequences for the individual? What are the pros and cons?

Could you open up a discussion with your peers or colleagues on whether it is right that someone who has mental health challenges and is legally capable of making decisions can be given psychiatric treatment against their will? What is the spectrum of views and can you distil a position?

FURTHER READING

Sayce, L. (2009) 'Risk, Rights and Anti-discrimination Work in Mental Health', in Adams, R., Dominelli, L. and Payne, M. (eds). *Practising Social Work in a Complex World*, pp. 99–113. Basingstoke: Palgrave Macmillan.

• Discusses the centrality of thinking about 'risk' in denying independent living, choice and control; and the need for a proportionate, rights-based approach to risk

Szmukler, G. (2010) 'How Mental Health Law Discriminates Unfairly Against People with Mental Illness', Lecture to view at http://www.gresham.ac.uk/lectures-and-events/how-mental-health-law-discriminates-unfairly-against-people-with-mental-illness

Mindfreedom: American organisation that campaigns against forced treatment, with resources and newspieces. At http://www.mindfreedom.org/

Just Fair (2014) 'Dignity and Opportunity for All: Securing the Rights of Disabled People in the Austerity Era', at http://just-fair.co.uk/hub/single/dignity_and_opportunity_for_all/

• An analysis of compliance and non-compliance with human right requirements in the UK, in the areas of independent living and social protection

Disability Rights UK. Organisation led by people with lived experience of disability or long-term health conditions, which campaigns and runs projects both to combat poverty and secure better skills and employment opportunities. Publisher of the Disability Rights Handbook. www .disabilityrightsuk.org

Bloggers on major debates amongst activists on the issues raised in this chapter:

Neil Crowther – see http://www.neilcrowtherconsulting.com/

Bendy girl – see http://benefitscroungingscum.blogspot.co.uk/

We Are Spartacus – see http://www.spartacusnetwork.org.uk/

5 | Social Models of Disability, Madness and Participation

Chapter Summary

- The liberation of the social model of disability
- Its application to people living with mental health challenges
- The limits of identity politics
- Evolution of the 'disability inclusion' model
- Human rights and capability theory
- Ditching the myth of perfection
- A social model of participation

If people living with mental health challenges are to become full, not partial citizens, then an approach that tackles head-on the patterns of discrimination that constrain citizenship might appear, logically, to have more chance of success than less directly targeted approaches, such as re-branding mental health conditions as biological brain diseases or needs for emotional growth (see previous chapters).

In Sayce (2000) I proposed the 'disability inclusion' model, which draws on the social model of disability to challenge discrimination and open up new opportunities. In this model, it does not matter what caused the mental health challenge – early trauma, economic and social inequality, faulty genes, spiritual crisis, anything else – or whether it is a real or a perceived problem in the first place. What matters is that people living with actual or perceived mental health challenges are excluded – 'disabled' – by society's behaviours and attitudes; and through campaigning for inclusion this can change. This model has the potential to unite people whatever they view as the cause of mental distress or madness.

When the disability movement developed the social model of disability in the 1990s it was revelatory, liberating:

> It is not a problem to me that I have no legs. My only problem is the fact that society denies me access to places because of its attitudes and the way it has built cities and buildings. (American disability activist, personal communication, cited in Sayce 2000).

Campaigners coined catchphrases to summarise opposition to discrimination:

> 'Piss on pity'.

Proponents of the social model argued that people are disabled not – or not mainly – by their *impairment* (that is, the physical, mental or emotional difference from the norm – actual or perceived) but by the barriers that society places in their way: of behaviour, attitude, structure, environment, law. The central idea that rather than 'having a disability' we are 'disabled' by the barriers society creates shifted the locus of the 'problem' – from the individual to society. Those involved talked eloquently about feeling freed from the sense that there was something 'wrong' with them, and excited by the prospect of tackling the true problem – by securing civil rights to break down barriers to full participation. They took inspiration from other liberation movements. If the black civil rights movement could make segregation (in universities, buses, lunch counters) a thing of the past, then disabled people could challenge segregation in institutions. Famously a group living in a Leonard Cheshire home in the 1970s got so fed up with being expected to be in their pyjamas by 5.30pm that they wheeled themselves to the pub – in their pyjamas – and started plotting better alternatives. Thus was the British independent living movement born. In 2000 I wrote about 'segregation within segregation' – the segregation of black people in separate wings in American psychiatric institutions, which in themselves segregated people with mental health conditions from the wider society. In the USA, the anti-segregation message had added potency.

There was also learning from the women's movement. If women could successfully challenge the essentialist claim that it was 'natural' that women had different and lesser roles than men (in the home, in supportive caring or secretarial jobs) – then perhaps disabled people could overthrow the idea that it was 'natural' that they would lead limited lives – in institutions, out of work, or in a distinct set of jobs, from piano tuner for blind people to 'industrial therapy' for people with mental health challenges – packing tea or airline cutlery, often for pay well below the minimum wage.

But was the social model of disability relevant to people with mental health challenges? Did it resonate as a liberating idea?

On this there was equivocation on all sides. For many living with mental health challenges, the archetypal image of a disabling barrier (steps) and accessibility (the ever-present wheelchair symbol) reinforced the feeling that disability rights were no help to them. Many feared that even within the disability movement, mental health issues were viewed as the less savoury side of disability – to be tolerated at best, 'othered' at worst – for fear the taint of madness would rub off on the more respectable side of the disability movement. Mad and distressed people, it was feared, would never be fully included. Where, for instance, was the disability movement's campaign to challenge the unethical use of coercion under the Mental Health Act? (see Sayce 2000).

For leaders in the disability movement, meanwhile, there was sometimes frustration at why everyone could not just adopt the liberating concepts of the movement and show solidarity. Why, for instance, talk of 'recovery' when the agreed language was 'independent living'? And why identify as 'service users' or 'survivors' rather than as 'disabled people'? When research in the early 2000s revealed that about half of people who would be covered as 'disabled' by the Disability Discrimination Act would not view themselves as 'disabled people' one activist commented 'if they don't identify as disabled, f*** 'em' (personal communication).

It is not difficult to find evidence to justify this mutual distancing. Some leading authorities on disability equality seemed to miss the mental health dimension.

A 2003 Scope report recommended that employers should make sure their application forms ask about disability – on the grounds that disabled people should not have to hide their impairment, and to give them somewhere to explain any additional needs (Daone and Scott 2003). This was *after* the mental health sector had successfully persuaded the Ministerial Disability Rights Task Force to outlaw questions about disability and mental health before job offer (though it took a decade for it to become law) (DRTF 1999). People writing about 'disability' (which allegedly included mental health issues) seemed not to understand the intense fear and actual prejudice experienced by people living with mental health challenges. Sayce (2010) found people with mental health conditions were four times more likely than people with physical conditions to be open to no one at work, for fear it would damage their career prospects – and were less likely to be in senior jobs. Where people were open it was normally to colleagues, not the boss or HR colleague with power over their career. Where people feel safe to be open, it can be massively powerful: a weight lifted, improved well-being and productivity. But it needs to be safe to do so. A report that advocates openness, to secure technical adjustments, without engaging with these fears is unlikely to be credible with a mental health audience.

Later disability writers still underplay the mental health experience. The launch of 'Secrets and Big News' (Nash 2014) opened up a new conversation, replacing words like 'disclose' with 'share' and argued powerfully for new breakthroughs to 'be ourselves'. It asked advice organisations to stop discouraging people from being open. But its own research found 60% of those not sharing were afraid of the repercussions of doing so; other research finds that over 30% of employers still view employing people with a mental health problem as a significant risk (Henderson et al. 2013) and that the proportion of people reporting that they concealed their mental health experiences went up from 2008–12, from 73% to 77% (Henderson et al. 2014). Encouraging people to have open conversations does not quite engage with the depth of historic prejudice and fear that lead to reduced promotions and ill-health retirement. A more systemic approach is required, including support for employee and employer to reduce fear.

The Greater London Authority routinely talks of 'deaf and disabled people' – a nod to the diversity of 'disabled people' that still does not feel inclusive to people living with mental or indeed physical health conditions, from depression to cancer.

The reason these are fairly significant omissions is that repeated studies find people with mental health challenges face particularly intense disadvantage even as compared to other groups of disabled people, for instance encountering a public that is not comfortable with them in roles such as boss, MP or babysitter (see Chapter 2). One might expect in-depth attention to mental health, instead of which some disability thinkers seem to echo lay perceptions of 'disability' as being mainly about people using technical adjustments or interpreters.

Conversely, where mental health and disability advocates have come together there have been significant advances. Chapter 2 described how Mind joined 'Rights Now', the umbrella lobbying group, campaigned alongside other disability activists and in 1995 saw the first ever law passed to debar discrimination on grounds including 'mental impairment'. It is highly unlikely this would have been achieved for mental health alone: it took 12 attempts to bring in a wider disability discrimination Bill before government finally succumbed; separate laws for different conditions would have been a step too far.

Some in the mental health world picked up the social model of disability to underpin thinking and campaigns in mental health:

> It is society that disables people … People who have been through the mental
> health systems or have otherwise acquired a psychiatric history often find their
> access to employment, housing and other necessities to a good quality life barred
> by others' subtle and not-so-subtle discriminatory behaviour (MacNamara 1996).

British lobbyists learnt from American colleagues who achieved civil rights law earlier (1990), through an explicit policy of unity in the face of attacks. Some opponents tried hard to divide 'deserving' from 'undeserving' disabled people. Senator Jesse Helms quizzed the proponent of the American bill repeatedly, asking 'does the bill cover' issues from paedophilia to schizophrenia, whether adoption agencies would still be allowed to take decisions based on diagnoses like schizophrenia – and ending by saying:

> If this were a bill involving people in a wheelchair or those who have been injured
> in the war, that is one thing. … But how did you get into the business of classi-
> fying people who are HIV positive, most of whom are drug addicts or homosexuals
> or bisexuals, as disabled? (for a fuller account see Sayce 2000).

In the face of this onslaught people with HIV, psychiatric disabilities (to use the American term) and other less popular groups agreed to operate a completely united front – to win or fall together. Survivor Judi Chamberlin travelled the US actively overcoming barriers between disability and mental health groups. She wrote:

We have grown closer to the disability community and discovered the common-
alities that we share. In the beginning this was difficult for both communities
because there were mutual levels of mistrust and of feeling that we did not have
the same problems. Many people with physical disabilities feared being lumped
in with 'crazy' people, while many former mental patients took the position that
'We're not disabled, we're just oppressed' ... What has happened has been a
process of mutual unlearning in which persons with both physical and psychiatric
disabilities have learnt to undo stereotypes and myths and see each other as the
individuals we are. (Chamberlin 1993).

In the UK the Disability Rights Commission (DRC), formed in 2000 to enforce and promote
the Disability Discrimination Act, set up a mental health advisory group made up of people
with lived experience, with an independent Chair Abina Parshad-Griffin. It published its
own disability rights agenda from a mental health perspective (DRC 2003). This included
rights challenges in areas from insurance to employment – and challenges to disproportionate approaches to risk, which jeopardised housing, led to removal of children and
compulsory detention – all on grounds of putative future risk not applied to other citizens
(see Chapter 4). DRC Commissioner Richard Exell and Chair Bert Massie spoke directly
about their commitment to address discrimination faced by people with mental health
challenges:

As someone with personal experience of depression I've been delighted to work
with users and survivors of mental health services from around Britain to help the
DRC address the particular types of discrimination we face. We are breaking down
fear and prejudice. (Richard Exell, cited in DRC 2002a).

We need to recognise that mental ill health is now operating as a badge of
exclusion from the labour market in the same way that race and gender once did.
(Massie 2006).

The DRC supported legal action taken by people facing discrimination on mental health
grounds and undertook formal investigations which made strong recommendations for
greater equality (see Chapter 6).

By 2013 the Government's disability advisory group Equality 2025 was chaired by someone
with lived experience – Rachel Perkins – and their 'Disability, Health and Employment
Strategy' had a distinct section on mental health: as Perkins put it, once mental health overtook musculo-skeletal problems as the largest group claiming 'incapacity' benefits, suddenly
policy makers intent on reducing the benefit bill became passionately interested in mental
health and employment (Perkins, personal communication).

Gradually some misconceptions about disability held in the mental health world were
dismantled. Sayce (2000) notes that the most common initial objections to the concept
of 'disability' are based on myths: for instance, 'but I am not born with my condition' (nor
are 98% of disabled people); or 'but my condition is not permanent' (nor are many physical
impairments from epilepsy to cancer). Papers and presentations shared the significance of
disability rights with mental health professional groups who became somewhat better able
to advise people using their services that they had some rights (see Sayce and Owen 2006;
Sayce and Boardman 2008).

May be change was in the air. Perhaps the 'disability inclusion' model could become the unifying rallying cry for people with mental health challenges – joining forces with disabled people more widely, as happened in America, to make rights real.

This model has a clear focus on full citizenship, it targets exclusion, it is rooted in disabled people's leadership ('nothing about us without us') – and we have begun to see disabled people's organisations tackling the particular discriminations that people with mental health challenges face within a wider disability rights agenda.

In terms of Link and Phelan's criteria, this model does challenge the negative loading of difference (criterion 2) – by arguing powerfully for equal respect and citizenship. It disrupts the separation of 'them' and 'us', by its focus on disabled people's rights to full inclusion in everything from education to employment; it challenges unequal life chances, through shining a light on material inequalities (employment, parenting rights and more); and it does all of this with attention to the power that drives both discrimination – and freedom from it. It turns to the power of civil rights law (see Chapter 6 for how this has been used and extended) and the collective power of people with lived experience to campaign and co-produce solutions with organisations (see Chapter 6). It is not tainted by sectional interests from pharmaceutical companies or particular professional groups promoting medical remedies – or indeed those challenging medical orthodoxies only to promote their own therapies, from CBT to psycho-analysis.

This model scores higher on subverting Link and Phelan's drivers of discrimination than the models explored in earlier chapters. But it is questionable whether it softens the line between 'us and them' – whether it does anything to meet the first of Link and Phelan's drivers – overcoming the process of distinguishing between and labelling human difference. Indeed it seems to require people to identify as disabled people in order to secure rights.

In 2000 I argued that it was necessary to emphasise difference, not downplay it – and it was therefore not useful even to try to subvert the first of Link and Phelan's components: we needed to be different and proud, not suppress difference or erase the power of collective action through common identity.

However, this argument may be more pertinent at some points in history than others. To fight against racial segregation in 1960s America, it was a sensible and perhaps essential strategy to bind black people together to fight for rights – under a common identity as African Americans. Similarly in 1990s Britain the Disability Discrimination Act was secured by forging a disability movement. However, developments since 2000 suggest the disability inclusion model has become overly entangled with identity politics for the current phase of history. It could evolve to be stronger for a new era.

Evolution of a model

If a model for equal citizenship relies on joining forces with the disability movement and sharing emancipatory ideas and language (social model, disabling barriers) – then the first problem is a pragmatic one: will it work? DWP (2003) found that 48% of people defined as 'disabled' by the DDA viewed themselves as 'disabled'; 52% did not. Follow-up research by the DRC with a sample of those who did NOT so identify found they viewed 'disability' as having a condition from birth, being permanently incapable, unable to do things for yourself and often 'bed-bound'.

Beresford et al. (2010) asked a fairly knowledgeable group of mental health service users their views on the social model of disability. Most knew of it but views were mixed. Some rejected it on the grounds that a mental health issue was not an objective 'impairment' like a physical impairment: this is probably another example of a misconception, in that the social model of disability presumes people face barriers because of perceived – not just actual – impairment. The key point is that mental health service users, in the main, even when knowledgeable about the social model, choose not to identify as 'disabled'.

The notion that people with depression or cancer are 'disabled people' does not seem to have reached the lay public – not even the 'disabled' lay public, who were the people engaged by the DRC and Peter Beresford. Moreover there is some evidence that numbers of people identifying as 'disabled people' is going down. DWP's 2003 research found – contrary to the common view that older people are less likely to identify as disabled, ascribing their impairments to the inevitability of ageing – that it was younger people who were least likely to identify. When DRC researchers went to schools seeking to interview 'young disabled people' they had no takers; once they changed the language and gave examples, young people with challenges from dyslexia to cerebral palsy came forward.

By 2013 the Office for Disability Issues published research that found the proportion of people defined by law as 'disabled' who identified as such had gone down – from 48% in 2003 to 24%. The numbers are not directly comparable, as numbers covered by (changed) legislation had risen – but this did not account for the scale of the change. The message was clear: three quarters of 'disabled people' did not view themselves that way and they were becoming less likely to do so.

This leads to a concern based on principle rather than pragmatism: why should people take on the identity of 'disabled person'? In the 1970s there was a move to encourage everyone of minority ethnic heritage to identify as Black. People of Turkish, Bangladeshi, Irish and other heritages were encouraged to shed or downplay those specific identities in favour of solidarity as Black people. Solidarity was important at a time when people were fighting for basic anti-racist protections (the Race Relations Act came in as late as 1976). However, the common identity did not hold. In time new terms – 'ethnic minorities', 'black and minority ethnic communities' came into being, to allow for greater recognition of difference; and the Census asked increasingly fine-grained questions about ethnic identity, for instance adding new 'traveller' and 'Arab' categories in 2011.

The effort to encourage over 11 million people living with a range of health conditions and impairments to identify as 'disabled people' is a similarly blunt tool. It runs counter to lay understandings of 'disability' and to the way people have developed their chosen self-identifications: as deaf people, or people living positively with HIV, or people who hear voices. In time the very idea that 11 million 'disabled people' live in Britain may seem absurd; a concoction of policy makers imposed against the grain of lay belief, rather than a reflection of how people live their lives. Nonetheless, many employers ask whether you are 'disabled' – perhaps with a definition in the fine print – and express surprise when few people tick the box. They might do better to list the type of impairment/condition first, asking whether people experience any of those – and only subsequently (if they wish) whether they consider themselves a 'disabled person'.

There are manifest risks in continuing to press for the 'disabled person' identity. Political commentators read it as a way of arguing for increased expenditure on a group they simply do not believe is as large as claimed. For instance, Alice Miles wrote in *The Times*:

The 11 million figure … includes those with mental illness, allergies, learning difficulties, stomach or liver problems, diabetes, epilepsy, bad digestion, 'bad nerves',
pain in the arms, head, shoulders, legs and feet, asthma, poor circulation and, the
highest category, back or neck problems. Oh, and 'other'. Which makes me disabled on at least four categories myself. It would be risible were it not for the fact
that the 11 million (or sometimes 10 million) is used to justify vast new interventions and therefore expense. Small business owners are told by the Government
that disabled people have £80 billion of spending power. The Disability Rights
Commission says it is £50 billion. £50 billion. £80 billion. A squillion billion. Take
your pick. You see how random it all is? (*The Times* 23 March 2005).

Businesses may resist the common message that the households of 11 million disabled
people have a spending power of £212 billion (DWP 2014) – because probing makes clear
that only by segmenting this market can a business fully benefit. There is no evidence that,
say, someone with depression would make consumer choices based on whether a counter has
a hearing loop; and if a hotel chain makes its rooms fully accessible to wheelchair users it
will realise a benefit (InterContinental Hotels showed a bottom-line benefit) – but since less
than 5% of the 11 million are wheelchair users, this act alone does not strictly speaking tap
into a £212 billion market, any more than a service that translates all materials into Bengali
taps into the whole black and minority ethnic market. More convincing 'business case' arguments segment the large market, remembering that many people have multiple impairments
and families and friends who will be deterred by lack of access (I recently had an argument
with a Westminster café that refused entry to my colleague's guide dog: after threats of legal
action they backed down, but lost my custom long-term as well as my colleague's).

To win a piece of legislation requires solidarity of 'disabled people', and to spark initial
business interest requires an overview of a large market. But the solid work of changing
institutions from hotels to health services requires a much more fine-grained understanding
of different people's experiences and aspirations.

There is a strong case for adopting a term equivalent to BME (black and minority ethnic) –
to signal differences of experience within a wider grouping. A couple of suggestions have been
tried. Radar used 'people living with IID' (ill-health, injury or disability); Disability Rights UK
used 'people with lived experience of disability or long-term health conditions'. These terms
are imperfect: strictly one could argue for 'lived experience of disability including [not "or"]
long-term health conditions' , since health conditions count as disability under legislation;
and none of these terms captures being disabled by society. There are, though, advantages:
these terms signal an inclusive approach, with no suppression of difference and no reduction
to a lowest common denominator (the problem of the wheelchair symbol for access). They
increase credibility of statements about the size, voting and spending power of the group:
the public and *Times* journalists are ready to believe that over 11 million of us – one in five –
are living with a health condition or disability, but not that one in five is a 'disabled person'
(given the bed-confined person or wheelchair user they have in mind). And these terms make
it easier for people to understand that rights accorded to 'disabled people' might apply to
them – as people living with HIV, schizophrenia, or cancer.

This questioning of group identification is happening in a context of growing unease
about a form of identity politics that 'boxes people in' to categories, as Fanshawe and

Sriskandarajah (2010) put it (see Chapter 3). They argue that as Britain becomes more super-diverse, people are ever less likely to identify primarily as 'black', 'Asian', 'gay' or 'disabled'. These categories tell us little about life chances – firstly because there are such differences within them (the employment rate of African men, for instance, ranges from 20% amongst Somalis to 80% amongst Ghanaians); and secondly because increasing numbers of people live in super-diverse families and communities, of mixed ethnic heritage, mixed religions. There is no such thing as the 'Muslim community' or the 'disability community'. And younger people are more likely to adopt fluid identities – for instance, having same-sex relationships without identifying as gay.

Campaigns adopted by young people tend to focus on issues (poverty, the environment) whereas campaigns of the baby boomer generation focused more on identities (gay liberation, the women's movement, the disability movement).

As Baroness Jane Campbell (2008) put it, drawing on the work of Nancy Fraser:

> There are risks of an overly narrow representation of disabled people, which denies the complexity of people's lives, the multiplicity of their identifications and the cross-pulls of their various affiliations. The rich diversity of disabled people has too often been reduced to the wheelchair symbol.

A 'disability inclusion' model may be rooted in a 1990s world that now seems overly to 'box people in', to require people living with mental health challenges to identify as 'disabled people' in order to benefit from inclusion.

Peter Beresford, conscious of this difficulty, has explored a 'social model of madness'. He encountered an initial lack of consensus amongst people with mental health challenges on the merits of 'madness', 'distress' or other terms of identity; but this work is developing. There is some ambiguity as to whether a social model of madness is concerned with the social barriers you encounter once 'mad' (akin to the social model of disability) or with the social causation of distress/madness: as described in the maxim that we should always ask 'not what is wrong with you, but what happened to you?', i.e. inquire about past trauma (Onken 2012). The latter could mean only challenging biological explanations of mental illness. Whilst useful on many levels (see Chapter 3), this would lose the potential of the original disability inclusion model to unite people whatever their understanding of causation, specifically to create full citizenship participation.

The social model of disability, which underpins the disability inclusion model, has been subject to critiques and changes. Some are helpful in bringing the model closer to mental health thinking. For instance, Carol Thomas (2004) has emphasised the importance of emotional encounters, as well as physical barriers – a particularly important development for people with mental health challenges; and Beresford's social model of madness has real potential. Others raise fundamental questions about the model itself.

It is unusual for a group of people to define themselves purely by the way they are oppressed – 'we are disabled by society'. More commonly, groups create an identification that embraces pride or positive possibility – being gay, or living positively (with HIV), for example. There is a risk that having thrown off the image of the 'tragic victim' of impairment, disabled people now become victims again – this time of discrimination. In the 2000s a leadership programme run by and for disabled people was met with the following view from some individuals: 'but we cannot become leaders; first organisations must remove barriers, only then can we participate'. The social model was being used as a prescription for passivity; the liberating idea that the 'problem' was external barriers had been turned into a new form of restriction, holding people back from engaging in a dynamic process of exercising leadership, being part of the change you want to see. Takala (2009) and Shakespeare (2014), whilst recognising the social model's achievements, argue that it has contributed to a culture of victimhood, with activists likely to emphasise oppression to the exclusion of recognition of progress.

In 2011 Radar published a document 'Making Disability Rights Real Now' which started by celebrating the achievements of the movement: creating centres for independent living, lobbying successfully for anti-discrimination law and progressive improvements to it, persuading companies to improve their practices. It noted that disabled people had become more likely to be open about disability, more likely to take up leadership roles, more likely to know their rights.

More often, paradoxically, disabled people's organisations downplay their own achievements – highlighting the horrors of discrimination and inequality. Shakespeare argues controversially that the big focus of disability activists on hate crime is a symptom of this tendency. Challenging egregious crimes on the basis of disability must surely be important, but needs to be done within an ambitious endeavour for positive participation.

Being defined by oppression can also obscure positive aspects of living with disability.

Positive models of madness and participation

In 2010 Radar undertook the first national survey of disabled people succeeding in their careers. Over 1,400 people responded, providing clear evidence on what enabled people to succeed (career-long senior-level support, and mentoring). A repeated theme from qualitative interviews was that the experience of living with a mental health challenge or other impairment brought transferrable skills. For instance:

> Most people with disabilities have extra coping skills ... Sell those. It sets you apart from the herd.

> My employer has used me as a mentor ... My disability helps me relate to my colleagues (Sayce 2010).

Numerous accounts by people with living with mental health challenges conclude that if they had the choice, they would not be without the experience. For example, Lady Gaga has spoken of how her extreme costumes are a way of expressing and dealing with her experience of hearing voices: it's how I feel about my insanity, she says.

Kay Jamison, a professor of psychiatry who personally lives with manic depression (her preferred term) has found through international research that people with this experience make more connections in their thinking, more rapidly, than others. If people are able to harness and edit this experience, it can lead to new business ideas, scientific or artistic thinking. Of her own experience, she writes that whilst the depressions leave all things dark and devoid of feeling, the highs leave cocaine in the dust – with ideas and feelings like shooting stars and the power to captivate others a known certainty. If she had the choice to be without her condition she would opt to have it (Jamison 1995).

Peter Chadwick, a psychologist with personal experience of schizophrenia, has written about the blurring of boundaries between self and others, self and environment – and the empathy and spiritual awareness this can bring:

> Schizophrenia, creativity and spiritual experience are all intimately connected ... Thinking in this way about the condition can help health professionals to realise that people with schizophrenia are kith and kin and that they have abilities that can be used to enhance the future of our world. (Chadwick 2002).

Mary O'Hagan, in her memoir aptly called *Madness Made Me* argues for a culture of madness, a valuing of mad experience (O'Hagan 2014, p. 113):

> My madness took me places I had never been. It showed me the universe without its clothes. It stripped my mind of all its chattels. It rubbed my nose in the divine. It turned the lights off all over the undulating continent of my brain. Many people pass through this territory at some time in their lives. Most manage to skirt their away around the edge of it and look on with dread at a distance. But those who are forced right into its belly come out with richer pictures of a being that has been lost and found again.

A life lived with madness may be awful, or wonderful, or mixed. It cannot be reduced to the experience of oppression.

Shakespeare (2014) favours a relational model of disability, which puts more emphasis on disabled people's action – escaping the trap of passivity. Van den Ven et al. (2005) propose a model of 'integration' with five dimensions, including 'trying to reach one's potential, which may need help from others' and 'being director of one's own life'.

There is a fine line between placing enough emphasis on the agency of the individual – and blaming the victim. The climate in Britain tends to the punitive: imposing benefit sanctions if you do not comply with the Work Programme with its 88% failure rate (Crowther and Sayce 2013) or do not apply for four jobs a week, however much job seeker and employer time is wasted in nonsensical applications. The rhetoric of empowerment should not be a cover for placing all responsibilities on the individual, when the state and employers are crucial to opening up opportunities. It is too easy to emphasise 'integration' in the sense of expecting the individual to fit in with existing social norms, with no scope to stretch those norms or even make adjustments so the person can meet requirements.

Nonetheless, with the strong proviso that the responsibilities of those with power must be met, an emphasis on individual agency is a vital corrective to versions of the social model that encourage people to wait for barriers to be removed. Waiting is particularly problematic in the area of employment – if people who are out of work wait until there are no barriers, their chances of working will reduce dramatically as each month passes.

Crowther (2014) has explored capability theory, as developed by Amartya Sen, to propose new approaches to achieving equal citizenship, articulating new responsibilities for the state as well as individual agency and control. He argues that public policy should invest in disabled people's capabilities – expecting people to participate and contribute, and equally according them the rights and supports they require to do so. This involves a major shift from a safety net to an investment state, from a deficit model to one based on strengths. It envisages disabled people living self-authored lives, exercising power over self-directed support or appointing advocates to do so. This places a much greater emphasis on strengths, generating resilience and enabling people to grow than the original 'strong social model'. It focuses hard on networks to do so – social connectedness that strengthens people's capabilities to participate. An example of a practical difference this would make is that, instead of 'safeguarding' policies to protect 'vulnerable' people, we would see supported risk-taking – in which people with mental health challenges secure support on their own terms to pursue the lives they want, managing risks in line with their priorities – not simply avoiding risks identified by professionals.

The relational model advocated by Shakespeare (2014) can fit with capability theory but there are questions of interpretation. Shakespeare cites Macintyre (1999) in arguing that we all have periods of needing to rely on others, to unpredictable degrees, and that therefore the interests of 'disabled people' are not the specific interests of one group, but of the whole of society – integral to our collective conception of the common good. This notion of mutual and changing dependence is helpful in widening the significance of support requirements – but it is vital that 'dependence' does not erode autonomy or power. A model implying that at times some of us are just 'looked after' because of our mental health problems and left powerless in our dependency would set the clock back.

Shakespeare favours giving more prominence to impairment (sometimes downplayed in Britain's 'strong' social model, with its hard focus on barriers), and wants recognition that impairment and the disabling society shade into each other. He recommends intervening at different levels – the impairment, the environment, the relationship between the two (rather than just removing barriers, as the social model might prescribe). It is helpful to stress that impairment and disabling barriers are intertwined, and many people with mental health challenges want treatments as part of the way they manage experiences from depression to hearing voices. For the specific purpose of opening up citizenship opportunities, however, there is a risk in focusing on impairment. An overwhelming paradigm in mental health policy is to focus on treatments as a means to social inclusion: witness the claim that 'improving access to psychological therapies' (IAPT) would lead to improved employment outcomes (see Chapter 1). A model to enhance citizenship must focus on the external environment and the individual actor within it. Focusing more on impairment would be a step backwards, to the discredited idea that clinical improvement itself brings greater social participation. Sadly it does not (see Chapter 1).

The so-called 'capabilities' approach is valuable for the citizenship participation of people with mental health challenges. The mental health sector has a huge amount to offer the wider world of disability rights in supporting 'capabilities' in this sense. Recovery, at its best, is all about being the author of your own life, securing support – including peer support, and connectedness – to build strengths and participation. This is a more dynamic understanding than much independent living theory, which is often more practically based (how to employ a personal assistant, how to take autonomous decisions). The recovery movement grapples with the sense of loss on acquiring a diagnosis (loss of the life you thought you would have) and the process of taking charge to build a life of meaning and purpose (Repper and Perkins 2003).

Whilst the name 'capability theory' is problematic (with unfortunate echoes of the work capability assessment), the theory offers a new evolution of the disability inclusion model. It is congruent with human rights – and therefore has the benefit of not requiring people to 'box themselves' in to a disability identity. It emphasises our common humanity and a goal of participation across our numerous, complex differences of experience.

In 2014 journalist Robert Fisk wrote about the wish of Jewish people to ensure the history of the holocaust was never forgotten, in part by retaining the word 'holocaust' as something qualitatively different from the genocide of, for instance, Armenians. Fisk, with the greatest respect, disagreed. He argued that it is only through recognising our common humanity that we stand any chance of remembering the 20th-century industrial-scale genocides: by recognising that 'these people were our people. Their fathers and mothers and brothers and sisters were our fathers and mothers and brothers and sisters.' In other words, whilst at times we need to demonstrate our group differences, ultimately discrimination will only wither through a deep recognition of common humanity.

In the disability field, rather than relying on group identity as 'disabled people', we should recognise that we are all likely to experience health conditions and impairments, it is part of the human condition – and it should not divide us.

The full participation of people living with any health condition or impairment is in everyone's interests because it makes policies and practices work for all. As David Cameron acknowledged in 2013: 'What hope do we have in this global race if we lose out on the talent and skills of one fifth of our population? It would be like competing with one hand tied behind our back' (Cameron 2013). Any recovery has to be inclusive simply to succeed.

In 2007 the DRC published the Disability Agenda, which articulated the point that most priority policy issues are disability issues, once probed; and can only be resolved through attention to disability, in all its diversity. At the time it was commonplace for disability organisations to emphasise that *children in families experiencing disability* were at least twice as likely to live in poverty as non-disabled children (a point that had resonance for people concerned about social justice and disability). The DRC changed the message by a simple reversal in the statistical base – by stating that a third of *all children living in poverty* had at least one disabled parent; only then did policy-makers realise they could not reach their main target to halve child poverty without finding solutions for families experiencing disability. John Hutton, then Secretary of State for Work and Pensions, stated 'child poverty is a disability issue'. On the same argument, it is hard to improve the nation's skills or the nation's health without an inclusive approach that supports the skills and health of disabled people.

In 2009 the UK ratified the UN Convention on the Rights of Persons with Disabilities (UNCRPD). It lays out rights to participation, inclusive employment and education, leisure, housing and more. It has the advantage of emphasising common humanity – whilst recognising specific requirements of people with mental health challenges and other experiences of disability. For instance, the UN Convention Committee visited Austria in 2013 and expressed concern at the way people with mental health problems were being detained – an issue that might not have risen to the surface in a completely generic assessment of human rights; the 'disability' convention gives focus, within a framework of rights for all.

Of course human rights frameworks can have their downsides: they may encourage nations only to reach the 'floor' of decent treatment – for instance, reducing torture and degrading treatment and never getting on to aspirations for equality. And in Britain they may be ignored – Britain is unusual in not using human rights as its main framework for considering equalities issues. In 2014 Conservative Home Secretary Theresa May said a future

Conservative government would repeal the Human Rights Act – prompting Liberty to take out press advertisements contrasting the commitment from the same Government *to* human rights abroad, *against* human rights at home.

Work has begun to reframe human rights, to link 'our' rights to the fundamental beliefs of the British public in fairness and protection from injustice, mobilising the power of both communications and law. Human rights have the potential – linked to 'capability theory' – to act as a framework for citizenship participation of people with mental health challenges that both links to others – disabled, not disabled, of any ethnicity, religion – and also gives some specific attention, through the UNCRPD, to the rights of people who are mad.

CONCLUSION

The original disability inclusion model that I described in 2000 was highly effective in bringing people together across experiences of mental health and other disability/health conditions to campaign for civil rights – under the banner of 'disability' rights. In particular, from a mental health point of view, this led to the Disability Discrimination Act 1995 (DDA) that gave the first-ever protection against discrimination on mental health grounds; to the DDA 2005, which gave improved protection to people with depression as well as cancer and MS; and to debarring employer pre-job offer health questions under the Equality Act 2010, achieved through expert collaborative lobbying by Radar, Rethink, National AIDS Trust and Macmillan.

The disability inclusion model is a highly credible approach to reversing the lethal drivers of discrimination articulated by Link and Phelan. It strongly revalues difference (criterion 2), challenges separation between disabled and non-disabled people (criterion 3) and uses power – of law in particular – to prevent unequal life chances (criterion 4).

It does not, however, address the first criterion – softening the line of difference between people living with mental health challenges and others: the model tends to expect large numbers of people to rally under the identity of 'disabled people'. Arguably the model itself is entangled with identity politics in ways that 'box people in' to a category, rather than respond to the fluidities of people's identities (including mental health aspects of identity). This renders the model in some respects less suited to the next challenges – securing rights and full participation in practice, beyond the statute book.

This chapter argues that for these purposes, we need both to take a more fine-grained approach that recognises super-diversity (the micro-differences between people living in families with so many combinations of mixed ethnicity, faiths, combinations of 'caring' and experiences of health problems). But we also need to go wider, linking our issues to a much broader experience – our common humanity, our common interests, and our 'human' rights, from which may flow an erosion of the distinction between 'us' and 'them'.

Other developments of the 'social model of disability' have proposed a shift from an identity based on being oppressed – 'we are disabled by society' – to relational and 'capability' focused approaches that build a more dynamic model of rights. Under this approach, the state's responsibility is to invest in people's participation rather than running a residual 'safety net', building on strengths rather than managing 'deficits', facilitating networked solutions – including peer support. People living with mental health challenges would have corresponding rights – to self-directed and networked support, to positive action to redress inequalities.

This would extend sources of power, from a narrow focus on legal rights, to the power of people to create change, seizing leadership and working with decision-makers to forge new 'mainstream' practices: demonstrating that the challenges of the nation, from skills to health, can only be met by attending to disability.

The term 'capability' theory may seem confusing, but the ideas are helpful, and linking them to human rights frames an approach which avoids both 'boxing people' in and embedding oppression into our identities.

This gives space for people to come together over specific issues, as younger people increasingly do – linking to new issues instantly online – rather than joining a common identity. It enables people to unite on mental health and disability issues when there is reason and motivation to do so. Equally, people may want to engage in issues from housing to culture, without seeing themselves as disabled, mad or distressed – without joining the category.

Because there are some shared issues between people living with different health and impairment experiences it would be useful to build agreement on a language to describe people living with any kind of health condition or impairment – to facilitate sharing and shared campaigns. The purpose is not to create an identity to 'join' – but to bring far more people together over common issues, without the hurdle of identifying as 'disabled'. Suggestions to date include 'people with lived experience of disability or health conditions' or 'people living with ill health, injury or disability (IID)'. Further debate is required.

Amongst issues in common is the necessary challenge to notions of 'perfect' humanity. As Leonard Cohen put it:

> Forget your perfect offering. There is a crack in everything. That's what lets the light get in.

The concept of a norm of a perfect physical or mental being is a myth. Humanity varies and we all experience health issues and disability in our lives. Working together, those viewed as different can push the bounds of those norms, stretch them, and assert our right to fully belong unconditionally, not by 'fitting in'. People may need support and adjustments to fully participate: by asserting our rights to independent living we create the conditions to be full contributors.

There is an irony in a society that describes people as scroungers whilst not providing the supports to enable us to contribute. Working together we can advocate for rights to independent living, for support to use our strengths. In 2014 Disability Rights UK brought independent living leaders together – including John Evans, who had 'escaped' from a Leonard Cheshire home in the 1980s and been instrumental in developing the first centres for independent living. DR UK with partners forged proposals for rights to independent living for the next historical period (www.disabilityrightsuk.org).

It is time to develop the disability inclusion model, to break its strong link to identity politics as well as retaining its great strengths in revaluing the human differences of mental health challenges and using power to stop separation and end unequal life chances.

This chapter has looked at the social models of disability and madness, and hinted at a social model of perfection, with people uniting to challenge the norms by which those who are mentally or physically 'different' are judged. But in the end the goal is equal human participation. We need a social model of participation that recognises a dynamic approach to

rights, with autonomous individuals accessing networks and self-directed support to participate fully, matched by strong and proactive duties of the state to prevent discrimination
and positively facilitate growth and participation. This could extend sources of power, using
law but also exercising leadership to channel the power of institutions to tackle mainstream
aims through inclusive approaches. This is firmly not about placing the burden of responsibility on individuals. But nor does it leave the individual as a victim of oppression. It loosens
the emphasis on identity politics to draw deeply on our common humanity and human rights.
For clarity we might call it a participation rights model.

Reflective Exercises

For someone experiencing mental health challenges, what may be the pros and cons of
considering yourself 'disabled'?

What do the core human rights to independent living, participation, equality and an
adequate standard of living mean in people's lives? How would a mental health service
demonstrably respect them?

FURTHER READING

Shakespeare, T. (2014) *Disability Rights and Wrongs Revisited.* Routledge: London.

- Book subjecting the social model of disability to scrutiny and analysing theoretical developments that
  can advance both thinking and practice in disability

Disability Rights Commission (2003) *Coming Together: Mental Health Service Users and Disability Rights.*
DRC: London.

- Written by a Mental Health Advisory Group (MHAG), made up of people with lived experience of
  mental health issues, this paper applies disability rights to people with mental health problems and
  sets out demands from a mental health viewpoint

Disability Rights Commission (2006) *Coming Together: Mental Health Service Users and Human Rights.*
DRC: London.

- Again written by the MHAG of the Disability Rights Commission, this paper lays out the human rights
  issues of most concern to people living with mental health challenges

Campbell, J. (2008) *Fighting for a Slice or for a Bigger Cake? 6th Annual Disability Lecture.* Cambridge:
University of Cambridge

- A lecture outlining a new approach to disability rights, with stronger emphasis on disabled people's
  full participation and leadership than in classic social model thinking

Crowther, N. (2014) *Refreshing the Disability Rights Agenda – a Future Imagined.* www.makingrights-
makesense.wordpress.com

Beresford, P., Nettle, M. and Perring, R. (2010) *Towards a Social Model of Madness and Distress? Exploring
What Service Users Say.* New York: Joseph Rowntree Foundation

- An exploration of views of a social model of madness amongst people living with mental health
  challenges

6 | Learning from Campaigns, Policies and Research: What has Worked?

Chapter Summary

- Drawing on the 'models' to effectively achieve more equal life chances
- Subverting the labelling of difference
- Revaluing difference – from messaging to 'mad pride'
- Overcoming separation: the importance of contact
- Equal life chances: systemic legal powers, citizen power, the power of incentives
- A long-term strategy: contact on equal terms in day-to-day life

Mixing and matching models

The last three chapters explored different models used in the well-motivated – but not always well-grounded – endeavour to improve citizenship opportunities. It tested them against their use of power in reversing Link and Phelan's (2001) four components of stigma/discrimination, especially the unequal life chances (component 4) that matter most to people: housing, jobs, income, freedom from crime and bullying, freedom from the fear of children being taken away, respect within mental health services (Sayce 2000; Social Exclusion Unit 2004; Corker et al. 2013). It found that some models should not be used, some had limitations and some had far more promise.

Addressing the four components need not be sequential (see Chapter 2): if action can get straight to the heart of overcoming discrimination without touching the other drivers, that can be effective.

The 'illness like any other' model did not address the drivers of discrimination at all. In particular it devalued rather than revalued difference (component 2): this message tends to increase the view that people with 'mental illness' are incapable, unpredictable and dangerous. It did not overcome separation or unequal life chances.

The 'individual growth' model softened the line between 'them' and 'us' (component 1); but tended to stop at encouraging people to seek help, with no impact on separation (component 2) or unequal life chances (component 4); and no effective use of power.

The libertarian model launched a direct attack on unequal life chances, in the form of unfair coercion (component 4) and used power of legislation and litigation to create change. But on its own it was not wide-reaching enough to create a sea change in behaviours and attitudes.

The social security protection model also intervened directly on unequal life chances, this time in terms of greater poverty (component 4), and used the power of social media to influence policy-makers; but it carried some risk of reinforcing notions of incapacity, which meant it did not fully revalue difference and could paradoxically limit opportunities for equal citizenship.

The participation rights model addresses all the drivers. It extends sources of power – seizing leadership as well as using law – to press for investment in citizen participation and policies that work for all. It matches individual participation with state responsibilities.

These models can be 'mixed and matched' depending on the objective, with three provisos. Firstly, the 'illness like any other' model should not be used; it is counter-productive. Secondly, for an overarching initiative to overcome discrimination and enhance citizenship, the participation rights model is the most promising. Thirdly, the selection of approach needs to be guided by purpose and external opportunities and challenges. For instance, in a time of austerity when activists are divided (see Chapter 4), the participation rights model may 'rise above the terrain' of disagreement and help build bridges.

The rest of this chapter is devoted to discussing 'what works'.

Softening the lines of difference

The most common practical approach to reversing the first driver of stigma – distinguishing between and labelling human difference – is through 'universal' policies that aim to make our cities, communities, workplaces and schools work well for everyone.

A games for all

In the lead-up to 2012, the London Legacy Development Programme committed itself to 'designing and building places that everyone – regardless of disability, gender, sexual orientation, race or faith – can enjoy confidently and independently with choice and dignity'. They wanted no disabling barriers, so everyone could take part without separation or 'special' treatment. Some initiatives focused on physical design – like lifetime neighbourhood standards, enabling people with mobility impairments, buggies or luggage to move around with ease – but they also committed to putting people at the heart of design. Housing developments aimed to 'design out' crime, to reduce the fear of going out for people who might be subject to hate crime. Thousands of volunteers welcomed travellers to the Games – which benefited people experiencing anxiety or confusion and lost tourists as Londoners caught the mood and started, rather uncharacteristically, to talk to each other and help out (London Legacy Development Corporation (LLDC) 2011).

Universal policies are also useful in the workplace.

A list of 'workplace adjustments' for people with mental health challenges (the equivalent of adapted chairs or technology for people with physical impairments) reads like a manual of good general management practice. Boston University's Center for Psychiatric Rehabilitation promotes evidence-based accommodations including:

Changes in supervision:

- Providing extra supervision hours
- Modifying the way feedback and instructions are given.

Flexible scheduling:

- Changes in the start or end of work day hours
- Part-time hours
- More frequent breaks.

It is a routine outcome of management training to understand the differing motivations, career stages and learning styles of employees, so managers vary the type and frequency of feedback and instruction: some thrive on maximum autonomy, others on frequent guidance; some on accountability against hard objectives, others on a more discursive approach to learning.

> To lead most effectively, you need to modify your management style to accommodate the needs of each team member. The flexible leader recognizes that there is nothing inauthentic about modifying his or her approach as needed. (Bywater 2012).

Flexibilities may be 'adjustments' for someone with a mental health condition – but can benefit all employees and enhance productivity, in a win-win. Flexible scheduling can work for someone doing an evening degree or supporting children or an older relative.

Asking all employees what will help them perform to their best

Some employers have taken a 'universal' approach to meeting diverse employee requirements. They abandoned the traditional approach of finding out who is legally entitled to a 'reasonable' adjustment and only then making it – and instead asked all employees whether there was anything they needed to perform to their best. If it fitted with business needs, then meeting the request was likely to increase motivation and loyalty.

BT managers were trained in identifying and managing stress in their teams – and given data on stress-related absence and helpful resources. This was not a 'special' arrangement for people experiencing mental distress but an organisation-wide approach to improving well-being and performance.

Health, work and well-being plans

Rachel Perkins set up a programme in 1995 that deliberately employed and supported people with mental health challenges within an NHS Trust, followed by a Charter committing them to employing people with lived experience in all jobs. By 2010 23% of all recruits had lived experience – and the proportion was higher the more senior the staff (31% at bands eight and nine, including Director of Nursing, Chief Executive, and a consultant psychiatrist who had been sectioned under the Mental Health Act).

To support people she introduced a 'health, work and well-being toolkit'. It rapidly became clear that it worked for everyone. It starts by asking you to specify what is important to your well-being at work: anything from getting home to see the kids, to being thanked when you do a good job or having opportunities to develop. It leads into planning what to do if you are having an off day – perhaps take a short break, talk to a colleague – or if 'the wheels come off'. Finally it encourages you to specify what your line manager can do to support your plans. The manager is pre-prepared by going through the same process him- or herself.

This tool is as useful to someone planning how to deal with their next psychotic episode as to the person considering how to deal with their anger at a colleague. The message is: we all have bad times; we can all benefit from tools to help us plan and manage them; and managers have responsibilities. A second toolkit helps plan for a return to work – after anything from time off with a mental health problem or bereavement to having a child – including how to talk to colleagues and get back up to speed (Perkins 2012a).

The philosophy of universalism is that everyone belongs. Some start from a young age. In 1988 Newham Local Authority set the following vision:

> The ultimate goal of Newham council's education policy is to make it possible for every child, whatever special educational needs they may have, to attend their neighbourhood school, to have full access to the national curriculum, to be able to participate in every aspect of mainstream life and achieve their full potential. (London Borough of Newham 2001).

By 2014 Newham continued to be the highest performing council in the country in terms of inclusion of children with 'special needs' (including behavioural and mental health issues), sending just two per thousand children to special schools, compared to seven times that in the worst performing authority (Centre for Studies in Inclusive Education 2014).

In the 2000s there were a number of legal cases supporting children to be fully included in the curriculum and life of the school. Lee Buniak, who had autism, was registered to attend a mainstream school – but was often left alone, and denied the chance to be in the school photograph and school play. His family took a case, supported by the DRC, and won – which led to heart-warming tabloid headlines about the need for all children to reach their potential. Nonetheless during the 2010s numbers of children in special schools went up – beyond the 100,000 mark by 2013 – due to a policy shift away from inclusive schools particularly after 2010.

Under a universalist argument, a successful economic recovery is aided by the skills and participation of all citizens. In 2014 business leaders sought to maximise the skills of all the population – reversing the structural increase in youth unemployment that pre-dated the recession – and to improve productivity, which lagged behind competitors (UKCES 2013).

In 2007 the Social Market Foundation estimated that if the skills of disabled people were brought up to the same level as non-disabled people it would boost the economy by £13 billion by 2020 (Evans 2007).

In 2014, Disability Rights UK produced guidance for both local authorities and disabled people's organisations on inclusive communities. They linked three components of citizenship participation to major local policy drivers:

1. Social citizenship. Increased social participation of 'disabled people' (including people with mental health issues) would contribute to the community's well-being and reduce isolation. These were major priorities of England's health and well-being boards.
2. Economic citizenship. Increased economic participation would support local growth. Hartlepool authority made a simple switch in employment support for people with learning disabilities from social services to the economic regeneration team. The employment rate of those known to social services reached double the national average (15% as compared to 7% – still low, but improved).
3. Political citizenship. In 2014 government, with the Local Government Association, encouraged more disabled people to stand as councillors, to meet a need for a bigger talent pool of councillors. This built on the Speakers' Conference work to increase diversity in Parliament (Speaker's Conference 2010) and included work with political parties to remove barriers and support aspiring leaders.

In 2007 the DRC launched the Disability Agenda (see Chapter 5). This argued that policies that enabled participation of disabled people were quite simply better policies. If social care could be turned from a safety net to a springboard for independent living, this could benefit disabled people, their (often female) informal family supporters, their (often female, often BME) paid carers – and the wider community, as people turned from recipient to valued citizen, fulfilling roles from grandparent to friend and neighbour (DRC 2007).

The essence of this 'softening the line' of difference is to accommodate differences, in win-wins for whole communities, whole workplaces – whole countries.

It does not happen on its own. It develops through committed champions and innovators – working outside and inside systems – and through the exercise of power.

The Greater London Authority's and LLDC's commitment to inclusive design was articulated as part of their public sector equality duty – a legal requirement on public sector organisations from 2006 to set out plans to positively promote equality; to act proactively and systemically – not just respond to discrimination after the event, as earlier race and gender law had done. The (revised) public sector equality duty under the Equality Act 2010 might entail engaging with disabled people, and monitoring employment rates, or health or policing outcomes: if this revealed inequalities between disabled people (or groups of disabled people) and other citizens, this could stimulate an action plan to achieve better outcomes.

Barclays, BT and others were ahead of the curve in ditching pre-job offer questions about health and disability. They did so partly because they were a waste of money – there was no correlation between a stated health condition/impairment and performance, so why waste money on occupational health questionnaires? But many other organisations still used them, leaving many with the awful quandary of how to answer questions on mental health history: tell the truth and risk being rejected without ever being able to prove this stemmed from discrimination, cover the career gap with a lie and you could later be sacked. In 2010 the Equality Act made pre-job offer questions on health illegal except in highly specified circumstances (for instance, to arrange for reasonable adjustments for interview) – which has given people with non-visible conditions increased confidence. If someone is now rejected on health grounds, it has to happen after job offer, be transparent, and open to challenge. The legislation spread good practice beyond the pioneering organisations that led the way.

Newham was ahead of legal requirements. Until 2001, when the DDA was extended, there was no protection against discrimination in education. Other authorities began to follow suit (although more recent policy has shifted away from the goal of inclusive education).

Work to develop an 'inclusive community' is guided by the Equality Duty and by accessibility requirements on all service providers – private, voluntary, public – see http://www.equality-humanrights.com/private-and-public-sector-guidance/public-sector-providers/public-sector-equality-duty. Making inclusion real is also influenced by the power of citizens. Pye and Sayce (2014) describe four levels of engagement to develop inclusive policy and practice: from tokenistic 'consultation' at one end, to full co-production and leadership by disabled people at the other.

Good customer service for all

When Intercontinental Hotels (which covers hotel chains from Holiday Inn Express to Crowne Plaza and Intercontinental) decided to be exemplars in accessibility, they trained all their customer service staff by reference to the example of a guest with a disability or health condition. If staff could demonstrate flexible, respectful and effective customer service to them, their skills could be transferred to all customers.

Inclusive towns and communities

When partners came together to develop dementia-friendly towns and communities, people living with dementia were involved as champions – offering peer support to others recently diagnosed, influencing local companies to become 'dementia friendly' and helping shape the work of organisations from banks to local authorities, as they changed their practices to make it easier for people with dementia to go out, manage their money, extend their social networks, find their way if confused – and have a good life (Local Government Association and Innovations in Dementia 2012).

Universalist approaches do not rule out the need for individualised adjustments. An excellent mental health at work policy will anticipate what is needed – but not address each individual requirement: for instance, if someone working on a till needs frequent toilet breaks because of medication effects, a manager needs to identify the rostering solution to make that work. The policy will commit to flexibility – but the specifics require a can-do attitude and imagination on all sides. Many adjustments cost nothing – for instance, more frequent feedback or a different start and finish time to avoid rush hour traffic; others may cost a few hundred pounds, for instance additional mentoring.

Universalist approaches rely on power – the power of legislation and litigation, the power of co-produced solutions, in which major organisations share their power with citizens.

The work to soften the lines of difference may address component 1 of work to overthrow discrimination and stigma. But legal powers and activism to change life chances (component 4) were a necessary precondition of much work on inclusion described here.

Revaluing difference

'I pledge to welcome and accept everyone on their own terms.' Thus ran one pledge amongst many made on the occasion of the 2013 global gathering of anti-stigma campaigns in London.

This message epitomises revaluing difference – unconditionally accepting people whose experiences may be different from many people's, not only if they 'act normal'. In practice this would mean someone who has just decided to be open at work would be treated with at least as much respect as before; that a waiter serving someone who was talking to themselves and seemed distressed might ask them if they were OK, but would not reject them. This is about communities becoming better able to accommodate ordinary human differences, not reacting with fear. It is about unlearning the tendency of families and communities to leave dealing with 'mad' people to the experts.

Practical examples can be very ordinary:

Knowing you belong

At a meeting, as introductions were made round the table, a government official gave her name and mentioned that if she were to get up and move around during the meeting, it was just because she was having particular difficulties with panic attacks and moving helped them; we could all just carry on. Everyone nodded and easily complied with the request. Whilst this kind of request is reasonably commonplace in Britain in relation to deaf people asking to give an interpreter a break or face them when speaking, it is unusual with people with mental health issues.

At an event for business disability networks in Canary Wharf, mental health was opened up as a topic by speakers. In informal discussion a woman from a major bluechip company chatted easily about how her manager had welcomed her back after she had been off with bipolar and how she had now talked with the whole team about what it meant, which had put them all at their ease; all had been supportive.

It is possible to imagine a world in which speaking about our mental health, and any adjustments we need, becomes very ordinary; where talking *about* people behind their backs is replaced by us all talking about our experiences.

It could of course be argued that extremes of difference are harder to accommodate. Yet there are many communities and families that do accommodate unusual behaviours: from the friendship groups operating a support rota for someone in crisis, to cafés which accept seemingly eccentric people who make one cup of tea last an afternoon. Britain has come some way since incarcerating large numbers of people in distant institutions. It is possible to extend communities' capacity to accept.

Societies will always decree some behaviours unacceptable; but we need to distinguish between madness and crime. If someone with a mental health condition commits a crime, it is reasonable for a community to respond in line with the rules of the day. Most crime, though, is committed by people with *no* mental health diagnosis (Institute of Medicine 2006); and crime is very different from unusual behaviour and conversations.

If the aim is to extend acceptance of difference, the question is what has worked best to achieve it.

The most compelling evidence is that contact – in particular circumstances – can significantly change behaviours and attitudes towards groups viewed as 'other'. Hewstone found that when non-Jewish Germans had Jewish friends in childhood, the likelihood of them rescuing Jewish people when the Nazi oppression started was 12 times higher than amongst people who had had no Jewish friends (Hewstone 2012). The kind of contact that changes attitudes is repeated or ongoing.

Hewstone, from a meta-analysis of over 500 articles, finds that 'meaningful' contact between different groups (across ethnicity, religion, psychiatric status and more) reduces prejudiced attitudes. Contact is more meaningful when it allows people to get to know each other, i.e. is more than just physical proximity. It is effective when the contact is on least equal terms (for instance, if the person open about a mental health problem is your boss, landlord or friend – not your patient or intern); if the contact involves cooperating on a common goal (for instance, playing in the same team or working together); and if the contact moderately disconfirms stereotypes. If the contact is with a superhero this may disconfirm the 'incompetence' stereotype so strongly that nothing is generalised: Stephen Fry's openness about his bipolar disorder may make people think 'yes but he is an exception – most people with bipolar are incompetent'. Even the person living with a bipolar condition may think 'yes, but I can never be like him'. If someone closer to your own world says they have bipolar – a teacher, a friend of the family – it is much more likely to change your attitudes to people with bipolar generally.

Whilst celebrities grab attention, it is 'ordinary' role models that are most likely to make you generalise the learning, to believe all people with bipolar disorder (say) may not be what you previously thought. When 'ordinary' people with lived experience share stories in schools, with colleagues or online, this is likely to have a particularly powerful effect.

Of course the contact does need, albeit 'mildly', to 'disconfirm' stereotypes: to replace images of incompetence with competence, of passive victim with active contributor. If a role model talks of having a biological brain disease, this is likely to convey unreliable judgement and incompetence (see Chapter 2).

There are many examples of people with lived experience drawing on their experience – without seeming 'perfect'. For instance, the Time to Change video 'schizo' builds up a filmic atmosphere of danger through black and white photography, images of a long dark corridor – which leads inexorably to a room, as the suspense builds. In the room is a gentle man who tells us about his life with a diagnosis of schizophrenia, whilst making a cup of tea. The film leads us towards a stereotype and then graphically disrupts it.

'Recovery stories' are growing: see for instance Boston Center for Psychiatric Rehabilitation's 'stories of success and inspiration', where people upload filmed stories – at http://cpr.bu.edu/resources/employment/personal/my-employment/success) – and stories shared through anti-stigma campaigns (like New Zealand's Like Minds Like Mine campaign). These showcase the lives of people who are contributing as parents, artists and more. Some do not airbrush out the challenges of mental distress. Accounts of finding ways to manage voices or a personality disorder are humanly gripping – and avoid the risk of implying you can be included as the acceptable face of mental distress, not like the 'really mad' people. Stories are increasingly drawn on to engender empathy amongst mental health practitioners (see, for instance, *Stories in Mental Health* by Nizette et al. (2012)) as well as to share encouragement amongst peers.

The way contact works is by reducing anxiety and promoting empathy. These are critical to replacing stereotypes with greater acceptance. The strongest way to do this is through actual human contact that is repeated or ongoing (Pettigrew 1998). There is a lesser effect – but still an effect – for indirect contact, for instance hearing from your sister about her colleague who has a mental health condition. One-off exposure to role models, or 'indirect contact' via watching or reading recovery stories, can be helpful as a backdrop – but is no substitute for being engaged in a common endeavour with people from the 'out' group.

Some anti-stigma campaigns have drawn on this evidence. Time to Change ran activity days bringing together people with and without mental health problems to engage in dance, sports, music; this confirmed that contact had a positive impact on perceived attitudes towards people with mental health problems (though not intended behaviour) (Evans-Lacko et al. 2013). Activity days by definition do not offer continuous or repeated contact. Whether a separate strand of funded activity to bring people together on a one-off basis is the most sustainable way of enabling contact to happen is open to question. A more scalable approach is likely to be to boost – and make the most of – natural contacts in the school, pub, club, mosque or workplace – wherever people have opportunities to meet and engage in common activities. Hewstone notes that contact is effective when people can get to know each other properly. One-off sports events are likely to be less effective than ongoing mutual engagement (Hewstone 2003).

Contact is more effective than just 'messages'. Information itself does not change attitudes: research shows that increased mental health 'literacy' and knowledge can go alongside rising trends in desire for social distance (Evans-Lacko 2013, p. 85). It is naive to think that informing people how common mental health problems are will generate improved attitudes. It is empathy and reduced fear that make the difference. As Alice Walker put it, 'facts expire; stories inspire' (2014).

Anti-stigma campaigns have increasingly taken an audience-based, marketing approach: starting from current attitudes and aiming to move them in a positive direction. The most fully evaluated example is England's Time to Change campaign. This targeted both the general public and specific groups, prioritised by people with lived experience: employers, medical students, trainee teachers, and particular demographic segments of the wider community, like people aged 25–45 in middle income groups. They used bursts of social marketing, delivered through TV ads and resources distributed through community and professional networks, as well as activities designed to promote contact. The campaign also aimed to influence the media.

The overall changes in extent of reported discrimination, and in public attitude and intended behaviour, from 2008–12 are discussed in Chapter 2: in essence the average extent of discrimination across life domains went down, although the proportion experiencing *any* discrimination did not; there were positive changes in public attitudes offset by entrenched beliefs about incapacity, with young people showing more negative attitudes on some indicators; and there were improvements in intended behaviour but not actual reported behaviour (although by 2014 there was an increase in public reports of living, being friends with or working with someone with a mental health problem, see Chapter 2).

Results published in the *British Journal of Psychiatry* in April 2013 and subsequent articles reflect on the impact of the Time to Change campaign on these changes. Learning included:

- Evans-Lacko et al. (2014) found a relationship between the Time to Change campaign and positive attitude change, but not intended behaviour.
- They found campaign awareness was a predictor of improvements in some attitudes (on the commonness of mental health problems, and on dangerousness); but there was no association between campaign awareness and the belief that people with mental health problems should be given no responsibility.
- They found improved attitudes on prejudice and exclusion but not tolerance or support for community care; and suggest the campaign may have been strongest in disconfirming negative ideas on exclusion, rather than enhancing positive attitudes (for instance, about support to live a full life in the community).
- TNS BMRB (2015) found no difference between those who had seen Time to Change adverts and those who had not in how comfortable they would feel talking to a friend, or family member, or employer if they had a mental health problem.
- Hamilton et al. (2015) found people in employment or who had retired reported significantly lower levels of discrimination compared to people who were unemployed or currently studying or volunteering.

On specific target groups:

- Henderson et al. (2013) found some improvement in employer attitudes from 2006–10 – for instance, employers became slightly less likely to think taking someone on with a

mental health problem was a risk, and less likely to think they would be unreliable. Employers became more likely to report making adjustments like reducing workload or hours.
- Medical student attitudes improved following an intervention, but this was not sustained (Friedrich et al. 2013).
- Media stories from 2008 to 2012 showed an increase in articles about mental health promotion; no increase in articles about injustice, or stigma; and no decrease in stigmatising articles (Thornicroft et al. 2013).

There are several points worth drawing out of these results.

Firstly, reduced median experience of discrimination, is hugely important and may have been at least partially attributable to the campaign; however initial gains in the proportion of people with mental health challenges experiencing *no* discrimination were not sustained (Corker et al. 2013; Evans-Lacko et al. 2014).

Secondly, there is a strong need to decide which attitude changes are the most important supporters of citizenship participation. Measures of positive attitude used by the Department of Health include agreement that mental illness is an illness like any other. Given the evidence (see Chapter 3) that this is associated with the belief that people with mental health problems are incapable, unpredictable and dangerous, this measure should be scrapped or used as a negative indicator.

The association between campaign awareness and improved attitudes on dangerousness is encouraging. The fact that campaign awareness was associated with knowledge of the commonness of mental health problems, but not with a reduced belief that those affected cannot be held responsible for their own actions, is of concern (though there was a decrease in the proportion of the public believing people with mental health problems should be given no responsibility – see Chapter 2). Belief in the ability to take responsibility is a far more important positive indicator than awareness of how common mental health problems are. By analogy, if people believe there are large numbers of people in their neighbourhood from Eastern Europe it does not necessarily make them less prejudiced – the opposite may be the case.

Improvements in employers' attitudes on 'risk' of employing people with mental health challenges are very important (see Chapter 4). On the specific point that employers became more likely to report reducing hours or workload as 'reasonable adjustments', this could potentially be a mixed blessing. The Office for Disability Issues (2013) found the most common type of discrimination reported by disabled people (generally) was being given too little responsibility. It is not impossible that employers were shielding people from full responsibility.

It is critical to decide which measures matter most – and focus on them.

Thirdly, the findings on media articles suggest discussion of injustice has not increased; but softer mental promotion coverage has. This raises the question whether the campaign has been able to influence a media tone drawing on the register of power, as a vehicle to challenge discrimination. It also finds – as have earlier anti-stigma campaigns – that improving positive media coverage does not insulate you from a continuation or even increase in negative coverage. Glasgow University found negative reporting of people with any disability as a 'burden' or scrounger was increasing: this counteracted efforts to promote positive media stories (Strathclyde Centre for Disability Research and Glasgow Media Unit 2011).

Some commentators have questioned the extent to which Time to Change, led by established charities, models power in being led by people with lived experience. This concern seems overstated in that people with lived experience are centrally involved in all stages of the campaign. Nonetheless, the tone may be slightly different from, say, the Swedish anti-stigma campaign which states 'this is not a campaign about people with psycho-social disabilities: it is run by a network of people with lived experience' (see http://www.hjarnkoll.se/In-English/).

Fourthly, the evaluation found that contact was a predictor of improved attitudes; but that improvement, for instance when medical students returned to the culture of their institutions, was not sustained. Systemic changes in institutions are needed: one-off training programmes are not enough. The 2014 Time to Change theme of 'time to talk' may be very helpful here, encouraging people to share the impact of powerful stories in an ongoing way. The New Zealand Like Minds campaign succeeded in increasing the number of families discussing mental health, and this appeared to be one factor in attitude improvement through the campaign (Ministry of Health and Health Promotion Agency 2014).

It is important to note that people in employment or retired were significantly less likely to experience discrimination than those who were unemployed, studying or volunteering. Explanations might include that the positive status of 'worker' helped neutralise negative stereotypes; and/or that people in employment were engaged in 'contact on equal terms' with non-disabled people, working towards a common goal in situations where they could get to know each other (i.e. contact was more than one-off). This suggests a particular significance to incentivising and supporting employment and other forms of ongoing, equal contact (rather than one-off contact or campaigns).

Finally, there has not been a consistent pattern of improvement in reported behaviour by the public. Even if attitudes are successfully changed, does this translate into changes in behaviour? Research suggests that the answer is 'not necessarily'. Increasingly academics working on stigma are focusing on how to change behaviour, not just attitudes (Sartorius 2014). There was also more progress on overcoming negative discrimination than in enabling positive participation, as outlined in Chapter 5.

Contact can influence behaviour as well as attitudes. Pettigrew (1998) argues that contact meeting the requirements above (such as being on equal terms) acts as a benign form of behavioural modification.

Media and film can be important backdrops to the power of contact, particularly through ongoing narratives as in soap operas, where they subvert the common stereotypes of incompetents or scroungers. In 2014 Time to Change worked with *Holby City* to secure a story line relating to someone with bipolar disorder; and Wahl has written extensively of both positive and negative portrayals of mental health in media, film and the arts (see Wahl 1995).

Mad pride

Mad pride started in the 1990s. Through festivals and writings, people have revalued their lived experience, using the message that madness is an asset. An example is the Largactyl Shuffle events: guided walks in London that celebrate the history of madness and contributions of mad people. See http://www.cooltanarts.org.uk/category/largactyl/).

Changing attitudes should not be the only or main goal of anti-stigma campaigns – what matters most is life chances. But attitudes are inter-twined with behaviours, and when they are measured, the measures should reflect the priorities of people with lived experience – not acceptance only if you 'act normal'. The picture should not be muddied by measuring people's views on how common mental health problems are or whether they are 'an illness like any other'.

Overcoming separation

To cite a famous American civil rights legal case, 'there is no such thing as separate but equal'. (In 1896 Plessy v Fergusson established that separate facilities and lives of black Americans could be equal, under the constitution; overturning this doctrine with Brown v Board of Education 1954 was a major civil rights landmark.) Groups facing discrimination have historically fought against segregation, demanding the right to be fully and equally included: not only protesting overt segregation, like occupying 'whites only' bus seats and lunch counters; but challenging subtler processes, like making gay men pre-1960s meet in secret for fear of being prosecuted.

People with mental health issues too have challenged separation from their fellow humans: campaigning against mass institutionalisation, special schools, sheltered work-shops. Separate means unequal – a culture of 'us' and a devalued 'them'.

These campaigns have met with some recognition. The UN Committee on the Rights of Persons with Disabilities (2013) stated that they were 'deeply concerned that Austrian laws allow for a person to be confined against his or her will in a psychiatric institution' for reasons including mental disorder. They also expressed concern that 19,000 Austrians were working in sheltered workshops outside the mainstream labour market.

In the UK institutions are under scrutiny following a new generation of scandals (see Chapter 1 on the scandals of the 1970s and 80s): abuse of people with learning disabil-ities at Winterbourne View, of older people in North Staffordshire, the death of Connor Sparrowhawk (Laughing Boy) in an assessment centre in 2013. Nonetheless numbers of people with learning disabilities in institutions were higher in 2014 than at the height of the Winterbourne View scandal a few years earlier. About 3,200 people with learning disabilities and autism remained in private or NHS-run settings like Winterbourne View (*Guardian*, 19 March 2014). More than 60% had been there over a year and 20% for more than five years.

Many disabled people who had gained hard-won independence feared going back into residential care, due to funding caps: Worcestershire, in 2013, won the right with safeguards to require people whose care cost more than £500 a week to accept the cheaper option of residential care.

The Joint Committee on Human Rights (2010) spelt out the right to 'independent living' inherent in the UNCRPD and found the UK government falling short; it recommended intro-ducing a right to independent living.

Separate workplaces are being phased out in a number of European countries including the UK, in line with the UNCRPD. In 2011 I led an independent review into employment support required by disabled people and recommended moving resources from separate, non-viable 'special' factories to individualised support that you could take with you from job to job, contract to contract. Young people no longer expect a job for life; and want the same chances as their peers of building skills and experience through a range of different opportunities. Recommendations included expansion and transformation of the Access to Work programme, with far more peer support and personal say over the support you need. The review was highly controversial due to the impact on Remploy workers of the proposals (see Chapter 4). At the launch the police were called – a serious over-reaction to a peaceful trade union demonstration – and at one point a demonstration involving a horse took place outside the offices of an organisation led by disabled people that supported the move away from separate factories. As with the closure of psychiatric hospitals, a change of direction that could be of long-term benefit to inclusion is resisted by people set to lose current security. Subsequent reports echoed the same evidence for 'what works' (National Development Team for Inclusion (NDTI) 2014). Nonetheless in 2014, under the Work Choice programme there were around 2,000 places in sheltered workshops. In theory these sheltered opportunities act as stepping stones – but in reality people do not step anywhere. The longer they are out of regular employ-ment the less likely it becomes that they will ever get back (Perkins 2009; NDTI 2014).

Work to replace more segregated services with individualised support is inevitably contentious in a climate of cuts: just as community care was viewed as a cost-cutting exercise, so reduction of day centres and sheltered workshops seemed a plot to with-draw support. Some progress was made with individualised employment support in the 2010s: the Access to Work programme, despite policy and operational problems prompting a 2014 inquiry by the Work and Pensions Select Committee, did see increased usage, after a dip during the recession; the proportion of its users with mental health conditions rose from a ludicrous 0.7% in 2010 to over 3% in 2013 – woefully low, but at least increasing. And all main political parties expressed interest in proposals for individual budgets to enable people to take control of their own employment support (see Crowther and Sayce 2013).

Evidence-based support to get and keep open employment

Individual Placement and Support (IPS) is more effective than traditional approaches to vocational rehabilitation for people with a mental health condition (Burns et al. 2007; Bond et al. 2008). It involves embedding employment specialists within clinical treatment teams so that treatment and employment support are integrated and simultaneous (help with open, competitive employment starts from day one rather than waiting for someone to be successfully treated: the longer the wait, the less chance of retaining or gaining employment). There are seven key principles:

1. Competitive employment is the primary goal.
2. Everyone who wants it is eligible for employment support.
3. Job search is consistent with individual preferences (people are more likely to succeed if they pursue a job that interests them).
4. Job search is rapid: within one month.
5. Employment specialists and clinical teams work and are located together.
6. Support is time-unlimited and individualised to both the employer and employee.

7. Welfare benefits counselling supports the person through the transition from benefits to work.

Rinaldi et al. (2006), in *Not Just Stacking Shelves*, show how people with difficulties like schizophrenia, bipolar disorder and serious depression have been supported with IPS to secure jobs including boatyard worker, events manager, administrator, labourer, teaching assistant, leaflet dropper, baker, interior designer, credit controller, bar worker, accountant, journalist – and many more.

Crowther and Sayce (2013) argued that failing government work programmes should be replaced by budgets given to individuals and employers to create bespoke solutions: a survey of disabled people found three quarters wanted to know what resources were available for employment support and to decide what would work best for them.

ALLFIE (Alliance for inclusive education) campaigned strongly for rights to inclusive education in this period, against government rhetoric on the need to reverse a supposed bias in favour of inclusion. If progress towards inclusive practice in schools stalls, there is no real 'choice' – since regular schools are under reducing pressure to offer effective teaching and environments for children with mental health issues. ALLFIE's aims include to ensure inclusive education as a right for all (see http://www.allfie.org.uk/pages/about/aboutindex. html#aims).

Segregation is not only about learning, working and living separately. It is also about ending up socialising only with others in your 'group' – meeting only other 'service users' and professionals. To overcome this requires more than challenging separation – it requires a positive approach to secure rights to participate.

Overcoming discrimination and unequal life chances

When the Disability Discrimination Act was passed in 1995 the mental health world assumed all the legal cases would focus on stripping away physical barriers – ensuring ramp access to restaurants, offices and the like. In fact, by the early 2000s, 23% of employment cases concerned people with mental health problems (Sayce 2003). Some were successful – people like Ms Melanophy, expected to leave her job as a successful customer service manager after being sacked whilst a psychiatric in-patient. Others were unsuccessful – like Ms Marshall, a Cambridge graduate offered a job as a finger printing officer, only to have the job offer withdrawn once her diagnosis of bipolar disorder came to light. She took a case and won, but the police force later appealed and won, in a case that sent shock waves through the mental health world. (Sayce 2003).

Through the 2010s, cases involving mental health continued to increase. Lockwood et al. (2014) note that they made up the largest category of cases reaching the Employment Appeal Tribunal (EAT).

Some cases offered justice:

But there were also weaknesses in the law.

Ms Crisp worked at Iceland Foods. She experienced panic attacks. When she had a period off sick, the employer implemented its unauthorised absences policy (although she had submitted sick notes) and refused her request for her husband or mother to accompany her to the disciplinary hearing. The company accidentally left a recording of an internal conversation on her answerphone in which they belittled her experience of panic attacks. The tribunal commented that their awareness of mental health issues was 'no less than woeful' and upheld Ms Crisp's claims for constructive dismissal, disability harassment, direct disability discrimination and failure to make reasonable adjustments. They awarded compensation including £7,000 for injury to feelings and required the company to implement disability discrimination training for HR and certain management roles. (Crisp v Iceland Foods Ltd ET/1604478/11 & ET/1600000/12)

Mr Rose applied for a used-car salesman job at the Alfreton branch of GK Group Ltd in 2011. Asked a standard question in the application form about why he was leaving the current job, Mr Rose explained that his previous employment was terminated because he experienced a major episode of depression, from which he had recovered. At one of his two interviews he was asked inappropriate questions about his mental health – for instance, how he would feel when his colleagues found out and 'took the piss'. He did not get the job. The Tribunal found this created a hostile environment for Mr Rose and he had therefore been subject to disability-related harassment. (Rose v GK Group Ltd ET/2802708/2011)

Firstly you had first to demonstrate that you were a 'disabled person', which required you to show that there was a substantial adverse and long-term impact on your day-to-day activities, before going on to argue that you could do the job. Sometimes the first undermined the second.

Secondly, under the original law, you had to show, only in the case of a mental health problem, that your condition was 'clinically well recognised'. This was designed to stop floods of people with minor stress bringing the law into disrepute – but it was clearly discriminatory, in that it did not apply to physical impairment, so was removed in 2005. Judges make clear that whether you are 'disabled' depends on the legal definition, not a medical judgement. In J v DLA Piper (2010) the EAT stated that determining mental impairment can mean getting bogged down in difficult medical or indeed metaphysical questions, because diagnosis in mental health is notoriously difficult. Therefore, providing there is an impairment recognised in a common-sense way by the effects that it has produced, it is not necessary to answer the question of diagnosis.

Thirdly, case law sometimes made securing justice harder. Under Malcolm v London Borough of Lewisham (2008) the comparator used to determine discrimination changed through a House of Lords judgement. Mr Malcolm had a diagnosis of schizophrenia. He sublet his council flat without permission and argued that this resulted from his mental health difficulties. Before this, the comparator to establish disability discrimination (as interpreted by the Court of Appeal in the case of Clark v TDG Ltd t/a Novacold) was someone to whom the disability-related reason for the treatment did not or would not apply. In Mr Malcolm's case he would only have had to show that tenants who had not sublet had been treated more favourably to establish a prima facie case of disability-related discrimination. The case would then be decided on whether the council had a valid justification defence. Instead the House of Lords used the comparator of a non-disabled person who had sublet: in effect arguing that discrimination did not take place if you were simply treated 'the same' as a non-disabled person. Following this case, provisions were put into the Equality Act 2010 with the aim of remedying this problem.

Fourthly, even if you won, there was often no impact for others – you might just get compensation. In this sense the case of Ms Crisp (above) was uncommon in requiring training.

The law and its interpretation are dynamic and legal work to establish helpful casework is ongoing.

Nonetheless, because of limitations of impact of individual casework, the Disability Rights Commission (DRC) in the 2000s placed a growing emphasis on strategic interventions, like formal investigations.

In 2006 the DRC published the results of its Formal Investigation into health inequalities experienced by people with mental health problems and/or learning disabilities. Drawing on the involvement of over 1,000 disabled people, an analysis of over eight million primary care records, active involvement of medical and nursing leaders, and a high-level Inquiry Panel chaired by a Barrister, it concluded that:

- People with mental health problems were more likely to get common killer diseases, more likely to get them young, and likely to die of them faster
- These illnesses included heart disease, stroke, chronic obstructive pulmonary disease, some cancers (for instance, people with a diagnosis of schizophrenia were more likely to get bowel cancer – a completely new finding)
- As a result they died at least 15 years earlier than other citizens, after accounting for suicide
- Yet this group was less likely to get some of the recommended tests and treatments for those very diseases
- Qualitative research revealed experiences of 'diagnostic overshadowing', i.e. putting reported symptoms down to aspects of the psychiatric problem.

The recommendations were strongly supported by medical leaders and the Department of Health and led to changes in commissioning of primary care services and to a major plank of government mental health policy being equal physical treatment. The investigation and joint work with Rethink and Mencap succeeded through a combination of hard evidence and stories, engagement of both service users and professional leaders, and bringing those responsible for policy and practice into the process of forging recommendations.

A second Formal Investigation focused on the 'fitness standards' required to enter or stay in nursing, teaching and social work. It found no consistency of approach and a set of standards and practices that could be discriminatory – for instance, using presence of a mental health condition as a signal of risk, triggering enhanced supervision, in the absence of any evidence of impact on practice. Professionals spoke eloquently about not being open about mental health difficulties for fear of losing their jobs or even professional accreditation. The investigation found a culture in which disabled people were more likely to be asked 'what's wrong with you?' than 'what can you contribute?' (DRC 2007a).

The Equality and Human Rights Commission (EHRC) held an Inquiry into targeted harassment and hate crime, prompted in part by high-profile cases of murders, for instance that of Stephen Hoskin, a man with learning difficulties who was tortured and then dropped from a railway viaduct to his death in 2006. Despite this targeted behaviour towards someone viewed as 'different', the case was not prosecuted as a 'hate crime'. The Inquiry raised the profile of the requirement on police and Crown Prosecution Service to investigate harassment as potential hate crimes.

The Inquiry gave added impetus to developments around the country to enable more disabled people – including those with mental health conditions – to report crimes, be believed, and be supported to give evidence.

Reporting hate crime

In Lancashire, joint work by DPOs and agencies including the police and Crown Prosecution Service led to increased confidence to report hate crimes and harassment. DPOs worked with multiple agencies to set up third party reporting sites, i.e. safe spaces for disabled people to report harassment and hate crime, coupled with training for 3,000 front-line police officers to respond to crimes as 'hate crimes'. Under section 146 of the Criminal Justice Act sentencing can be tougher if a hate crime motive is established. This led to an increase in reporting from 64 reports of disability hate crime in 2012–13 to 172 in 2013–14. Keys to success were a multi-agency approach and peer-to-peer reporting, where disabled people are trained as volunteers to take evidence and write reports of hate crime that the police take seriously. Disability Rights UK brought DPOs together to share good practice and produced guidance for individuals, families and DPOs. See: http://www.disabilityrightsuk.org/how-we-can-help/publications/lets-stop-disability-hate-crime-guidance

---

These examples use the power of law to instigate systemic change. The law itself, though, was still primarily based on the model of seeking redress only after the event of discrimination. Legal theorists like Sandra Fredman, the late Caroline Gooding and Nick O'Brien argued that systemic legal instruments were needed – positive, proactive public duties, to act in advance of discrimination, to promote equality. Their ideas were shared with campaigners, and together they influenced government to introduce proactive public sector duties to promote equality.

The Duty was used by public organisations in myriad ways, starting from the priorities of disabled people and evidence of inequalities. Action covered issues from improving support for students at university, to tackling community safety (Radar 2009).

This systemic, proactive duty is a realisation of the participation rights approach with its emphasis on positive participation – not just being a victim of discrimination. Positive equality duties provide a framework for engagement, analysis, action planning and review.

The 2010 Equality Act modified the public sector duty – removing, for instance, the requirement to produce a disability equality scheme (with the aim of reducing bureaucracy) and potentially 'watering it down'. The duty remains a tool to generate systemic change. There are powerful arguments for further strengthening systemic legal powers, discussed in Chapter 9 – for instance, requiring employers to say, transparently, how many disabled people they employ (rather as they currently report on the number of women on their boards); and much greater use of the huge public sector commissioning budgets as levers to require contractors to apply good practice in employment and services. This was done during the Olympics: organisations simply did not win contracts if they could not demonstrate inclusive practice.

In 2009 the UK ratified the UNCRPD. In much of the world disability policy is framed in terms of human rights. Not so in Britain, where human rights is often viewed as special pleading by prisoners or an imposition from Europe. Yet it offers opportunities. Comments by the UN Committee suggest that England and Wales's mental health law and mental capacity law are non-compliant; the attempt by Northern Ireland to create one fair, non-discriminatory legal framework is an encouraging development (see Chapter 4).

Challenging unequal life chances requires using power and smart collaborative partnerships to achieve lasting change. Just legislation is not enough – history is littered with examples of laws that are not implemented, not least the 1944 requirement on employers to employ a quota of 3% of disabled people. But law, with systemic power for positive action, matched with collaboration to make things happen, can create changes in people's lives. Even just knowing your rights can make a difference, with no need to go anywhere near a court room: for instance, when Ms B was faced with being retired on ill-health grounds after a period in hospital with depression, she both cited the Equality Act and explained that she would be able to return to work with a short period on shorter hours – and her job was secured.

Law is not the only type of power. People with lived experience can have power as providers of peer support in the everyday business of asserting rights to participation – deciding whether and to whom to be open, negotiating for jobs and college places, getting out and taking part in life (see next chapter). Networks can bring people together as campaigners, consumers, voters, to exert collective influence. And there are levers other than law that can be brought to bear on organisations. For instance, 'Trading for Good' aims to offer a kite mark to companies that demonstrate their social responsibility in areas like employing disabled people – making it a selling point.

Has this approach to overcoming discrimination worked? The DRC commissioned an evaluation of its work which found it had achieved its objectives over six years, building partnership support and reputation, using legal powers strategically and achieving outcomes (Fletcher and O'Brien 2008). Nonetheless legislation is contradictory, we live in an era of de-regulation, and the powerful narrative of win-wins through universal design is under threat from government policy that 'protects' a few 'really disabled people' rather than supporting equality for disabled people overall; and from campaigns that, in reaction to cuts, aim to preserve old-fashioned and often disempowering services. Growing impact is uncertain.

CONCLUSION

There is evidence to draw on, to learn what works to soften the line of difference, to revalue that difference, to end separation and to overcome unequal life chances. The most promising evidence is on the significance of contact, on at least equal terms, to change both attitudes and behaviour. This requires an end to segregation. It requires positive rights to participate, with levers of power.

Participation would bring a massive power of increased contact on a daily, routine basis.

Those rights seem best pursued through a blend of systemic legal powers, levers to influence business and partnerships between people with lived experience and those with power to achieve change. Networks amongst people with lived experience (bonding capital) can provide a springboard for wider participation (bridging social capital). Together these approaches could open up significantly more citizenship opportunities, with developments based on universal design in mainstream policies and practices: a win-win for all.

Anti-stigma campaigns have been important to raise awareness of the challenge and start chipping away at the extent of discrimination. They have had most success where they target behaviour as well as attitudes, and where they are clear about the narratives they are seeking to create to overturn stereotypes.

It is possible to extend community acceptance, and soften the lines of difference – with recourse to the power of participation rights. There is no need to work through all four 'components' of stigma: for instance, if more and more people with mental health challenges were in regular education and workplaces, and open to others about their experience, we would have ongoing contact on equal terms; the bounds of community acceptance would be stretched, as people became known as fellow students and colleagues and treated increasingly with empathy, without fear, through contact. The research finding that people with mental health problems in employment or retired are less likely to face discrimination is highly promising in this respect. Experiences of mental health challenges would became more ordinary.

A take-out message is that ongoing contact will make most difference – and the easiest and most effective way to achieve that is by boosting and making the most of all the natural contacts in workplaces, schools, faith organisations and more; backed by the power of participation rights to make it happen on the basis of equality. This matches the evidence for ongoing contact on equal terms. It is not a universally held view amongst experts, who sometimes favour discrete anti-discrimination interventions. The next chapters look at future ways forward, rooted in the thinking of global leaders on combating stigma and discrimination.

Reflective Exercises

Workplaces, communities and whole societies that are inclusive of people with mental health problems tend to work better for everyone. Can you think of examples where you could draw on this to make a compelling argument to make a change in your own community or workplace or practice?

Contact on at least equal terms between people with different experiences (from ethnicity to religious belief) can influence attitudes and behaviours. Has contact ever affected or changed your attitudes? How might you draw on this in relation to attitudes towards people with a diagnosis of mental illness?

Well-being plans are useful for everyone. Try making a plan for what will keep you on an even keel. Look first at:

- What supports your well-being? (it might be talking with friends or partner, or the exercise you like, or anything else)
- How will you build this into your regular life?
- What helps when you are having a really bad day?
- How will you plan to make sure that is in place?

How might that exercise be useful more broadly to people facing mental health challenges?

FURTHER READING

DR UK (2014) *Inclusive Communities. Report and Guidance for local authorities, and for disabled people's organisations.* www.disabilityrightsuk.org

- This report and guidance draw on a literature review, conceptual analysis and examples in practice to guide DPOs and local authorities to change whole local communities to be more inclusive

Perkins, R. (2012) *A Health Work and Well-being Toolkit.* DR UK: London.

- The toolkit can be used by employees in the context of an organisational commitment to improve well-being

DRC (2007) *The Disability Agenda.* DRC: London.

- An agenda that puts disability at the heart of mainstream policy issues

EHRC (2009) *From Safety Net to Springboard.* EHRC: London.

- Re-conceptualising social care, from 'caring for' people to enabling people to lead full lives

EHRC website www.equalityhumanrights.com

- Contains summaries of legislation, Codes of Practice, guidance and reports on equalities and human rights issues

LGA and Innovations in Dementia (2012) Developing Dementia Friendly Communities: Learning and guidance for local authorities. Local Government Association: London

- Guidance on how to engage people living with dementia as champions and to bring together local businesses and agencies to make the community more inclusive

DRC (2006) *Equal Treatment: Closing the Gap. A Formal Investigation into Health Inequalities Experienced by People with Mental Health Problems or Learning Disabilities.* DRC: London

- This investigation included a report, guidance for individuals, commissioners and providers, and a DVD. It made practical recommendations to reduce premature death and physical ill-health

FOUNDATIONS OF
MENTAL
HEALTH
PRACTICE

7 | Ways to a Better Future: Starting Personal

This and the following two chapters discuss how to take a participation rights approach, at an individual, service and societal level.

These three levels are inter-connected. It may be tempting to think that changing policy will create change on its own, but history is littered with examples of policies not being implemented. In one NHS organisation, the CEO piled government guidance he had received on the floor. As it rose above his desk he posed the question, 'which of these are our priority?' Change comes from concerted action by different players and levers to sustain progress. The work needs to start from a deep commitment to the right to participate.

> States Parties to this Convention recognize the equal right of all persons with disabilities to live in the community, with choices equal to others, and shall take effective and appropriate measures to facilitate full enjoyment by persons with disabilities of this right and their full inclusion and participation in the community. (UNCRPD Article 19).

By 2015, the time was right to propose fresh approaches. Some leaders of anti-discrimination work were calling for a complete re-think. Professor Bruce Link said biologically based messages had not worked and that an effective approach still lay ahead (see Chapter 3). Professor Norman Sartorius gave a lecture entitled 'Postulates of anti-stigma work re-examined' (Sartorius 2014), in which he subjected all the common tenets of anti-stigma work to critical scrutiny, knocking them down one by one: for instance, should we aim for changes in attitudes? (no, changes in behaviour are what matter); will increased knowledge of mental health reduce stigma? (no, it can increase it).

Anti-stigma campaigns such as 'Time to Change' and 'Like Minds Like Mine' had made some important gains, but results were complex and nuanced, as the *Guardian* put it (3 April 2013) – rather than sweeping.

Austerity measures had polarised views amongst writers and activists: with some fiercely opposing cuts, even to services people hate; others arguing that we should 'never waste a crisis', that turbulence is an opportunity to transform services into networked, humanised, empowering support. A very few people squared the circle. In 2014 Graeme Innes, outgoing Disability Commissioner at the Australian Human Rights Commission, criticised the government's talk of 'lifters' and 'leaners' (the Australian version of the UK's 'strivers' and 'skivers'); agreed the best form of welfare is a job – but argued the mantra was backed by no jobs plan, only a welfare plan. He objected to policies of austerity and also proposed solutions within budgetary constraint.

I asked seven people with deep expertise in participation and equality to articulate their top priorities for effective work for the next phase of history: leaders with lived experience from the UK, USA, Australia and New Zealand; academics specialising in equality and stigma; and policy analysts. They were:

Peter Beresford (UK): Professor of Social Policy, Brunel University and Chair, Shaping Our Lives, a national disabled people's and service users' organisation.

Mark Brown (UK): set up the UK's only mental health magazine written by people with lived experience and is a director at Social Spider Community Interest Company, which helps people make change happen.

Andrew Imparato (USA): Executive Director, Association of University Centres on Disabilities; previously President and CEO of the American Association of People with Disabilities.

Bruce Link (USA): Professor of Epidemiology and Sociomedical Sciences, Columbia University; has published widely on stigma, mental health and inequalities in health.

Lyn Mahboub (Australia): Strategic Recovery Advisor, Richmond Fellowship Western Australia; and Lecturer and Consumer Academic, Curtin University.

Mary O'Hagan (New Zealand): International Mental Health Leader and Consultant, with experience including Mental Health Commissioner for New Zealand, Advisor to the UN and first Chair of the World Network of Users and Survivors of Psychiatry.

Graham Thornicroft (UK): Professor of Community Psychiatry, Institute of Psychiatry, Kings College, London; has published widely on discrimination, stigma and mental health.

All identified achievements in the quarter century since the first anti-discrimination law (the Americans with Disabilities Act 1990), and surge of anti-stigma activity from the 1990s. For example:

- 'The growth of the survivor movement' (Peter Beresford, UK)
- 'CRPD (Convention on the Rights of Persons with Disabilities) – although the impact is not fully realised – because it is a major advance in mental health law' (Mary O'Hagan, New Zealand)
- 'A small but growing movement of people being "out at work" with their mental health conditions' (Andy Imparato, USA)
- 'Time to Change – measurable reduction in stigma and discrimination' (Graham Thornicroft, UK).

They also registered differing levels of disappointment at various setbacks:

- 'No improvement in life outcomes such as employment, income, relationships and physical health because these outcomes matter to all humans' (Mary O'Hagan)
- 'The culture continually reinforces stereotypes in ways that are not widely recognised and proceed unchecked' (Bruce Link, USA)
- 'The lack of critical engagement around the construction of "mental illness"' (Lyn Mahboub, Australia)
- 'The impact of neo-liberal ideology and politics – creating ever more out-groups' (Peter Beresford).

They identified challenges and opportunities:

- 'Building wider alliances, recognising inter-sectionality' (Peter Beresford)
- 'Discriminatory mental health legislation needs to be repealed because it is the legal cornerstone of discrimination rather like the old sodomy laws' (Mary O'Hagan).

Riding the waves of challenges and opportunities

Without attempting to find a crystal ball, it is worth considering the implications of relevant future trends. They include:

- Rising inequality (discussed below)
- Changing family structure, with more divorce, childlessness, living alone and risks of isolation. This may call for concerted peer and community support to enable everyone to exercise the right to participate
- An ageing society, with greater prevalence of age-related impairments including dementia and depression
- Likelihood of long-term fiscal constraint, given considerable mainstream political consensus on the need to throw out the post-war agreement on redistribution and replace it with a smaller, enabling state. This points to the need for novel use of public finance and mobilising human and new financial resources: for instance, scaling up peer support rather than meting out tiny parcels of highly rationed professional, one-to-one time
- Reduced public trust in major institutions including politics, the media, faith organisations and charities. This calls for new leadership to gain trust – including from people with lived experience
- Changing attitudes: a growing public belief that social security claimants are responsible for their plight (see Chapter 2). Younger people are far more likely than older to take equality for granted on grounds including ethnicity and sexual orientation, but likely to disapprove of behaviour deemed lacking in personal responsibility, with relatively low tolerance of people who are not working. This suggests a need both to ride the wave of support for equality – and to unsettle the tendency to blame the poor, in part by drawing a clear line at unacceptable behaviours: bullying, harassment and hate crime (see Chapter 6)
- Technological change. The mobile phone is 40 years old. The next trends may include personalised manufacture – printing out products to personalised designs; further reductions in customer service staff (as everything from supermarket check-out to ticketing is automated); and ever-new uses of social media. As well as threats this may suggest opportunities for connection in mutual support: uploading and sharing personal solutions, self-organising projects and campaigns rather than going through formal organisations. A minority even of young people will not be online and there will remain a need to guard against digital exclusion
- De-regulation. There may be opportunities to remove oppressive legislation (such as community treatment orders) or paternalistic approaches to 'safeguarding'; or for 'red tape challenges' to strip away unnecessary bureaucracy faced by individuals – who are assessed again and again.

Poverty and inequality

Whilst absolute poverty has declined sharply since the Second World War, Clark and Heath (2014) use large datasets to argue that since the financial crash of 2008 absolute poverty has grown again in the UK and US, once debt and housing costs are taken into account. A quarter of UK households had no or negative financial assets. Mary O'Hara, in *Austerity Bites* (2014) notes a rise in theft of nappies; and ever-growing use of food banks.

Clark and Heath (2014) found a drop in real-terms income and dramatic rise in wealth after a third of a century in which the egalitarian assumptions of the post-war settlement have slowly rotted under the surface' (p. 28). As Britain went into recession, the allocation of wealth and opportunity were skewed to those who had both; and this trend accelerated, leading to a corrosion of optimism. People in social class ABC1 were more positive about many aspects of life – family relationships, friends, sex – than people in social classes C2DE.

Relative poverty, as AC Grayling puts it, 'entails functional exclusion' (Grayling 2014, p. 6). Rowan Williams argues that 'the opposite of poverty is not so much wealth as participation, the appropriate degree of sharing in a common social project' (Williams 2014, p. 9). People avoid going out altogether because of being the one who cannot pay. Clark and Heath found markedly reduced social participation since 2008, and reduced volunteering – 'the small society', with reduced social networks.

This was not simply a result of unemployment: the UK was unusual in having relatively high employment even in recession (UKCES 2014). There were major problems of in-work poverty and under-employment: the number of unwilling part-timers rose in a decade from 600,000 to 1.4 million, higher even than the numbers unemployed (Clark and Heath 2014).

Disabled people, including those with mental health challenges, were hit harder than others by increases in absolute and relative poverty. Reed and Portes (2014) found impacts of tax and benefit reforms were more negative for families containing at least one disabled person. In 2015 the new Conservative government (despite a stated commitment to protecting disability benefits) announced that from 2017 new claimants placed in the 'work related activity group' on Employment and Support Allowance would receive 30% less than current claimants (a drop from around £5,000 per year to nearer £3,500 – a significant difference to someone out of work).

This suggests a need to focus on anti-poverty work, with allies. Joseph Rowntree Foundation (JRF) has developed an overarching UK anti-poverty strategy, which addresses the cost of essential goods and services, whether people are able to reach their potential, the nature of jobs at the bottom end of the labour market, and individual choices as well as the state's response.

It is important to consider what would give people living with mental health issues more of a foothold. By 2014 jobs were coming on stream, albeit not in all areas or communities (and not sufficiently for young people, who faced structural unemployment predating the recession (UKCES 2013)). Disabled people in work appeared to be afforded a degree of employment protection during the recession of the 2010s (Hogarth et al. 2009). However, there was no progress in enabling the millions on ESA to gain work, due partly to failures in effectively contracting Work Programme providers, termed a scandal by the Work and Pensions Select Committee (Work and Pensions Select Committee 6 November 2014).

Promising approaches to reducing poverty of people with mental health challenges include:

- Inclusive education – ensuring people do not lose out if they acquire mental health problems. Educational qualifications are even more protective for disabled people against unemployment than for non-disabled people, the more so the higher the qualification (Office for Disability Issues 2013).
- Youth employment. Strenuous efforts are being pursued by business-school partnerships and some individual companies to open up apprenticeships, traineeships and good work experience to more young people (UKCES 2013). Ensuring those with mental health challenges benefit, with intensive support if needed, is important.

- Employment support. Putting control of employment support in the hands of individuals and employers would be more effective than incentivising welfare to work providers (Crowther and Sayce 2013).
- Career progression. Whilst the growth of part-time work, zero hours contracts and self-employment can be useful for people living with fluctuating difficulties, for some these trends and the 'disability pay gap' mean getting 'stuck' below your earnings potential or self-employed for lack of alternatives (Sayce 2010). Career development and mentoring are important: see DR UK's leadership academy programme at www.disabilityrightsuk.org.
- Changes in tax and benefits. Given a UK cross-party consensus on constraining benefits expenditure, it may be difficult to rely on social security change as the primary anti-poverty mechanism, but radical change in the Work Capability Assessment, sanctions regime and other specifics would reduce hardship (Massie 2014; see also www.disability rightsuk.org).
- Transform housing policy, so affordable housing is matched to where jobs are available.

There are two broad ways of thinking about reducing poverty amongst people living with mental health challenges. The first is to push for freedom from inequality specifically on mental health grounds. This is eminently worth doing: if qualification, employment and pay rates were the same even as for disabled people in general, we would see the employment rate of people with mental health conditions more than double. The downside is this only gives people the chance to be somewhere on the spectrum of inequality – when inequality is growing. Arguably to break the vicious cycle of mental ill-health and poverty (each stimulating the other) requires tackling growing inequality per se. This requires much broader alliances than just mental health or disability campaigners.

The rest of this chapter is devoted to what individuals can do to promote participation rights.

Individual action, personal support

Individuals are not islands. They can contribute to wider changes – drawing on power as campaigners, consumers, leaders. They are subject to systemic forces, for good or ill. For instance, when endeavouring to combat discrimination it can be highly problematic that sources of advice are in decline (see below).

But any strategy to achieve participation must include the strategies and powers of individuals. Starting with the impetus of positive aspiration is important – for the individual to decide what they want and work out what it will take to pursue it. This proactive approach matches recent developments in disability theory, legal and clinical arenas:

- People living with health challenges or disability cannot be defined by being 'victims' of our condition or of discrimination ('disabled by society'). Under the participation rights model we can be the change we want to see – getting into colleges and workplaces and changing them, with others and with support (see Chapter 5). Far from being just 'victims' many people living with mental health difficulties bring assets from resilience to creative problem solving (Radar 2010).
- In the early days of anti-discrimination law, the emphasis was all on redress: having your day in court after facing discrimination. This was the basis of Britain's first equality laws,

on race and gender, from the 1970s. It encouraged a retrospective, adversarial approach that put the responsibility on the individual (the 'victim') to take action – otherwise discrimination went unchecked. From the 1990s the emphasis shifted towards positive action: first through the concept of 'reasonable adjustments' (i.e. positive steps to enable people to have an equal chance to participate), and then to public sector equality duties (see Chapter 6) (Fredman and Spencer 2006).

- Clinical thinking has increasingly moved from helping people to reduce symptoms and deficits, to enabling people to build the life they want, mobilising strengths (Repper and Perkins 2003).

Much has been written by people with lived experience about how to steer your own journey to participation, creating the life you want, finding the support that helps. See for instance:

- Pat Deegan's 'Recovery and the Conspiracy of Hope' (1996 Presentation presented to the sixth annual mental health conference of Australia and New Zealand)
- Stories of recovery loaded on to the Scottish Recovery Network website: (www. http://www.writetorecovery.net/)
- The National Empowerment Center's audio stories at: http://www.power2u.org/recovery-stories.html.
- People speaking out about their lives at: http://www.time-to-change.org.uk/talk-about-mental-health.

Stories mobilise and inspire: that is why management consultants often propose stories to motivate workforces.

If an individual's motivation is to get into employment after a gap, then learning from others who have done just that – how they explained their career gap, negotiated adjustments, talked with colleagues, dealt with the benefits system – enables them to move forward rather than allow the very thought to be paralysing.

This is why disabled people's organisations (DPOs) can often support people to move into employment more successfully than companies offering standard approaches like CV writing courses (Crowther and Sayce 2013). These providers have not 'been there' and do not understand how to negotiate the pitfalls of entering work with a mental health condition in the way that fellow travellers do.

Peer support for employment

Manchester-based DPO Breakthrough UK offers personalised employment support on people's own terms: 'we'll work with you, not make decisions for you'. Support is designed around the individuals' employment goals and needs and delivered by other disabled people who have lived experience of the barriers of prejudice, environment and lack of support. Policy and practice is based on the social model of disability and clients learn to understand how barriers can be removed to enable them to work in any role or workplace.

Peer support and mentoring can result in people feeling better able to try new experiences. This is why funders invest in them with 'marginalised' groups: see the video career stories at I Could (at http://icould.com/watch-career-videos/enable) and the spread of peer mentoring amongst ex-offenders and people with drug/alcohol difficulties. St Giles Trust, for instance, enables ex-offenders to share their skills and experience to help others in their journeys.

Repper and Carter's (2011) evidence review finds peer-support workers are more successful than professional services in promoting hope, belief in the possibility of recovery, empowerment, self-esteem, self-efficacy, self-management, social inclusion, engagement and increased social networks. On clinical outcomes, whilst studies are few, they found peer-led initiatives were as effective. Advantages can include empathy and a softening of the power imbalance so prevalent in mental health services.

Drawing on lived experience takes numerous forms – from informal natural support to peer support within services or whole peer-led services. It can be face-to-face: for instance, when the first person you meet on admission to hospital is a peer-support worker, who can empathise, show you the ropes. It can be through sharing online stories, or through social media: see for instance Social Spider at http://socialspider.com.

There has been a big expansion of peer support in the USA, Canada, Australia and New Zealand and some development in the UK.

There are many books, planning tools and resources written by and for people with lived experience: see Nottingham's plan, which covers how to keep well, manage crises and pursue your dreams and ambitions (www.wlmht.nhs.uk/information-and-advice/personal-recovery-plans/); and handbooks on 'taking charge' of your life (Disability Rights UK 2015).

A psychiatric diagnosis feels like a major loss, of the life expected. An important first step in recovery is to feel you can take charge, to plan life in new circumstances, with peer support.

It can help to think in terms of rights to participate. The UNCRPD expects governments to take action to comply with articles covering independent living, housing, transport, inclusive education, employment, health and more. Disabled people have the right to choose where they live and with whom: no one should be unlawfully forced into a particular living arrangement, like a care home, against their will. It includes having the same right as anyone else to marry and start a family.

These rights overturn, at least in principle, centuries of exclusion: segregated education or no education at all; prevention from having children (you will be 'unfit parents' or pass on the condition); being in institutions for lack of decent alternatives. If these rights were fully realised the effects would be profound.

The EHRC has guidance on the UNCRPD, written by and for disabled people – at http://www.equalityhumanrights.com/publication/united-nations-convention-rights-people-disabilities-what-does-it-mean-you.

If individuals draw on a deep sense of entitlement to human rights, it can give strength. Practical realisation of those rights is extremely partial (see below), but knowing the rights that are internationally recognised can help in formulating what you want, and overcoming any internalised sense of not 'deserving' equality.

Negotiating participation

Moving from planning participation to doing it can present a plethora of barriers. Ideas from others can help: for instance, if you need flexibility at work, knowing what others have done can help you decide what would suit you, what would work in your job and negotiate for it.

Examples of workplace adjustments for people with mental health issues

Changing hours and working patterns

- Changing the start or end of the workday to avoid travel in the rush hour or accommodate side-effects of medication
- Taking more frequent breaks
- Taking time off for appointments for mental health support
- Working part-time or job-sharing
- Working 'annualised hours', i.e. working when well, across the year.

Changed support and feedback

- Being able to call someone from work – a (peer) support worker, a friend – for support when needed
- Changes in management feedback on work performance, and recognition of achievement: more regular feedback, or support for greater autonomy
- A 'return to work' plan after any time off, which might include updates from colleagues, and a daily action plan in the first week.

Physical and technological support

- Agreeing with colleagues how best to receive instructions – for instance by email rather than verbally
- Use of GPS or organiser functions to manage anxiety
- A separate office or partitioned work area to reduce distraction.

Changed objectives or jobs

- Having minor job duties eliminated – for example, assigning 'fill-in' duties to another employee – freeing you to focus on your primary responsibilities.

Adapted from Center for Psychiatric Rehabilitation Potential Accommodations on the Job – at http://cpr.bu.edu/resources/reasonable-accommodations/jobschool/potential-accommodations-on-the-job

What is considered a 'reasonable' adjustment legally depends on factors like the adjustment cost, size and budget of the employer, and whether this adjustment will address the need effectively.

One common challenge is, do people want or need to be open about mental health issues?

Being open, like 'coming out' as gay, is not a once-and-for-all decision: it is made repeatedly, each time you encounter new people or situations, about whether to be open, who to, when, using what words. If someone decides to be open to their manager, it is very different saying 'I have a serious mental illness' than 'I have a mental health problem; I'm managing it but it would really help me if I could change my shift pattern to start a bit later in the day'. The first may leave the manager afraid that you will be unable to do the job. The second shows the manager what he or she can do and indicates that you are actively managing the situation. It is possible to take control, to choose whether to speak, and what to say.

'Doing Careers Differently' (Radar 2010) is a guide including tips like 'Come with answers, not with issues, prepare your solutions, but be flexible'.

Sayce (2010) found people with mental health problems were four times more likely to be open to no one at work than disabled people generally; and particularly fearful of being smothered with low expectations and stopped from doing anything 'stressful' if people at work knew their 'secret'. Where they were open, it was more likely to be with a colleague than a manager or HR professional, i.e. anyone with power over their career.

To be open at work?

- Losing the weight of a secret, the fear that someone may 'find out', can be liberating
- You can move on from worrying about what people know – to getting on with life. This is good for well-being – and productivity
- You can ask for any adjustments you need – it's hard to ask without being open
- Being open could encourage others to be open too. Humanity is varied and a strong workforce is one where people are not afraid to mention health experiences, differences of culture, faith or sexual orientation. You could play your part in modelling a 'stretch' in what is considered ordinary
- With more openness, attitudes and behaviour will change – since it is contact, on equal terms, working on common goals that changes them (see Chapter 6).

But people might stereotype you and view you as less capable.

- You may be able to influence that by how you convey your experience, who you talk to and gain support from
- You have rights: it can give you confidence that if an employer rejects you because of a mental health issue that is against the law. If they do not meet your need for an adjustment, you could mention that it is just like a hearing loop for someone who is deaf ('disability access' applies to people with mental health issues too)
- If you encounter a bad reaction you may be able to get support from a trade union, a disability network at work, friends, a mental health support network or a colleague.

Being open beyond the workplace – in a mother and toddler group, at the pub, mosque or church, with a new friend or partner – poses similar dilemmas and potential benefits. Gowar (2014) found that for a local community to be inclusive, inclusion must be unconditional: with greater space to be different than in a traditional homogeneous community. The idea that a community is either strong (united around similarity) or diverse is a myth. The contemporary community is only strong through being diverse – with diversity expressed. For instance, people with dementia should not need to stay at home because they behave 'strangely'; dementia-friendly communities have shown that businesses, champions living with dementia and public organisations can together make the community more accommodating, so more people with dementia go out and participate in anything from fishing to shopping (Local Government Association and Innovations in Dementia 2012).

Hamer (2014) studied what people with lived experience felt about inclusion. Participants felt 'othered', rebuffed and denied full citizenship opportunities. They often had to 'act normal' to be included – but even then were often not fully accepted. They wanted more acceptance of difference, celebration of creativity and eccentricity. Some operating within services had found ways to 'bend' (not break) rules in the interests of inclusion.

One response to being 'othered' is to hide your difference. Another is to adopt the identity of 'mental health service user' almost to the exclusion of other identities: if it seems impossible to be a mother, engineer or waiter with (open) mental health problems, then perhaps being a mental health service user is the one identity left. In the 1980s the few people who were open tended to be 'professional' mental health service users – working in 'user involvement' and advocacy. By the 2010s there were more mothers, engineers and waiters who were open (see Time to Change stories, above). Perhaps it is becoming easier to choose the weight to give in your identity to having mental health challenges: whether to be out and proud as a 'mad' person (as a primary identity), or primarily a mother or engineer, who experiences madness as one aspect of life.

The hope is that as more people are open, inclusion will become less conditional. History tells us equality is sometimes achieved at the expense of difference: when gay people became defined as 'born that way', wanting the same marriages as everyone else, equality flowed; it was perhaps harder for those challenging heterosexist norms and forging new types of community and relationship.

The more that individuals stretch the bounds of the 'normal' the more that risk is averted. Mary O'Hagan calls for a development of mad culture, a positive revaluation of the experience (see Chapter 5) which could fundamentally support that stretch of norms.

Knowing your rights can be important for negotiating community as well as work participation. Rights are not (for most people) about going to court; they enable you to discuss from a position of knowledge the adjustment you need at university, or the support from health and social services that will enable you to lead the life you want. You may be met in any setting by rules, fears and prejudices that risk keeping you out. It is useful to draw on the power of your own solutions and, where needed, the language of rights.

UK rights in brief

- Under the Equality Act 2010 you have rights including to be free of direct discrimination in areas from housing to healthcare and insurance; freedom from indirect discrimination, harassment, and victimisation; and a right to reasonable adjustments in education and employment. Employers do not have the right to ask you about your health or disability before job offer, except in highly specified circumstances (such as asking if you need adjustments at interview). See: http://www.equalityhumanrights.com/your-rights/equal-rights/disability

- Under the Criminal Justice Act 2003, amended in 2011, you have a right – if someone commits a crime motivated by hostility towards a disability or perceived disability – to have that crime recognised as a hate crime. This means the crime is viewed as more serious and the sentence can be raised. The Crown Prosecution Service (2010) states they will always take seriously people with mental health problems or learning disabilities and 'we will not make assumptions about your reliability or credibility'. A guide for disabled people is at http://disabilityrightsuk.org/how-we-can-help/publications/lets-stop-disability-hate-crime-guidance, with Easyread version

- The Human Rights Act 1998 gives core rights including to life, private and family life, personal freedom, freedom from torture or inhuman or degrading treatment, free expression, and freedom from discrimination. All these rights can be qualified – for instance, the Mental Health Act allows for compulsory detention despite the 'right to personal freedom' – but this law does enshrine basic rights and freedoms for all. The British Institute for Human Rights has a guide for disabled people http://www. bihr.org.uk/sites/default/files/bihr_disabled_guide.pdf

- The Self Directed Support (Scotland) Act 2013 and Care Act 2014 in England offer rights: for instance, in England the local authority must consider the physical, mental and emotional well-being of the individual and build care around the person, through personal budgets
- The NHS Constitution sets out rights including: to receive treatments recommended by NICE (National Institute for Health and Clinical Excellence) if clinically recommended, to choose your GP practice and be accepted unless there are reasonable grounds to refuse (in which case you should be informed of them), to be treated with dignity and respect, to access your health records and correct inaccuracies, to have any complaint properly investigated, and not to face unlawful discrimination. See http://www.nhs .uk/choiceintheNHS/Rightsandpledges/NHSConstitution/Documents/2013/the-nhs-constitution-for-england-2013.pdf
- There are some rights under mental health law – for instance, to have your detention reviewed by a mental health review tribunal – but the law itself denies rights (see Chapter 4).

There are numerous examples of people using rights to propose solutions:

> There has absolutely been an increase in students and parents knowing their rights and talking to us about adjustments. (Further Education College, personal communication).

> The DRC advised me on how to approach my employer, and when he didn't understand they wrote a letter on headed paper explaining my rights. Then they made the adjustment so I could contact my support worker when I needed to. (Individual with mental health problems, personal communication).

The DRC (2000–7) used 'rights-based mediation' within a framework of legislation. Solutions were brokered that met good practice under the law and satisfied both parties. This avoids the risk of someone with a mental health condition settling for too little.

There are some examples in mainstream media of sharing stories of using rights. A 2014 *Guardian* letters page included the following:

> Joanna Hall's GP is wrong not to refer her to a sleep clinic ... I too have the syndrome and after a lifetime of unhappy mornings, diagnosis was a relief. It meant I could ask my employer for an occupational health assessment, which led to a 'reasonable adjustment' to my schedule – I was allowed a later start in the working day. My productivity improved, as did my quality of life. (K. Flynn, *Guardian*, 23 August 2014).

However, there is potential for far greater knowledge of rights and how to use them, spread through peer support, social media – and mental health workers (see below).

Don't hold back – go for it

It is easy to be put off from trying to participate for fear of rejection or failure, in what Patrick Corrigan and colleagues have called the 'why try?' syndrome. They found people who live in cultures that stereotype people with mental health problems anticipate discrimination, and internalise the devaluing stereotypes. This damages self-esteem and self-efficacy, which in turn means people do not try to participate in employment or independent living – even though they could have succeeded. This can lead to passivity and hopelessness.

Corrigan et al. (2009) found that people who are righteously indignant at the stereotypes have a greater sense of power than those who take them as valid; and that this power can be achieved by solidarity and mutual support. This enhances self-efficacy and reduces the tendency not to try.

People are sometimes right to anticipate rejection (see Chapter 1). It is useful to anticipate not just the rejection but how to deal with it. For instance:

- The Health and Safety Executive is clear that health and safety should not be used as a false excuse to deny disabled people opportunities. They publish guidance, with examples (see http://www.hse.gov.uk/disability/casestudies.htm). Taking the 'reasonably practical' steps required by health and safety legislation to avoid harm is consistent with making 'reasonable adjustments' under the Equality Act. If someone suggests a job is 'too stressful' for you, you could draw on this guidance to challenge them.
- Good practice dictates that you should be involved in your own risk assessment. In 2004 JRF published research arguing that people using services were not involved enough in risk assessments, but did recognise risk and could co-design solutions (Langan and Lindow 2004). The Royal College of Psychiatrists (2008) argued that services had tilted too far towards risk aversion and recommended user participation in risk assessments. Disability commentators have argued that 'safeguarding' can be used as an excuse to deny autonomy: it must be implemented with the disabled person, rather than the state deeming the individual 'vulnerable' and stepping in to 'protect' them, entrenching disempowerment.

It is worth thinking through:

- What support would help if you encounter rejection or discrimination: for instance, from a friend, or others who have encountered similar challenges
- Are there people who may *not* be helpful – a friend, relative or mental health worker who you find over-protective or discouraging – and are there ways you can minimise their influence?

Stories of recovery often emphasise breaking away from shame, gaining strength to lead the life you choose.

> I believe deeply that fear and shame are dominating factors in many of our lives and often because others have engrained those feelings in us. I know that is true for my life. I do still have fears. I fear loss, I fear regret, I fear unknowns ... I fear myself because, like so many other patients, I have been

taught to fear myself. I have been fortunate to learn that, while I may very well be unable to control my thoughts, I am able to control my behavior with maturing precision. (Amanda Back's Recovery Story, National Empowerment Center website at: http://www.power2u.org/articles/recovery/recovery_stories/amanda-back.html).

I have been able to talk to and be around people who could understand where I have been and what I am still going through. It is so important to be believed and validated as a person, as this kind of support from psychiatric services is often not there ... I have suddenly felt a relax in my thinking and my criticism of myself ... My peers have helped me regain my dignity and my self-pride and their belief in me means that I am going to continue my fight for my full recovery. (http://www.power2u.org/recovery13578-stories.html).

Sharing stories can build confidence to get over the 'why try' phenomenon – and go for it.

One of the fundamental things is the right of marginalised communities or excluded communities to speak in their own voice and to break away from the sort of dependence in terms of which intermediaries become the main spokespeople. (Justice Albie Sachs, South African civil rights judge 2007).

Tackling discrimination and human rights breaches

The power of legal rights lies in sometimes using them: otherwise they are seen as an empty threat (see Chapter 6). If faced with discrimination or a breach of human rights, it may be possible to seek justice.

> The London Borough of Kensington and Chelsea changed Elaine McDonald's care plan and expected her to use incontinence pads at night rather than have a carer to support her to go to the toilet. This denied her dignity. Ms McDonald, a former ballerina, decided to fight. The European Court of Human Rights found that, when making decisions about cuts, authorities have to consider the dignity of the person affected. Elaine's needs were reassessed. She still did not get the support she wanted – but she did get some compensation and the case opened the door for more people to challenge care decisions. It has shown that when we use care services we all need our human rights to make sure we have privacy, dignity and independence. Authorities cannot ignore these rights in the drive to save money. (From Equally Ours statement 2014, at http://www.equally-ours.org.uk/cuts-care-found-breach-human-rights/)

Human rights law has also been used in mental health in areas including rights to privacy and family life, for instance marriage for people in secure settings. Sometimes the law is little help:

The case of Obrey v DWP (2013) concerned three people with mental health problems who had a pattern of being detained in hospital under mental health law followed by periods when they returned home. All had been detained for periods of more than 52 weeks. The rule they challenged was that after 52 weeks Housing Benefit is lost because the person is no longer regarded as being 'temporarily absent' from their home. This meant their homes were at risk of repossession. They argued that the rule failed to take into account the different position of those who are compulsorily detained. The first tier tribunal (Social Security) found the Housing Benefit Regulations breached the European Convention on Human Rights. This case could have supported housing security, and peace of mind, for others; but unfortunately in 2013 it was overturned on appeal (Obrey v DWP 2013 EWCA Civ 1584)

Equality law has been used with both positive and negative results for people with mental health problems (see Chapter 6).

By 2014, the number of employment tribunal (ET) cases generally had dropped significantly, due to the introduction of fees to bring discrimination claims. In the first quarter of 2013 there were 63,715 ET cases; in the same quarter in 2014 only 10,967. Disability discrimination claims had dropped by 47% (Rubenstein 2014). In 2014 Unison applied for a Judicial Review of the Order that introduced the fees – but was turned down.

There were other restrictions on seeking justice:

- A deregulation bill introduced in the UK Parliament in 2014–15 included provision to remove the power of ETs to make recommendations for wider action by employers as a result of a case. For instance, in Ishaq v London Borough of Ealing, a contract worker was called an 'Asian monkey'. The Tribunal recommended mandatory equality training with conscientious monitoring of participation. This kind of systemic change was to be stopped.
- Advice, especially legal advice, was becoming harder to obtain. The Low Commission into tackling the advice deficit in 2014 found increasing demand (due for instance to changes in social security and housing), and a sector struggling under cutbacks. They cited cuts to advice centres, waiting lists and new restrictions on legal aid. They recommended simplification, early intervention, a blend of easy-to-use helplines and websites and embedding advice where people regularly go – GP surgeries, community centres. They proposed local advice and legal support plans, backed by a new Fund.
- Legislation enacted from April 2013 removed legal aid from cases concerning employment, housing (except in cases involving homelessness or risk to health and safety), debt (except in cases relating to certain proceedings where the home is at risk), and most welfare benefits cases (except appeals in the Upper Tribunal and higher courts). Legal aid remained available for some types of cases including judicial reviews – see: http://www. disabilityrightsuk.org/sites/default/files/pdf/judicialreview.pdf.

In a few areas work was improving access to redress: for instance, moves towards a more coherent approach to NHS complaints (see: http://www.healthwatch.co.uk/complaints).

The upshot is that seeking redress is not easy. Nonetheless, there are advice agencies in some areas, lawyers offering pro bono or 'no win no fee' support, networks of people prepared to share personal and legal knowledge to help decide whether to mount a legal challenge, and some capacity in the EHRC to support strategically significant cases. In 2014 the Open University held a seminar on the history of women's mental health work: one woman spoke eloquently of how she had brought to justice a psychiatrist who was ultimately found guilty of sexual assault; as a result she was contacted and offered support to others experiencing abuse by mental health workers.

As ever in social change, ingenuity and resilience are required. Even in tough economic and policy times, groups of disabled people challenged issues including the Work Capability Assessment's sensitivity to people with mental health problems (a Judicial Review found it was not sensitive enough), the closure of the Independent Living Fund and the Bedroom Tax. Whilst legal outcomes were mixed, the challenges created a buzz and showed people were prepared to fight.

The end of the DRC in 2007 led to a reduced emphasis on strategic disability litigation. There is a case for creating a litigation strategy amongst mental health and wider disability organisations, raising funds to challenge discrimination and human rights abuses strategically, linking the challenges to campaigns.

What can friends and family do?

Friends and family members often want to help the person they are supporting to build or rebuild a satisfying life. Support to have hope in tough times is massively appreciated in the literature of people with lived experience.

> It was very positive to be around people who were so supportive of me ... and it gave me a lot more joy and spark for the future. (Lapsley et al. 2002).

However, families and friends may not know how to help and, unsurprisingly, may hold the same fears and low expectations as any other member of the public. They may, with the best of intentions, be over-protective: people with lived experience speak about being held back by people who know them, who presume they need 'looking after' rather than support to move forward.

It is very helpful to read recovery stories, and learn what can be achieved:

> My wife was very worried about our son going to university. Would he be able to cope? We had been so involved in looking after him. Then I heard a presentation about how a degree radically improves the employment chances of people with all kinds of disability – and that convinced us. (personal communication).

It is also useful to understand rights – to be allies in using power for participation.

At the same time families and friends may be grappling with major changes in their own lives: are they a 'carer', and what have they lost as the person close to them has developed difficulties?

The Scottish Recovery Network website includes powerful examples of families and friends pursuing a journey of recovery – for themselves, and in support of their loved one.

Identifying as a 'carer' can have drawbacks, in the context of rights to participation, for three broad reasons:

- The preferred language of people with lived experience. Nationally, many people experiencing mental health challenges have objected to the idea that a key relationship – as daughter, spouse, friend, father – should be renamed as a one-way street of care, with them as the recipient (Sayce 2000; Repper and Perkins 2003). Some find this demeaning, because it seems to strip them of their own identity and to ignore the contributions – emotional, practical – that they make to families and friends. It can be one example among many of feeling stripped of a significant role – being viewed as 'unable' to work or study or parent.

> I've never told my daughter I go to a carers' group. She would be horrified. I'm her mother. She doesn't think of me as a 'carer'. (Focus group participant, cited in Richmond Mind 2013).

- The views of 'carers'. Whilst some family members are relieved to understand their status as carer – which can offer recognition, and access to rights and resources – others do not readily identify as 'carers'. They may view the support they give as simply a part of their family responsibility. They may view 'caring' as physical tending, whereas what they are engaged in is more emotional and personal. If mental health services use only the term 'carer', many families and friends who could benefit from support can be missed.
- The equalities dimensions to the debate. The way that support in families and friendship circles is understood differs, between people from different communities and experiences. For example:
  - Older and disabled 'carers' may be particularly likely to see the relationship as reciprocal, not one-way:

> I support my partner – but I'm also a user of mental health services, so when I'm bad she supports me. We support each other. (Richmond Mind 2013)

  - Networks of people using mental health services offer mutual support, sometimes in the absence of contact with families of origin – and do not split the network into 'carers' and 'cared for'.
  - In some black and minority ethnic (BME) communities people do not identify with the term 'carer' at all, viewing the responsibilities simply as part of family life.
  - Some lesbian, gay and bisexual people talk of their friendship networks as 'families of choice' – and may offer networks of support rather than a single 'carer'.
  - Parents who experience mental health challenges may be particularly reluctant to see their child defined as a 'young carer': with their parenting abilities potentially under scrutiny because of their psychiatric diagnosis, the last thing they want is language that suggests they are no longer parenting, but rather being cared for by their child (see for example Morris 1996).

The term 'carer' can seem to entrench a power difference – when, for the person going through mental health difficulties, having power is key to having confidence to 'go for it'. Even if the person seems to lack capacity, it is possible to work on the basis of their preference – not just what you think is in their 'best interests'.

Flexible language – families, friends and carers – can maximise relevance to the widest range of people. It better reflects the reality of people's varied, complex and reciprocal relationships than the shorthand language of 'carers'. Inclusive language makes it most likely that discussion, and services, will reach the widest number of people engaged in the important task of supporting those living with mental health challenges.

The most helpful role is to support the person close to you to rebuild their life – to follow their aspiration, feel in charge of their life, have support that works for them.

Being an ally for participation rights makes an incalculable contribution.

What can mental health workers do?

Mental health workers have technical expertise and can also be allies for participation rights.

Some keys to achieving this are to:

- Start from empathy. Always think about what the person is experiencing, from their point of view
- View it as your job to enable the person to have power and to participate. Link people to helpful resources to pursue their ambitions
- Learn about discrimination and the impacts it has. For instance, if someone you are working with seems very passive, consider that this may be as a result of the 'why try' response to anticipated discrimination (see above), rather than a 'symptom' of the 'illness'. Understand the impact of actual discrimination and be ready to support people who experience rejection to decide what to do
- Root your work in a commitment to everyone's human rights – the right to participate, to live where you choose, to have justice
- Know about actual rights – in broad terms – so you can share resources and signpost to sources of information, advice and peer support
- Give space if people want to talk about specific dilemmas like whether and how to be open
- Do not parcel out your time as if it was the one answer to people's support needs. Instead support people with managing their own personal budget, linking into peer support, getting inspiration about how to use that budget. Think of people's networks, new or established – family, peer support, online support, friendships...
- Be alert to issues of poverty and signpost people to good independent information on benefits and other finance issues (see Disability Rights UK's *Disability Rights Handbook 2015*). But do not inadvertently 'protect' people by encouraging them to secure benefits but not opportunities. Think also about what might enable the person to participate more fully in social and/or economic activities
- Enable people to think about risk and contribute to their own plan to manage it. Do not take a risk-averse approach to safeguarding. If someone may be suicidal, don't fall back on compulsory treatment or detention for lack of talking through what might generate hope
- Put your expertise at the disposal of people you work with, rather than deciding for them – be 'on tap not on top' (Perkins 2012, p. 17)
- Consider being mentored by someone living with a long-term mental health issue as part of your own learning
- If you have your own experience of mental distress, consider drawing on it to dismantle the 'us and them' divide.

The eminent South African anti-apartheid activist and civil rights judge Albie Sachs told the following story:

When I'd just got back from exile I spoke to a group called 'Concerned social workers'. It was wonderful to see a large hall filled with social workers who saw their role as being more than just to help people with needs – it was to help the transformation in society. A few days later I spoke to 'Disabled People of South Africa', and to them the social workers were almost the biggest impediment – the blockage, the people controlling the funding and speaking on their behalf ... I felt torn and very divided but that was an important moment for me. ... I said [to the disabled people] well, what you must do. Then all of a sudden I stopped and said No what we must do, what we must do ... That was the first time I used the term 'we' in that particular context and I felt very proud that I could identify with the community. (Sachs 2007).

Mental health professionals can choose to be open about their own lived experience. They can, like the South African social workers, lead change themselves; or be allies, working for the greater power and voice of people with lived experience, and their greater participation in every aspect of society.

CONCLUSION

Participation rights offer a framework for individual recovery and for support from families, friends and mental health workers. It is a framework that emphasises power, deep knowledge of common human rights, understanding of the tools of rights and the power of peer support and networks to achieve participation.

Individual action both influences and is influenced by wider systemic issues, which are the subject of the next two chapters.

Reflective Exercises

Can you think of an example where peer support has enabled you or someone you know to take a new risk? What are the implications for people living with mental health challenges and those who support them?

How can mental health services ensure that 'risk assessment' is not used to stifle freedom and opportunity?

What are the major rights you would want to be aware of in relation to discrimination or harassment on mental health grounds – and what are some of the keys to pursuing those rights in practice?

FURTHER RESOURCES

Scottish Recovery Network

• Includes stories of recovery at www.scottishrecovery.net/

Center for Psychiatric Rehabilitation

- Includes examples of workplace 'accommodations' for people living with mental health challenges at http://cpr.bu.edu/resources/reasonable-accommodations/jobschool/potential-accommodations-on-the-job

National Empowerment Center

- Includes stories of recovery at: http://www.power2u.org/recovery-stories.html

Equality and Human Rights Commission

- Has guides and codes of practice on human rights and equality at: www.equalityhumanrights.com

Disability Rights UK

- Publishes online factsheets, guides and books on 'your rights' in relation to independent living, careers, benefits and human rights at: www.disabilityrightsuk.org

British Institute for Human Rights

- Publishes guides on human rights at: www.bihr.org.uk

National Survivor User Network

- Publishes guides on involvement and co-production at: www.nsun.org.uk

8 | Ending Discrimination within Mental Health Services

Chapter Summary

- Continuing discrimination within mental health services
- The desire for change
- The nature of discrimination
- How to create change
- Leadership in services
- Wider transformation

Continuing discrimination within mental health services

Over 30% of people with mental health difficulties surveyed for the Time to Change evaluation in England in 2011 reported negative experiences of discrimination from mental health staff – higher than in most other life domains, like finding a job, or encounters with police, housing or education. Whilst discrimination from friends, family and social life declined from 2008–11 (with fluctuations thereafter, see Chapter 2), there was no significant decrease in discrimination from mental health staff. David Brindle (2013) noted that one group – extraordinarily – seemed resistant: mental health professionals.

This chapter explores how services might be transformed from a site that can reinforce the discrimination of the wider world to a zone that gives power and equips people to pursue their ambitions and challenge injustice.

The desire for change

When I asked leaders in anti-discrimination work what they thought the next priorities should be for anti-discrimination work (see previous chapter), several mentioned transformation of mental health – and wider health – services. Graham Thornicroft placed in his top two priorities tackling discrimination amongst health service staff and driving down premature mortality. Mary O'Hagan argued for fundamental service change, realigning funding away from clinical crisis provision to supporting people to regain their personal power and social and economic opportunities. For her, this required major legal and professional change:

> Discriminatory mental health legislation needs to be repealed because this is the legal cornerstone of discrimination, rather like the old sodomy laws ... [and] Psychiatry and the professions need to publicly acknowledge the harm the professions and the state have done to people with mental distress now and in the past – to role model the unacceptability of discrimination.
>
> (Mary O'Hagan)

Peter Beresford advocated self-organisation amongst survivors – to challenge prevailing medical paradigms and develop 'social model' approaches and new forms of support. He saw revolutionary potential in the growth of survivor-led research and professional training – including accreditation of social work courses only where they demonstrate user and carer involvement. These developments could be built on, with greater support for the survivor movement and new overarching thinking, through the development of 'mad studies', learning from Canada (Le Francois et al. 2013). In 2014 for the first time the international disability studies conference held a whole stream on 'mad studies' (http://madstudies2014.wordpress.com/).

In 2014 the Time to Change campaign commissioned Disability Rights UK to undertake a literature review (Watson et al. 2014) and scoping study on discrimination within mental health services, and to host a round-table discussion at which survivor, professional and service leaders expressed commitment to tackling this in-house discrimination.

There appeared to be recognition in the mental health sector that action was needed. This does not necessarily imply consensus on what exactly should be done. Ideas in literature range from influencing the attitudes and behaviours of staff within existing services, through to de-commissioning those services in favour of an approach governed by a quite different paradigm, with more power accorded to survivors and – for some – removing discriminatory mental health law and systematically reducing coercion in services, year on year. The Norwegian government has set requirements on services to demonstrate progressive reductions in use of seclusion, compulsory detention and treatment – unlike in the UK, where (at least in England) we see year-on-year increases (see Chapter 4).

There are changes to existing services that could be built on.

Merseycare Mental Health Trust decided to put human rights at the heart of their whole service in the Rathbone Centre in Liverpool. They aimed to extend choice and decision-making as far as possible even where there are constraints and to recognise in practice individual rights to respect and equality. http://equally-ours.org.uk/putting-human-rights-heart-mental-health-care-2/

There are also developments designed to create peer-led alternatives, quite separate from statutory services. NSUN (National Survivor User Network) and the charity Together set up Peer2Peer, offering mutual support amongst groups of people with lived experience, aiming to mobilise the power of peer support and offer guidance on setting it up successfully. Together commissioned a consultation that warned of some dangers of 'professionalisation' of peer support by employing peer-support workers within mental health services (Faulkner and Kalathil 2012).

Before analysing different approaches it is useful to understand more about the form that discrimination within services takes.

The nature of discrimination

There are examples of studies, both internationally and in the UK, that find positive and empathetic staff attitudes and behaviours. For instance Gräusgruber et al. (2006) found that mental health staff were less likely to attribute mental health problems to 'weak character' than were the general public and less likely to see service users as dangerous. These studies are counter-balanced by a far larger set that find more negative attitudes and behaviours.

Some studies inquire into staff attitudes and behaviours by asking the staff. Hansson et al. (2011) found that mental health professionals would not want to date someone with mental health challenges and would be reluctant to let them look after their children – the very desire for social distance that lies at the heart of many definitions of 'stigma' (Thornicroft 2006). Research has also found that mental health professionals would perceive stigma if they themselves were diagnosed with a mental health condition (Sriram and Jabbarpour 2005). Attitudes appear to be particularly negative from staff members based in inpatient settings or treating psychosis (Hansson et al. 2011). In a survey of 187 mental health nurses, Linden and Kavanagh (2012) found those working in an inpatient setting held significantly more socially restrictive attitudes than those based in the community, indicating that they felt individuals with a diagnosis of schizophrenia were dangerous and should be avoided.

Some studies find clinicians hold pessimistic views of recovery: in a national survey of Australians' attitudes, Caldwell and Jorm (2000, 2001) found that only 2% of psychiatrists and 3% of clinical psychologists believed someone with a diagnosis of schizophrenia could recover fully, even with professional help, compared with 9% of mental health nurses, and 30% of the general public. Magliano et al. (2011) found that medical students who identified a case vignette in terms of a diagnostic label held more pessimistic views about the possibility of recovery, and believed that people with mental health diagnoses were unpredictable.

Warner (2009, p. 375) notes that 'one of the most robust findings [about schizophrenia] is that a substantial proportion will recover completely or with good functional capacity, with or without modern medical treatment'. This evidence appears from research not to be widely understood by clinicians.

Whilst there may be reasons for this pessimism – for instance, clinicians tend to see people in crisis, not when they are managing well – there are major risks that if professionals do not truly believe people can resume positive, valuable lives, they will convey this gloomy picture to the individuals they serve.

This is borne out by studies that investigate discrimination by asking the people who use services. People have reported feeling reduced to their diagnoses and disheartened by the implicit and explicit message that they would never recover or might commit suicide (Mancini et al. 2005). They report feeling excluded from important decisions, being spoken to as if they were children, and feeling humiliated, coerced or punished (Wahl 1999; Link et al. 2008; Lyons et al. 2009). Corrigan (2005) found that people with mental health problems often felt staff members assumed that they lacked the capacity to make important decisions about their lives. People with mental health challenges have consistently identified mental health professionals as fundamental contributors to the process of stigmatisation (Pinfold et al. 2005; Arboleda-Flórez and Stuart 2012).

In 2014 the McPin Foundation reported on early qualitative findings from the Viewpoint study, exploring experiences of stigma and discrimination (see http://mcpin.org/viewpoint-survey). Themes reported by people using services included not being listened to, not being understood, and lack of support.

The literature also reveals an 'unspoken threat of coercion' – as one person put it:

> I felt very upset, resentful, but I wouldn't show it because I knew if I did, they would section me.

For African and African Caribbean people, services can be characterised by containment, cultural insensitivity – or service avoidance. The Care Quality Commission (CQC) (2011) reported no material change in ethnic differences in admission, compulsory detention or seclusion since 2005, with numbers still disproportionately high for those communities. In addition, people with no right to remain in the UK were in 2014 being discharged after a crisis direct to the streets – since they had no entitlement to public support.

Other dimensions of identity also appeared to correlate with compound discrimination, for example lesbian, gay, bisexual and trans people continued to report that their sexuality is judged or pathologised; and people with forensic or drug and alcohol difficulties were perceived as having caused their problem and therefore less entitled to a sympathetic response. There is also evidence of structural ageism in services: older people receive a lower quality, less well funded service when they hit the age of 65 (Royal College of Psychiatrists 2011).

There appeared from the literature to be some differences in attitudes and behaviours between different parts of the mental health system. Primary care staff appeared to hold the most negative views, followed by forensic staff, inpatient care staff and psychiatrists.

The messages from research match what is being found in English mental health services. The CQC (2013) found 'evidence of practices and attitudes at all levels of some mental health service organisations that are neither informed by, nor respectful of, individual rights and needs'. On some CQC visits to hospitals, patients raised concerns about their interactions with staff including 'complaints of staff rudeness or disengagement; patients being made to feel inferior or not taken seriously by staff; and allegations of name calling and bullying. In a minority of these, allegations were made of physical abuse of patients by staff'. Overall, the CQC reports that too often mental health services have a culture of containment and control, rather than treatment, care, support and recovery. They note that far too few people are meaningfully involved in decisions about their own care and treatment: over a third of care plans showed no evidence at all of patients' views; many told the CQC they had no idea what was in their care plans (CQC 2013). (See: www.cqc.org.uk/content/monitoring-operation-mental-health-act).

Perkins (2014) has commented on the physical manifestation of the 'them and us' culture, including 'the separates': separate toilets, separate crockery and so forth. This conveys a message that you are 'lesser' and need to be kept separate. Devaluing someone and then separating them off are two key components of the process of stigmatisation (see Chapter 3).

How to create change

Earlier chapters established that the most promising approach to reducing discrimination in society is through a 'participation rights' approach, i.e. a focus on full participation, backed by power. The same applies within mental health services. As Mary O'Hagan puts it (above) there is a need for funding that 'supports people to regain their personal power and social and economic opportunities'; power, and opportunities to participate.

Tackling discrimination in services is not simply about mental health services playing catch-up with the wider society in terms of the odd initiative to improve attitudes and behaviour of staff. Rather it is about modelling participation and a fundamental shift in power: showing the wider society how people living with mental health challenges can participate, contribute and lead; and actively enabling individuals to seize opportunities (for friendships, relationships, education, sport, employment or anything else).

How might that be achieved?

The literature on reducing discrimination within mental health services includes evidence on the value of contact on equal terms (exactly as in wider society). Contact that goes beyond the 'professional/patient' relationship has mainly been evaluated in relation to training – where professionals or students are trained by people with lived experience. There is some evidence for the value of people having more control over their own support and for wider 'user involvement' and co-production, in terms of impact on service provider attitudes.

Much of the literature concerns itself with 'interventions' – particularly training. The problem is that one-off interventions are unlikely to have a lasting effect. The literature on training shows why. Training by people with lived experience is linked with improved attitudes among medical students (Spagnolo et al. 2008; Kassam et al. 2011; Friedrich et al.

2013); nursing staff (Dearing and Steadman 2008; Sadow and Ryder 2008), occupational therapy students (Beltran et al. 2007), psychology students (Bizub and Davidson 2011) and pharmacy students (O'Reilly et al. 2010; Gable et al. 2011).

However, the evidence also shows that one-off training is not sufficient to generate lasting change; not sufficient to counter-balance wider cultures within professions and services (Roth et al. 2000; Sadow et al. 2002). The Time to Change END (Education Not Discrimination) intervention involved training medical students, using testimonies from people with lived experience, role plays and an educational component. This led to improved attitudes (for instance, fewer students agreeing that 'it is frightening to think of people with mental health problems living in residential neighbourhoods'), improved intended behaviour (using a measure relating to living with, working with, living nearby or continuing a relationship with someone with a mental health problem) and increased empathy. However, six months later these changes were not sustained (Friedrich et al. 2013).

This suggests, firstly, that one-off modules within professional training are not enough to embed changes in attitude and behaviour: there is a need, even if only considering training, for people with lived experience to influence professional training right through the curriculum, systemically – to encourage respect and empathy – rather than inserting modules into existing courses. Equal contact, backed by messages reflecting respect, need to be inbuilt and ongoing.

Secondly, it suggests that training may be an inadequate way of implementing 'contact on equal terms'. Whole service cultures need transformation. However much professional training is changed, medical and other students go from training into service environments. If these do not reinforce equality and respect – if indeed they embody a 'them and us' culture – then the shift of power and respect embedded in training will have no enduring impact.

Changing 'them and us' cultures

It is useful to consider different levels of change and their impact on culture and practice. Several writers, starting with Arnstein 1969, have described 'ladders of participation' to explain how citizens can participate in decisions. The ladder – which has been much adapted to the participation of children, disabled people and others – starts with the most tokenistic level, where people are consulted on a fait accompli, and goes through to full co-production and leadership by citizens. Gowar (2014) and Pye and Sayce (2014) describe different levels at which people living with long-term health conditions or disability can participate in local communities: at the highest level, standing for elected office or leading initiatives jointly with public agencies.

> When Gavin Harding, who has a learning disability, was elected as a local councillor in Selby, Yorkshire, he brought to the role a history of activism both on behalf of people with learning disabilities and on behalf of the whole community. He was able to contribute beyond disability rights issues, moving into a position of wider influence.

Some local authorities have built the participation of people living with disability or health conditions into planning, decision-making, governance and scrutiny: for example, the

London Borough of Hackney engaged young disabled people in scrutiny, not by expecting them to attend formal meetings but through councillors going out to engage young disabled people directly in scrutiny; and NSUN (National Survivor User Network) engaged people with mental health challenges directly in being champions for improved health and social care:

Mental Healthwatch

National Survivor User Network (NSUN), led by people living with mental health challenges, recognised that when people with lived experience are properly involved in shaping their services and communities, their own health and the support available usually improve. NSUN therefore designed the Mental Healthwatch scheme – supporting people with lived experience to get involved with Healthwatch, the health and social care consumer champion, being trained to do 'enter and view' visits to local services and advising on service improvements. By 2014, 150 volunteers and 50 local Healthwatches had got involved in the programme (NSUN 2014).

Some organisations led by people with lived experience work in new partnerships to change whole systems: for instance, working with LEPs (Local Enterprise Partnerships) to open up improved employment opportunities for disabled people (Pye and Sayce 2014); or working with police and crime prosecution service to improve reporting of hate crime (see Chapter 6).

The 'ladder' is a useful metaphor to consider how to change the 'them and us' culture and practices of mental health services into zones of support for participation rights. The simplified 'ladder' below contains just three divisions or 'rungs' – although further sub-divisions are possible (Pye and Sayce 2014).

Within all these processes it is important to consider the power of people from different backgrounds and communities. For instance, people from transgender, LGB, gypsy and traveller and other communities have pressed the Department of Health to build intersecting experiences into its equality strategy.

---

300 Voices is working in partnership with Birmingham and Solihull Mental Health NHS Foundation Trust and the West Midlands Police to reduce the stigma and discrimination that can exist in statutory mental health settings and the police. The project brings together staff from mental health services, the police and young African and Caribbean men who have experience of mental health problems to jointly develop a toolkit that improves the experience for young African and Caribbean men using mental health services and empowers them to speak out and help change things for the better.

Rung 1: Constrained power

At this level of participation, the individual has some say in their own support – for instance, through personalised planning – but does not actually decide on their own services or on how resources are used. S/he still risks being subject to the pendulum swing between a service response when in crisis, and little support on her/his own terms in between.

There may be opportunities for 'involvement', i.e. feeding into the policies or plans of mental health organisations, but leaving the purpose and configuration of services the same.

This 'involvement' can be an exercise in participation – but it is constrained. For instance, it might focus on exactly which therapy and social groups should be held on a ward (rather than whether 'groups' on a 'ward' are the best response to people in mental distress). It may involve presenting people using services with a ready-framed proposal for service change, to which only small adjustments are possible given prior decisions on budgets or priorities. Discrete opportunities for influence are better than no opportunities, but they are limited.

There may be opportunities to get involved in training staff or students; but at this first rung of participation, this may solely mean 'telling your story' – confined to the role of 'case study' rather than commentator on services and how they could be run.

This can at least show that people using services are more than their ill-health:

> If the only time they see you is when you are your most vulnerable, in a crisis situation, then that colours how they view you at other times. They don't see you just getting on with your life in a day-to-day kind of way. So they always talk to you like a patient or like you are pathetic.
>
> (From Branfield 2009, p. 8)

Several sources suggest that the power of the service user narrative in training is becoming increasingly recognised and that service user involvement can enable students to connect with the values underpinning 'recovery', i.e. people pursuing their own journeys to the life they want (e.g. Tee et al. 2007; Stickley et al. 2009, 2010). The emotional impact of the person's narrative, coupled with their power – through the teaching role – are important to this learning (Rush 2008). This can offer transformational learning.

Direct contact has been found to be preferable to indirect, film-based contact – although powerful film content can have some value. In a randomised controlled trial of nursing students, participants were assigned to one of three groups: watching a live presentation given by a person with lived experience, watching a DVD of a similar presentation, or attending a lecture (as a control group participant). The study found that although both the DVD group and live presentation group showed improvements in attitudes, the live group showed more favourable attitudes toward social contact and greater overall enjoyment of the session than the DVD group (Clement et al. 2012). Other studies have found that real-life contact with people who are living a positive life with mental health problems changes staff attitudes in ways that exposure to taped materials, books and other resources does not (Sadow and Ryder 2008; Nguyen et al. 2012).

However, one-off training is not sufficient to transform attitudes and behaviour in the longer term (see above).

Rung 2: Substantive power

Beyond training, there are other ways that people with lived experience and staff can have contact with each other, on equal terms, working to common goals, in joint endeavours.

Amering et al. (2012) have described 'trialogue' groups that bring together people using services, family members and mental health workers in an open forum located on 'neutral terrain' – outside any therapeutic, familial or institutional context – with the aim of discussing the experiences and consequences of mental health problems, going beyond role stereotypes and constraints. In German-speaking countries well over 100 trialogue groups are regularly attended by approximately 5,000 people.

Where people with lived experience take leadership roles in particular programmes – for instance, expert patient groups – this can influence the attitudes of professionals, who may change their view of the capabilities of people once they see them leading initiatives (Lawn et al. 2011; Vaidee 2012).

The composition of the workforce may begin to change, with some people with lived experience employed in the service – as 'peer-support workers' or simply as people who happen to have a mental health condition. But they may not yet reach a 'tipping point' of influencing cultures. At a 2014 round-table some staff talked about the fear of being open at work in terms of 'not bleeding while there are sharks about'.

There may be opportunities to offer training to students or staff that goes beyond 'telling your story'. Training by service users is growing. It has been a requirement of social work training since 2004. Good practice is increasingly viewed as engagement across the curriculum, with involvement in the assessment of students and management of the overall course. See: http://www.scie.org.uk/publications/ataglance/ataglance19.asp. SCIE explored people's perceptions of such training from the point of view of user-trainers and found a belief in its value; although some academics note that the evidence for impact is still not extensive (Molyneux and Irvine 2004). Repper and Breeze (2007) reviewed literature and found two studies showing improvement in empathy and communications skills, but otherwise little evidence of impact; they comment that consumer engagement needs to be systemic.

Finally, there may be opportunities to participate in decision-making on focused programmes or services. Studies of collective approaches to 'user involvement' in planning or evaluating services have shown these can be useful in promoting social inclusivity, as well as improving service delivery (Rogers and Pilgrim 2000; Tait and Lester 2005).

The 'rung 2' types of participation do deploy contact, with people beginning to break down the 'them and us' divide by working to common goals. But they focus on specific interventions (such as trialogues) or programmes. They are not about transforming whole systems.

Rung 3: Systemic power

To truly change the 'them and us' service culture and create zones that model and support full citizenship requires profound, integrated changes in services. It begins with purpose.

A small number of mental health services have re-stated their purpose as being to support human rights (see Merseycare above) or to enable people living with mental health challenges to lead the lives they choose and to enjoy the same rights as other citizens (as South West London and St George's Mental Health Trust did in the early 2000s). These developments exemplify two linked changes:

- Changes inside mental health services: changing the power balance, through citizens' rights and
- Changing the boundaries with the wider world, to enable people as a core purpose to seize opportunities.

This is a long way from symptom reduction or 'cure' as a purpose. It is doubtful that any statutory organisation has fully achieved this transformation of purpose in practice – but there are indications of how to approach it.

'Recovery' has become a controversial topic – with critics arguing that what had once been a liberatory discourse invented by people with lived experience has been mainstreamed, professionally co-opted and aligned with both neo-liberalism and a requirement to work (Rose 2014); and that it may give insufficient space for people experiencing the trauma of discrimination to grieve and work through past discriminations, as in the legacy of slavery and racism on multiple generations (Kalathil 2007, 2011). Yet 'recovery' as originally conceived by survivor activists Pat Deegan and Judy Chamberlin is all about building the life you want, grieving for the life you might have had, taking power through civil rights, mobilising peer support and seizing social and economic opportunities. Recovery proponents have strongly warned against professional co-option: in 2012 Perkins and Slade argued that in the hands of a powerful system, recovery ideas can be distorted and accommodated within existing paradigms. This suggests it would be unwise to throw out the liberatory concept and its potential application; but vigilance is essential to ensure it serves participation through power, not the status quo.

To implement the opportunity for 'recovery' as described by Deegan, right across services, requires systemic change: single interventions, like training, are categorically not enough. Whitley et al. (2009) studied implementation of recovery across 12 community settings and identified four factors that are important when they act together: leadership, a culture of innovation, supervision and training. Perkins (2012) outlines the cultural changes needed in whole services, for recovery-focused practice to be embedded. She describes a shift in purpose – from treatment and symptom reduction to helping people live the lives they choose. This requires five key elements to be met:

- A different role for mental health services and professionals – moving from one 'expert' to two, valuing the expertise of lived experience; with professionals being 'on tap' not 'on top', putting their expertise at the disposal of people who may want to make use of it
- Different relationships between mental health workers and those they serve – breaking down the 'them and us' divide, working from our common humanity – with professionals using both their professional expertise and lived experience to facilitate recovery
- Redefining user involvement – moving to co-production in service design, delivery and development
- A different kind of workforce that includes the expertise of lived experience, through employing peer-support workers – perhaps aiming for 50% of the workforce to be made up of peers
- A different relationship between services and communities: replacing a clinical approach to 'fixing' people, so they fit in, with a focus on changing the external world so it includes you. It involves the 'right to live independently and to be included in the community' (as the UNCRPD puts it). On this model, individuals have a right to the assistance necessary for inclusion and to prevent isolation and segregation.

This represents a significant change in the balance of power and requires major organisational change. Repper and Perkins (2013) have produced guidance on how this can be achieved at team level (the Team Recovery Implementation Plan) by empowering teams and utilising the skills and resources of everyone at the front-line to develop innovative ways of promoting recovery environments. Iles and Sutherland (2001) find that the most effective process for stimulating sustained organisational change is to develop plans, monitor and review them, formulate new plans, with further review and revision. This 'plan-do-study-act' cycle was found to be most effective at producing sustained organisational change. Sainsbury Centre for Mental Health (2008) find this requires leadership from the top (Board level) as well as commitment from middle managers and the front-line. Front-line staff need to be empowered and equipped to take forward the principles of hope, control and opportunity – and staff can also share in the benefits. For example, in a forensic ward in West London, a team approach involved co-production of ward house rules, collection of recovery stories and other joint initiatives; this improved the experience of the ward for both service users and staff. Hours spent in seclusion went down, as did staff sickness and physical assaults on staff (Repper and Perkins 2013).

The leadership required is not only hierarchical – it is the leadership of ward managers, trade union representatives, influential service users, professionals who people listen to.

> There are many leaders, not just one. Leadership is distributed. It resides not solely in the individual at the top, but in every person at every level who, in one way or another, acts as a leader. (Goleman et al. 2003).

The shift from 'involvement' to 'co-production' is important: rather than involve people using services in contributing to 'our' plans, the idea is to plan and work together, enabling everyone to have the information, support and explanation of processes needed to contribute equally. SCIE (Social Care Institute for Excellence) has published guidance on the power of co-production – showing the value of planning and designing projects and services from the outset, within an equal relationship (SCIE 2013).

A further key is employment of people with lived experience – so people are engaged in a common pursuit quite simply by working together. This could be achieved by investing in organisations led and staffed by people with lived experience. There is a very strong case for this, given evidence for the importance of user-led organisations to act as a springboard: developing social approaches to recovery and cultures of madness that revalue experience; supporting each other to take power and participate. It could also mean employing a critical mass of people with lived experience in mental health services.

In mainstream services, peer support in conjunction with an organisation-wide emphasis on recovery-focused practice may provide an effective combination of contact and education to facilitate attitude and behavioural change of staff.

The introduction of peer workers is one powerful way of driving forward a recovery-focused approach within a team (Repper and Perkins 2013). 'Peer support workers' (PSWs) are trained and employed to draw on their personal experience of emotional distress to support others going through similar experience. This involves developing mutually empowering relationships, sharing their experiences in a way that inspires hope and offering support as an equal. For mental health staff, the presence of a critical mass of PSWs challenges the 'us and them' beliefs held by many staff members in a natural rather than forced way (Slade 2009). Just as peer workers provide hope and inspiration for others experiencing mental health problems, they challenge negative attitudes of staff and provide an inspiration for all members of the team. In drug and alcohol services the influence of people with lived experience has proved to dramatically improve staff attitudes (Rao et al. 2009). Peer workers also facilitate a better understanding between the people providing the service and those using it (Repper and Watson 2012). For the mental health system, peer-support specialists can be 'carriers of culture'. There is thought to be less need to train and maintain a pro-recovery orientation in 'consumers', because of their own lived experience (Slade 2009).

Research from the United States suggests peer support workers 'embody' hope which inspires both service users and service providers to believe in the possibility of recovery (Mowbray et al. 1998). In their meta-synthesis of studies of peer support, Walker and Bryant (2013) conclude that staff develop increased empathy and understanding toward people in recovery as a result of working with peer support workers.

As well as working in mental health services, people with lived experience can be influential in staff selection. There is a strong case for services recruiting on the basis of attitude, as many retailers do: specific skills can be taught; lack of respect may be impossible to overcome.

Recovery colleges are growing in the UK and beyond and embody a completely changed purpose for mental health services, replacing a therapeutic model with an educational one: peers and professionals co-lead courses on a wide range of topics, from getting a good night's sleep to spirituality and mental health or anger management (and more). This models the different types of expertise everyone brings and enables participants to grow and develop sources of power (of knowledge and solidarity).

Learning sets and training for staff can be useful when part of systemic change, and when initiatives are led or co-led by people with lived experience, developed and evaluated in processes of co-production. Lindsay Oades has been part of a research team that has trained over 600 mental health clinicians in 12 organisations across four states of Australia in recovery-based practice (Slade et al. 2008). Crowe et al. (2006) have reported significant improvements in staff attitudes through this training. Specifically, attitude domains included increased beliefs that recovery is possible for people with serious mental health challenges and can occur even if symptoms are present. Overall, the study found that after completing the training, people demonstrated higher levels of hopefulness and belief regarding the ability of people with serious mental health problems to define and achieve their goals. For these impacts to endure, the participants must be able to use them in contexts that support a refreshed purpose for mental health services – one focused on leading a life (not losing a symptom), and people having power over their own lives and support.

One manifestation of this kind of systemic power is individuals becoming planners and purchasers of their own care and support, in a move that radically changes the power balance. Through personal budgets, individuals can in principle decide exactly how to use the resources available for their support (whether or not they choose to manage the cash, through a direct payment – there is no obligation). For this to work effectively requires strong information and peer support – so people can learn from what others have done, feel supported not alone, and imagine 'what's possible'. Then people can use personal budgets to do the things they want to do: have support to go fishing with their mates, pool budgets with others to put on their own recovery group, use the budget to have a break by the sea to fend off a crisis and avoid admission. This is very different from choosing between a narrow menu made up of existing services. When personal health budgets were introduced, a common complaint was that they would not work for people with more complex needs or 'vulnerable' people like those using mental health services. In fact, an evaluation of personal health budgets has found them to be effective, with particular benefits for people with more complex needs including those with mental health challenges (Forder et al. 2012). It is easy to patronise and under-estimate people and thereby deny them opportunities. However, implementation of personal budgets requires vigilance about support, information, peer support – and options that go beyond the service provider telling you what 'day services' you can access, as sadly still occurs.

To change mental health services so they embody participation rights requires change within individual organisations – like mental health trusts, or large voluntary organisations – and in commissioning, so the whole configuration of services changes.

This requires widespread availability of support for participation, including evidence-based support to get education, employment, leisure, family life, relationships. There is good practice to build on (Sayce 2011; Crowther and Sayce 2013; NDTI 2014) but too often evidence-based inclusion initiatives are 'nice to haves' rather than lying at the core of services. NDTI found that only a third of resource spent on employment support of people with mental health problems was evidence-based, i.e. following the 'individual placement with support' model that 16 randomised control trials have shown to be dramatically more effective than 'traditional' employment support. Yet still people are offered sheltered work, or 'stepping stones' that help them step nowhere, or standard courses like CV writing that engage not at all with the challenges of seeking work with a mental health problem. In the Netherlands, by contrast, 'personal re-integration budgets' are offered by 40% of municipal authorities, to provide disabled people with support that they choose to get and keep a job. This was found to be more cost effective than traditional approaches (Alakeson 2014). In the UK government and services do not appear to trust people enough to hand over power – and get better results.

How might inclusion become central?

There is a vigorous debate as to whether peer support is best offered through user-led organisations or through embedding it in statutory and mainstream private and voluntary organisations. The answer is both. There is a strong case for significantly expanding and strengthening user-led organisations, turning them from a relatively informal and fragile 'add-on' to being the heart of the service; and for transforming a range of statutory, private and voluntary services (see above).

It is essential that co-production extends not just to planning and delivery in individual provider organisations – but to commissioning. If two thirds of employment support commissioned for people with mental health problems is likely to be ineffective (see above) we need radically altered commissioning that supports social and economic participation.

SENDPO (2014) produced guidance for commissioners and disabled people's organisations in how to work together to improve services for disabled people. Pye and Sayce 2014 argue that as Health and Well-being Boards, in England, define local 'needs' which underpin commissioning strategies, it is imperative to co-produce needs analysis and commissioning. Disability Rights UK worked with user-led organisations to develop user-driven commissioning, including pooled budgets and more systemic co-production with commissioners, under the 'win-win alliance' of user-led organisations (see www .disabilityrightsuk.org).

One challenge is that often user-led organisations hold less quantitative data on 'need' and 'effectiveness' than do professionals influencing commissioning (from public health to clinicians). This points to the importance of people with lived experience controlling more of the theory and evidence base. The introduction of mad studies is a promising start. The more the evidence base can be built and shared to demonstrate the most effective types of peer support, user-led services, recovery support, social and economic inclusion and organisational transformation the better.

There is also a case for change in whole professions, which is why the commitment from professional leaders (see above) to taking action is particularly welcome. When professional leaders have spoken strongly against discrimination in services it can be very powerful. For instance, Professor David Haslam, then President of the Royal College of General Practitioners (RCGP), spoke out about the avoidable early deaths of people with mental health difficulties or learning disabilities:

> Too often we have tended to rationalise the dreadful health outcomes of these groups ... I will never, ever forgive the GP who attended when my much loved sister-in-law who happened to have Down's syndrome died suddenly of meningitis. His first words to her grieving mother? 'Well I suppose it's for the best isn't it?' (President RCGP, cited in Sayce 2008).

His words, repeated in talks and articles, had more effect on professionals than any number of speeches and articles by campaigners.

CONCLUSION

Mental health services need not – and should not – look like they do today. There is a need to think long and hard about the following questions:

- Can statutory services fully model power and participation?
- Can peer support/survivor-led alternatives be more than marginal?
- How can commissioners move to a set of services that DO model participation rights?

Commissioning could and should be radically influenced by people with lived experience. This means both commissioners co-producing their analysis of need and commissioning plans with people with lived experience; and individuals becoming micro-commissioners, driving commissioning directly through personal budgets and pooled budgets to meet common goals.

This could shift where the money is spent – with more going on alternative, user-led services and support for inclusion, in areas like social life, support for parents with mental health issues, education.

The professions need not be as they are today: they could focus on rights and recovery, with people with lived experience shaping the theory and knowledge and designing both services and skills acquisition for staff.

Changing services from places that reinforce 'them and us' attitudes to zones of mutual support and sources of power from which to look outwards to social and economic opportunity, cannot be achieved through a knee-jerk decision to put on 'training'. To be sure training can have a place – but only when services and whole commissioning strategies have a renewed purpose, rooted in human rights, based on sharing of power and co-production, aiming for equal social and economic participation.

Evidence tells us that to change attitudes and behaviours there is great value in contact (on equal terms, working to common goals, where stereotypes are mildly disconfirmed), and in education and training where they are integrated into professional and culture change. But single interventions must be part of wider organisational transformation, which erodes the 'them and us' culture, brings benefits to both service users and staff, and is led from the Board and from leaders at service level. The presence of staff – including senior staff – who are open about their own lived experience is an important part of this cultural change; as is a workforce that contains a critical mass of peer workers.

At present there is a fundamental problem with our mental health services. It must be a cause for significant concern that people with mental health challenges name mental health staff as one of the major sources of discrimination in their lives – rather than allies in participation rights. This is why 'parity of esteem', touched on in the next chapter, is a very partial response to the challenge: we do not simply need greater access to existing mental health services, or shorter waiting times. If the services are experienced as compounding discrimination or make people feel there is a deep 'them and us' divide, then more of the same will not help. We need a different balance of power and radically changed services. Henderson and Thornicroft (2013) note that there is an irony in anti-stigma campaigns encouraging people to seek help – yet when they do they encounter stigmatisation. Until this changes, mental health professionals should not lead anti-stigma campaigns. They have a vital role in supporting them as allies.

To achieve service transformation – and also to achieve the ambitions of the previous chapter, to enable individuals to secure rights in practice – requires wider systemic changes, that go beyond what mental health services can do.

The next chapter turns to that macro level of change.

Reflective Exercises

Can you design a co-production exercise, involving people living with mental health challenges and a service provider or commissioner? What would be the most important components of the process?

What might be the best measure of cultural change in mental health services – breaking down the 'them and us' divide?

RESOURCES

National Survivor User Network puts people in touch with groups with lived experience in different regions and enables people to get involved in shaping policy and services: see http://www.nsun.org.uk/groups/

Sainsbury Centre for Mental Health (2008). *Implementing Recovery: A New Framework for Organisational Change*. London: SCMH

- Works through changes in purpose, staffing, culture and processes to support recovery-focused practice

Repper, J. and Perkins, R. (2013). *The Team Recovery Implementation Plan: A Framework for Creating Recovery-focused Services.* London: ImROC

Provides a framework for change at team level

In Control (2014) The Poet Surveys. http://www.in-control.org.uk/media/168340/poet%20health%20 report%20oct%202014.pdf

Surveys the experience of using personal health budgets, showing the benefits and also what is required to make them work effectively: for instance, peer support and brokerage

Repper, J. and Carter, T. (2011). *Using Personal Experience to Help Others with Similar Difficulties: A Review of the Literature on Peer-support in Mental Health Services.* London: University of Nottingham and Together

Summarises evidence on the effectiveness of peer support

9 | Macro Changes Across Society

Chapter Summary

- The leadership of lived experience: social movements and control of knowledge
- Working with allies, beyond identity politics
- Setting priorities
- Measuring progress and holding governments to account
- Framing for a movement
- Levers for change
- Power for those most excluded
- Channelling energies to the right to participate

his book argues that the most promising approach to overturning discrimination is 'partici-
ation rights'. It galvanises action by accentuating the positive, it mobilises the power of
eople and rights and creates opportunities for 'contact on equal terms'. This generates a
irtuous circle: as more people with lived experience participate in communities, workplaces,
chools, so 'contact' does its work in changing attitudes and future behaviours, making
articipation that bit easier for the next people who show up. This final chapter looks at the
nacro changes needed to make this happen.

The leadership of lived experience: social movements, controlling knowledge and power

When I asked seven experts for their top priorities for anti-discrimination work (see Chapter 7),
hey overwhelmingly mentioned leadership by people living with mental health challenges.
everal saw the survivor movement as the critical achievement of the last 25 years:

The most important achievement?

The survivor movement. And in particular, building and sharing survivor experience and
knowledge, the beginning of links with the wider disability movement, the development
of survivor research and survivor involvement in training professionals – which has revolutionary potential and sometimes impact. (Peter Beresford)

People have become more knowledgeable about mental health issues ... More important perhaps has been what I might call the beginnings of a social movement aimed at
changing stigmatizing attitudes and behaviours. The inclusion of people who identify as
having had a mental illness in this movement is particularly critical. It still has a lot to
achieve but in my opinion that is the best hope for sustained change. (Bruce Link)

This has not been straightforward. Survivor organisations have often been fragile, which
as limited their impact compared to other players.

Who has the power in debate?

I think that the psychiatric survivor/peer/ex-patient movement in the US has suffered
from in-fighting and from attacks from well-funded critics like Fuller Torrey. The Murphy
Act[1] is a good example of a mental health bill that was written without any meaningful
involvement of mental health consumers/ peers/ survivors and that constituency had a
difficult time influencing the bill (Andy Imparato)

Nationally, there is a dominance of large mental health charities as spokespeople
and they are in a qualified position – sometimes hesitant to speak out as they have
to seek contracts. In 1990 we would not have expected that by 2015 the main voices
would still be the same charities; and they have become more incorporated. (Peter
Beresford)

> Recently there was a Trans person on Question Time – their movement has progressed very fast. Where is the person living with mental health difficulties on Question Time? We need public figures beyond the individual 'telling their story' (followed by wordy commentary from a charity) – beyond the tragic, beyond the celebrity. (Mark Brown)

Funding of survivor organisations has been hit:

> I think peer-led advocacy groups ... are at risk of folding if their government funding goes away. (Andy Imparato)
> There is a weakening of user advocacy (Mary O'Hagan)

This is due both to general 'austerity' policies and a failure to move resources to survivor led work:

> It is vital to re-align funding for people with mental distress away from clinical crisis funding to funding that supports people to regain their personal power and social and economic opportunities. (Mary O'Hagan)
> The few funders that pay attention to mental illness have not been very good about lifting up first person perspectives or cultivating leaders with lived experience. (Andy Imparato)
> The big charities have stepped back from supporting local campaigns. Some anti-stigma campaigns, like in New Zealand, have got money out to grassroots organisations. In England they have tended more to suck the money in. (Mark Brown)
> The 'parity of esteem' proposition is ridiculous. It calls for shorter waiting times, better access to existing mental health services – rather than changing them. The more money is spent on those the less there is to develop our own services. The Chief Medical Officer Report 2014 requires investment where there is a strong evidence base: but we don't have the resources to produce that evidence base. It leaves micro-enterprises and grass-roots organisations marginal. (Mark Brown)

Parity of esteem is designed to beat discrimination, ensuring equal standards for menta and physical services, and some experts I spoke to supported it strongly: 'It's time fo the government to actually act on parity of esteem and not just talk about it' (Graha Thornicroft). But without a thrust to spend resources quite differently, others thought i could mean entrenchment of the power imbalance between survivor-led and mainstrea services.

The relative lack of public power of people with lived experience may make it harder t embed effective concepts into anti-discrimination work.

> For me the main disappointment is the lack of critical engagement around the construction of 'mental illness' and the consolidation and legitimisation of so called stigma-busting organisations such as Sane Australia and Beyond Blue. Their mantra – that

'mental illness is just like any other illness' or 'is just like diabetes' – is an insidious ideology that has taken root. As Thachuk (2011) argues 'Likening mental illnesses to physical illnesses (1) reinforces notions that persons with mental illnesses are of a fundamentally "different kind," (2) entrenches misperceptions that they are inherently more violent, and (3) promotes overreliance on diagnostic labelling and pharmaceutical treatments' (p. 140). I argue that regardless of the so-called advances in combatting stigma and discrimination that 'the mentally ill' identity is still a spoiled identity (after Goffman) ... [It] creates the conditions for limitations on autonomy and self-determination and citizenship due to diminished capacity and competence – this reductionist argument renders invisible all areas and spaces where decision making and self-determination can occur. (Lyn Mahboub, Australia)

[There has been] an over-emphasis on trying to reduce stigma and discrimination by putting forward the idea that the illnesses are biologically based – just like any other illness. Conveying accurate information about mental illness is important of course but thinking this would eliminate stigma and discrimination was a misstep. (Bruce Link)

We need more work to develop social model approaches. This is what survivors want. The first ever 'mad studies' stream at the Disability Studies Conference in Lancaster in 2014 is a great start. (Peter Beresford)

For the future, the seven experts hoped for strengthened networks and influence of people with lived experience; many called for more powerful discourse, replacing bio-medical assumptions with a focus on the social context that drives discrimination.

The big opportunity I see is for the new generation of young leaders with mental health conditions to assert themselves and take the movement to another level. In the US, Stephanie Orlando (appointed by President Obama to serve on the National Council of Disability) and Anupa Iyer (a lawyer with bipolar disorder who works for Chai Feldblum at the Equal Employment Opportunity Commission) are good examples. This younger cohort seems more entrepreneurial and more interested in cross-disability and cross-movement collaboration and I think they have the potential to 'break through' in a way that their predecessors have not really been able to do. (Andy Imparato)

We should become more self-conscious about developing a social movement to advocate and make things better ... It needs to be a coalition ... People who identify as having had mental illnesses, people who have not but are sympathetic and ready to act, research that conceptualises relevant issues and provides useful evidence. Push hard ... don't expect immediate results ... but keep eyes on the goal to make things better. (Bruce Link)

For social contact – the most active ingredient to reduce stigma – this means service users taking the lead with support from other sectors. (Graham Thornicroft)

We need to work together, not survivors on our own. Alliance is feasible and does happen, with cross-perspectives and overlapping identities. (Peter Beresford)

> The big challenge will be to work to unsettle the taken for granted assumptions about mental distress within the public domain and minimise the othering of difference. Vehicles such as Recovery Colleges can work ... to create the space for forming 'positive' identities such as student rather than patient. However, it will remain to be seen if such edifices can extricate themselves from the biomedical / bio-determinist ideology. (Lyn Mahboub)

Mark Brown noted that for the newer generation to mobilise requires bridging a radical break between two generations of activists – a break not based on chronological age, but timing of first involvement. For those who do not remember the fight against community treatment orders in the early 2000s, let alone earlier campaigns, the tradition of fighting for rights, rooted in 1970s struggles for black, gay and women's liberation, can seem alien; as can the practice of joining committees and inspection teams. Involvement has instead become structured through anti-stigma campaigns, in particular 'telling your story'.

> This is partly an artefact of the major mental health organisations that have decided stigma is the big issue, not policy, law, local campaigns or test cases. This leaves a hole in what people are campaigning for. The assumption is that as attitudes change, other changes will be easier to bring in – but this is untested. It's unclear what people can get involved in after they have told their story. Who is pitching to the hungry, growing world of people with mental health problems who want to do something? They often don't know the history, don't have a narrative on stigma and discrimination. We need the earlier generation to share experience and learning – to be communicators not only academics. (Mark Brown)

Brown argues that the newer generation coalesce around questions, ideas, issues – rather than an identity as 'service users' or 'survivors'. Broader conversations and alliances therefore matter. And they are not necessarily aligned with progressive or left-wing politics. Social media generates a growing debate that no longer belongs to established organisations. It is not an 'asset' to be used by those that control discourse. It can be influential, as when Spartacus (a group of disabled people) produced reports on welfare reform that gained media and political attention: self-selected groups can move fast, say things organisations cannot and influence discourse. 'Crowd sourcing' ideas may be promising, aggregating up ideas expressed through social media.

This discussion raises important pointers for the next phase of participation rights work:

- Leadership by people with lived experience is critical – but this does not mean leading alone. When activists secured the Americans with Disabilities Act in 1990 they secured support from trade unionists and business leaders, from democrats and republicans. As disability activist and now Baroness Jane Campbell (2008) put it, 'we must not let "nothing about us without us" become "nothing about us". We must reach out!' Andy Imparato noted that pan-disability organisations – like the American Association of People with Disabilities and National Centre for Independent Living – were well placed to lead the next phase of development, bringing mental health and disability activism together

- Investment in organisations led by people with lived experience is imperative. As Gowar (2014) puts it, groups of people facing similar challenges offer nurturing and a springboard for activism, participation and innovation. But formal organisations are not the only route to influence: self-organised networks can 'break through' into public discourse
- Whilst precise views may differ, all the seven experts, in line with evidence, favoured moving away from underpinning anti-discrimination work with the 'illness like any other' message. A discourse based on the demand for participation needs far more force.

A critical mass of leaders with lived experience and allies in all sectors – setting new debates, modelling participation – could offer new impetus.

Leadership support

- Radar (now Disability Rights UK (DR UK)) developed a leadership programme led by and for people living with mental health issues, HIV and other visible and non-visible experiences. Demand was strong: over 500 people took part over four years. Over 80% said the programme made them more likely to pursue their leadership aspirations and the Muslim Council of Britain recognised the programme's effective reach to young disabled Muslims. Sharing was powerful – on how to exercise leadership, how and when to be open, how to draw on lived experience as part of your authentic leadership style. Many went on to become trustees, school governors, youth leaders and more – influencing others through 'contact on at least equal terms'. DR UK went on to establish a Leadership Academy, offering career development programmes.
- The American Association of People with Disabilities offers leadership and mentoring opportunities, including shadowing and internships with politicians.

A social movement or looser set of networks needs power and resources; power can derive from funded organisations, positions in companies and politics or mass engagement; and can be networked rather than centrally controlled.

Priorities

Whilst evidence on combatting stigma and discrimination finds approaches need to be multi-level and multi-faceted (in order to get sustained change) (Thornicroft 2006) any social movement does need focus. A sensible approach is to be focused on the issues, more multi-faceted in the methods.

Many effective movements for change have worked both to outlaw the most egregious discrimination (i.e. bringing people up to a 'floor' of rights) and to push the boundaries of participation. For instance Stonewall, in the 2000s, campaigned successfully to get every discriminatory piece of legislation off the statute book: Section 28 (which stopped schools from 'promoting homosexuality as a pretend family relationship'), the unequal age of consent, unequal rights to adoption, unequal pension rights. They also pushed positively for equality at work and school, equal marriage – again successfully in terms of legislation, with more work in train to turn it to practical reality.

In similar vein, Mary O'Hagan argues that 'discriminatory mental health legislation needs to be repealed because this is the legal cornerstone of discrimination rather like the old sodomy laws'. And she also argues for a campaign focus on full inclusion, regaining personal power and social and economic opportunities:

> Governments need to treat social inclusion activity with the same urgency as they address smoking and car deaths because they will resource it well.
>
> The fact that people can be forced to be 'treated' in this day and age is a violation of human rights that would not be tolerated in any other form of medicine. (Lyn Mahboub).

Positive participation has the potential to replace stereotypes of 'violent madman' or 'scrounger' by 'contributor' – which then raises questions about why capable, contributing people are being forced to take treatment against their will (see Chapter 4). The Time to Change and Scottish See Me campaigns may have shifted opinion a little towards understanding our common humanity, which creates a platform to raise these questions.

To move forward on participation, a number of strong themes emerge:

Independent living – choice and control in everyday life

O'Hagan notes that one of the biggest achievements of the last 25 years was 'the closure of psychiatric hospitals, which made it more possible for people to experience a valued role in their communities and probably diffused the "location" of discrimination'.

A right to independent living includes living where you choose, with whom you choose; having friends and social networks you want; and living free of harassment and hate crime, confident in the criminal justice system.

Justice for LB (Laughing Boy) is a social movement aiming to draw on the death of Connor Sparrowhawk (known as Laughing Boy) to work for change. He was a healthy young man, who loved buses, London, Eddie Stobart and speaking his mind. He had autism and epilepsy. He drowned in the bath in a specialist unit in Oxford. Justice for LB has generated blogs, an animated film, a draft law (to make sure people can live at home) – challenging the damage of institutional life. But it is not an organisation. It is a social movement. Anyone can join in. It has achieved reach into parliament and media. It exemplifies both the commitment to replacing dysfunctional services with independent living and the type of 'social movement' that brings in allies.

The following website extract (https://lbbill.wordpress.com/draft-lb-bill-v-1) gives a flavour of the work:

> A dad called Mark took his local council to court. He wanted his son to be able to live at home. Mark said 'if you want to stop someone living at home, you must go to court. You must prove why the person cannot live at home.'
>
> We think that sounds a good idea.
> We think it will stop people dying like Connor died.
> We want it to be the law.
> We want the law to keep people close to home.
> We want people to get the support they need where they live.

A campaign for independent living might have as its targets:

- A home of our own. An end to people living in institutions (challenging behaviour units, distant residential schools, nursing homes) against their wishes (except in narrowly defined circumstances, for instance where a serious crime has been committed); and an increase in numbers having a secure tenancy or mortgage

- Friends and social networks. Reduced isolation, year on year
- Being and feeling safe from harassment. Year on year reductions in the incidence of hate crime and harassment; fear of crime; and increased confidence in the criminal justice system. This could be promoted through networks of safe spaces to report harassment and crime (akin to rape crisis centres) and alliances with police, prosecutors, and other groups subject to harassment.

Economic and social power, through education and employment

> Disabled people's employment was not disproportionately affected by the downturn ... And now employment is growing as the economy begins to recover. Disabled people and people with long term health conditions should benefit from this recovery. This is why if campaigners genuinely want to tackle poverty and ensure an adequate standard of living ... they will use the occasion of the 20th anniversary of the Disability Discrimination Act to launch a major campaign on the right to work and employment. (Crowther 2014a)

Campaigning against cruel sanctions regimes – applied when people do not comply with (often absurd) work-related requirements (see Chapter 4) – should not stop campaigns for the right (not requirement) to work. The two have become confused and require untangling.

A campaign for rights to education and employment could be led by people with lived experience, mobilising those with similar interests and with power to act: other disabled people, employers, trade unions, colleges, universities, training providers, apprenticeship services and government. Demands might include:

- Effective education: every year a reduction in school exclusions of young people with mental health difficulties; and improvements at all ages in securing the qualifications and work experience/traineeships/apprenticeships that lead to job opportunities
- Fair employment and pay: every year, an improvement in the rate of employment and pay of people living with mental health conditions – in each local area and nationally – compared with the population as a whole.

Demands would be set by people with lived experience working with chosen allies and might include new flexibilities, support to end work-based discrimination, careers rather than just entry-level or insecure jobs, and affordable housing where jobs are more numerous.

Repealing discriminatory mental health legislation

There is a compelling case for repealing mental health legislation and replacing it with improved Mental Capacity legislation, as is developing in Northern Ireland (see Chapter 4); and for government immediately to set requirements on mental health services to reduce year on year the number of people subject to coercion or seclusion, as is done in Norway (see Chapter 8). This should be monitored by equality dimensions including ethnicity, faith and gender, with an expectation that unequal use of compulsion should diminish as overall numbers come down.

The Mental Health Alliance in the 2000s tried and ultimately failed to mobilise a wide range of interests to challenge unfair coercion: community treatment orders were brought in against widespread opposition. This setback led to a retreat from activity in this area. With the 2016–17 examination of the UK by the UN Committee on the Rights of Persons with Disabilities – which takes a strong interest in non-compliant laws like the UK's (see Chapter 4) – and the development of potentially more progressive law in Northern Ireland, the time is right for a further push. Creative thinking about alliances is important: for instance, high-profile advocates for race equality, human rights and social justice. The previous alliance was very strong in having academics and progressive psychiatrists producing unanswerable analyses and legal drafting (Szmukler 2010); an additional aim might be to escalate the issue to a national scandal, drawing in the more libertarian strands of conservative and liberal traditions as well as social democratic commitments to justice, raising the issue politically to a level equivalent to the focus on institutional abuses as at Winterbourne View. In the 2000s, the DRC argued that mental health law was discriminatory per se; when replaced by the EHRC in 2007 that momentum was deflected. Organisations such as the EHRC, Liberty and the Law Commission may be potential allies.

The priorities above – removing egregious discrimination at the same time as pushing the boundaries of social and economic participation – are suggested as a set, but are not prescriptive. They are designed to prompt people to adopt or improve them. Other specific targets could be chosen – reducing premature mortality, improving choice and control in everyday life, ensuring stronger rights to parent, full access to everything from sports to arts. Whichever specific priorities are selected, it is important to be clear on the goals – so different people can aim for them from their different perspectives, positions and resources.

Measuring progress against goals

The first step is to be clear what success would look like.

It is not enough to get attitude change, because behaviour and real participation may fail to follow. If anti-stigma initiatives like Time to Change have opened a door, the next step is to decide on the freedoms and choices we want to lie behind that door. Success needs to be measured in terms of freedoms to enjoy participation.

The UNCRPD provides an overarching framework, against which progress has to be measured by Government, with regular inspections by the UN Committee, with input from the formal monitoring body (the EHRC in England and Wales, Human Rights Commission in Scotland, Equality Commission in Northern Ireland) and opportunities for civil society organisations to produce shadow reports and give evidence.

There is no shortage of stark statistics on the inequality experienced by disabled people (in general) and people with mental health conditions (in particular) (see Chapter 1). The EHRC (2010) published 'How Fair is Britain?' setting out the evidence of inequality in Britain and identifying major priorities for action. Its findings included the following.

- Education. At school, young people with disabilities or special educational needs are most at risk of being bullied (higher even than young gay students or those from BME communities). Those who report being bullied in England did 15% worse at GCSE, and were twice as likely to be not in education, employment or training at aged 16.

- Pay. Disabled men experience a pay gap of 11% compared with non-disabled men, while the gap between disabled women and non-disabled men is 22%.
- Access to justice. People with mental health problems are more likely to report abuse than other disabled people. They are disproportionately likely to spend time in prison. Young people with limiting long-term illness/disabilities are significantly less likely than those without to believe the criminal justice system is fair, or that it meets the needs of victims.
- Power and choice. People with a disability or a long-term limiting illness are less likely than those without to say that they can influence local decisions. Whilst 81% of non-disabled people reported having choice and control over their life, this was true of only 74% of disabled people.

A framework like this can be influenced. It contained many gaps: for instance, where is the evidence of what people with mental health challenges contribute, as parents, carers or entrepreneurs? In 2013 the Office for Disability Issues did cite the statistic that disabled people (generally) are twice as likely as non-disabled people to be 'carers' for relatives or friends. Far from being the passive beneficiaries of care, disabled people are more likely to offer support. Testimony indicates how people who have lost strong relationships with family or friends support each other, helping people get through tough times. Should these contributions not be tracked – as well as barriers?

There are also questions on how EHRC framed its priorities. For instance:

> Under economic participation, EHRC selected as one of 15 priority challenges reducing pay gaps by gender, faith and ethnicity; but on disability the challenge selected was just to close the employment gap. This reinforces the tired view that the employment agenda for disabled people is 'welfare to work', getting a job – any job – rather than a decent career with equal pay. Does it implicitly assume disabled people will not be capable of senior roles?

And under the challenge to 'close the power gap' the aspiration is set out to increase the number of women and BME MPs – but not the number of disabled MPs (also shamefully low).

By 2015, the EHRC had perhaps listened to concerns, and included in its 2015–16 Business Plan work on pay gaps experienced by disabled people, alongside women.

Finally, on many indicators the data is not broken down by different impairments, missing an opportunity to track the experiences of people with mental health challenges.

The Office for Disability Issues set out indicators under its Fulfilling Potential programme in 2013. Areas important to people with lived experience were covered – choice and control, education, employment (including, this time, levels of employment). In one or two cases the indicator might not have been the choice of disabled people, however: under education, there is no indicator on school exclusion – but there is one on 'unauthorised absence from school'; and under health there is no measure on premature mortality or health service discrimination but there is an indicator on 'managing of own health condition'. These indicators are somewhat redolent of the tendency to place responsibility on the individual (to attend school, to be healthy) rather than on powerful organisations.

It would be useful for people living with mental health challenges and allies seeking macro change to:

- Agree one set of statistics that is most important to track on the top priorities
- Influence the measures used by bodies including governments and the EHRC, with the aim of covering effectively the main bases of the UNCRPD.

Of course, the mental health sector can commission its own research and monitoring. But an advantage of bodies like EHRC or the Government doing it is that it provides such powerful context and wider relevance, for instance:

- Almost three quarters (71%) of permanent exclusions in England involved pupils with some form of SEN in 2008/09 and
- People with mental health conditions are more likely than those without to die during or following police custody (EHRC 2010).

These statements extend relevance way beyond people interested in the human rights of people with mental health difficulties – to people interested in broader policy questions of deaths in police custody, or school exclusion. It prompts them to think that to reduce (say) deaths in police custody will require understanding of the mental health dimension: they won't tackle deaths in police custody without addressing mental health.

Making inequality statistics relevant to people with broader policy interests was a core strategy of the Disability Rights Commission's Disability Agenda (2007). The Government of the time was committed to halving child poverty by 2020. Disability commentators had long quantified the proportion of families with a disabled child or a disabled adult who were living in poverty. The DRC changed the story and said 'a third of children living in poverty has a disabled parent'. The minute we changed the statistical base – from the number of disabled families to the number of children in poverty – we held the interests of policy-makers. Secretary of State John Hutton announced shortly afterwards 'Child poverty is a disability issue'.

By making 'our' issues widely relevant the door is opened to new allies. A campaign on the right to employment could include unemployed groups, trade unions, different equality 'strands', business leaders intent on filling skills gaps, colleges and universities driven by employability outcome payments.

Framing for a movement

The seven experts thought we had made some progress in reframing mental health issues but more work was needed:

> I believe we have helped to reframe mental health/ mental disability issues as in part issues of human and civil rights and not just issues of diagnosis and treatment. (Andy Imparato, USA).

In 2013 Crowther drew on the work of George Lakoff to argue for narratives that appeal to and ignite responses based on deeply held 'frames' in the public mind. These frames might include:

- Fear, a concern for safety
- Hope, a desire for equality, compassion.

Equally Ours, a coalition of rights-based organisations, set about testing human rights messages that were carefully framed with reference to this thinking. They came up with tested messages that used universalist language, including:

> This is about making human rights real for everyone, every day.

Without saying so – as this might ignite fears – this universalism moved the focus away from the more uncommon human rights abuses (of people in prison or accused of terrorism) to issues that everyone can relate to.

It is important to consider unintended consequences. High-profile communications about hate crime – complete with gruesome tales of torture and degradation – can make people with mental health conditions frightened to go out and can make everyone else see them as victims. More effective messages include that we can stop hate crimes and there are safe places to report any problems.

A participation rights movement or network needs to think carefully about framing. Campaigning for independent living could readily mobilise support from people driven by hope and equality; but those concerned with control might prefer 'difficult' people to be away from local communities. Messages could be tested, such as 'treating people fairly keeps us all safer' or 'we are working to reduce discord and conflict'.

The more that people with lived experience set and lead a new discourse the more powerful it is likely to be. In Britain, 20 years ago the only people 'out' in public debate were a tiny number of 'professional users' and a few comedians, like Spike Milligan, prompting the comment that comedians were expected to be crazy – but what about bank managers? (Sayce 2000)

But gradually people in the public eye who might not be expected to be as eccentric started to be open – famously Alastair Campbell, Tony Blair's Communications Director, but also regular actors:

> 'It's really important to talk about it because the more you bury it deep inside you the more you start to believe it's just you – and it isn't just you' (Rebecca Front, actor. Comment at http://www.time-to-change.org.uk/news-media/celebrity-supporters).

> Graham Thornicroft notes that the UK is unusual in having so many people in the public eye prepared to speak out.

The task ahead is to forge and promote new narratives about rights to participate, framed to have resonance, breaking through into public discourse in new ways. It is important to avoid co-option or dilution by organisations calling for more resources for services, more access to treatment, more 'hype' to encourage donations, or less stigma simply to increase help-seeking (see Chapter 3). The trick is to build new connections, new alliances, new routes into cultures through social media, mass media and arts.

It is also useful – as Bruce Link put it – to 'monitor the use of mental illness words – "crazy", "insane" etc for one week and you will see how often they are used and what they are used to explain eg terrorism'.

Complaints about media and advertising have a long history amongst mental health advocates, but despite winning some battles – for instance, ASDA apologised for its 'psycho' Halloween costume in 2013 – the war is ongoing.

A more powerful act might be to create a 'break' from normative assumptions: for instance, pressing for an apology for institutionalisation (as Paul Gibson from the New Zealand Human Rights Commission has done) or for 'psychiatry and governments ... to publicly acknowledge the harm the professions and the state have done to people with mental distress now and in the past – to role model the unacceptability of discrimination' (Mary O'Hagan). These 'big' statements would use rhetorical power to mark a moment of break from the past.

The task is to create new associations between 'madness' and participation. Whilst there is a place for protesting against the damaging discourse that equates 'madness' with evil, in the end pointing to it may inadvertently reinforce the connection. Lakoff notes that when Nixon said 'I am not a crook' people started to look at him as a crook. Crowther notes that saying 'there is very little benefit fraud' makes people think of benefit fraud.

The more powerful approach to changing discourse is to inject new associations – not just challenge the old ones. It is no easy task and will rely on all the entrepreneurial, new energy that Andy Imparato, Mark Brown, Peter Beresford and others identified as a hope for future change.

Levers for change

Making material changes like reducing the number of people living in institutions against their will cannot rely just on changing the discourse, important as it is.

For each of the goals selected for change, the important questions are whose behaviour needs to change and what would incentivise them to do so. Take employment. Intermediate targets, to close the employment and pay gaps, could include:

- *Changes in employer behaviour*: changing the world of work so that some people with fluctuating difficulties can work when well (monitoring outcomes, not times of work); creating workplaces that support well-being for all, modelling openness about human challenges, with good management feedback and support; implementing a wide range of individual flexibilities and adjustments; changing entry requirements to apprenticeships and jobs where these indirectly discriminate (for instance, where it has been hard for someone acquiring a mental health problem in adolescence to achieve the requisite set of high-grade GCSEs there can be other ways to demonstrate potential)
- *Changes in support available to individuals and employers*: replacing failing mandatory testing and work programmes with investment in support that works: personalised, streamlined support throughout education and employment; support that the individual chooses, using a personal budget (this has been found in the Netherlands to be more cost effective than traditional employment support); support for employers as well as individuals (Crowther and Sayce 2013).

A blend of carrots and sticks could be deployed to help make these changes happen:

- Positive incentives and policy levers. 'Go with the flow' of policy initiatives: for instance, at the time of writing LEPs (Local Enterprise Partnerships), co-owned by local authorities with businesses, universities and others, were responsible for economic development. Some DPOs and service providers worked with them to secure employment opportunities as jobs came on stream.

Essex Coalition of Disabled People (ecdp), a DPO, engaged with the South East Local Enterprise Partnership (LEP), with the aim of putting people with lived experience of disability at the centre of local enterprise development. ecdp Works is an award-winning peer-enabled employment training and work placement programme, delivered in partnership with business and the private sector.

Lobby government to incentivise and support employers – for instance, to employ people with fluctuating conditions, some of whom require time off but want to work when well. Access to Work could be made available for temporary cover, so the employer knows they will not bear the financial cost of someone needing disability-related leave.

• Transparency. Require transparency from large employers on how many people they employ with different experiences of disability, including mental health conditions, at different levels in their organisation. Draw on consumer power to praise those that do well, boycott those that refuse to say or have low figures. Lobby government to require transparency – as has been done in relation to the numbers of women on corporate boards. If employment of disabled people is so important to government, expect them to hold employers to account.

When the CEO of Australian department store Myers stated that his customers might not want to pay an extra cent in every dollar for the new disability insurance fund (to pay for personal budgets), Graeme Innes of the Human Rights Commission challenged him to reach a 10% rate of employment of disabled people. His petition was quickly signed by 37,000 people.

• The power of contracting. Lobby large business and government to use the power of contracting to require transparency and good practice. In the lead-up to the 2012 Olympics and Paralympics, all contractors were required to demonstrate inclusive employment practices – they simply would not secure contracts without them. Some large organisations drive change through their supply chains. And there is potential to mobilise consumer power, as has been done with environmentally friendly products and services. Trading for Good is a tool for small businesses to demonstrate their corporate social responsibility – including showing how they employ disabled people, young people and others with low employment chances. The goal is that the public would be able to select their window cleaner or removal firm by seeing whether they have the 'trading for good' stamp.
• Re-directed employment support resources. Lobby local and national government and NHS to divert resources from ineffective vocational services to support for people with mental health issues to achieve economic and social power. Sayce (2011), Crowther and Sayce (2013) and NDTI (2014) have shown that large sums of public money are spent on employment support that is ineffective. See Chapter 6 for how personalised support, peer support, support for employer as well as employee, could significantly enhance access to a wide range of employment opportunities.

- The power of strategic litigation and interventions. Build a test case strategy. Several of the seven experts saw strengthening legislation and legal cases as crucial:

  A significant achievement has been the Equality Act – so that one does not need to disclose mental health issues at application or interview for jobs. (Graham Thornicroft).

  Starting in 1992, thanks to the Americans with Disabilities Act, people with psychiatric disabilities are protected against discrimination in the workplace and are entitled to time off to see a therapist or a flexible schedule ... On litigation, we struggled for years with narrow ADA employment decisions from the US Supreme Court, but we were able to overturn those decisions in 2008. (Andy Imparato).

  We need a test case strategy. (Mark Brown).

  Chapter 6 gives examples of legal cases and interventions taken by people with mental health challenges and the dynamic process of legislative amendment and interpretation of law in the courts and tribunals. This is a vital area of strategic influence and people with lived experience, lawyers, the EHRC and others could between them generate more significant test cases than currently. The EHRC can also undertake strategic interventions – as it did in relation to harassment and hate crime. It might use its systemic, statutory powers to press for increased use of effective levers, like expecting public bodies to use the Public Sector Equality Duty to mobilise the power of commissioning and procurement to achieve equality.

- Individual rights. Make it easier for more people to know and negotiate for their rights, know what 'adjustments' are, take cases and secure changes in organisations – not just compensation. Chapter 7 identified a significant need for rights-based advice and advocacy, following the recommendations of the Low Commission. There is also a need for policy change to ensure the scope for Tribunals to require organisational changes.

This overall approach mobilises different forms of power – consumer power, commissioning power, the power of law, the power of transparent data – and targets those power sources on the people whose behaviour needs to change. Similar thinking needs to be applied to other priority objectives selected.

On reducing coercion in mental health services, transparency could be effective: demanding league tables of all services and their use of coercion and seclusion, making it public locally and nationally, praising and shaming services using different levels of coercion, influencing the inspectorates and consumer champions like Healthwatch to demand changes. On the back of publicity, mounting a challenge to mental health law per se by proposing and 'showing' effective alternatives.

On ensuring no one lives in an institution against their will, test cases and systemic legal interventions could be used:

  Using the Olmstead v LC US Supreme Court Decision, advocates have been able to use the ADA to push for home and community-based alternatives to congregate settings for people living with psychiatric disabilities. (Andy Imparato).

The power of commissioning may also hold promise. SENDPO's report on commissioning suggests ways that user-led organisations could both influence commissioning and position themselves to be part of local service configuration – offering a powerhouse of peer support and navigation. DR UK's work in partnership with Shaping our Lives and others on user-driven commissioning shows the power of different models: from micro-commissioning to pooled budgets and impact on whole commissioning strategies, to align services more closely to the social and economic aspirations of people for whom the services are theoretically designed (http://www.disabilityrightsuk.org/policy-campaigns/health-and-social-care-reforms/strategic-partner-updates-2013/strategic-partners). Influencing commissioners to fund strong survivor networks and organisations, some linked with wider disability groups, would help create a base of power, new thinking and expertise. Crowther recommended in 2014 a campaign to set up access centres in every area, backed by a national organisation to share good practice and technical support (Presentation to DR UK independent living conference July 2014).

Influencing commissioning of public services is not just about more money, or parity with physical health services. It is about new forms of organisation, with completely new purposes, cultures and staffing. O'Hagan emphasises the significance of recovery – because it 'promotes citizenship (in theory) and is a direct challenge to traditional and biological psychiatry'. Lyn Mahboub notes that recovery colleges have the potential to move to an educational model – if they can throw off the bio-medical paradigm. Guarding against professional co-option and distortion of concepts like co-production, recovery and independent living is essential.

It is also about supporting social networks and inclusive communities, rather than meting out ever-shrinking units of professional time. There may be opportunities by 'going with the flow' of future policy. For instance, health and well-being boards set up in every area of England were by 2015 focusing on issues such as reducing isolation. The time might be right to push for 'inclusive communities' that increase social networks and social capital. DR UK cites a number of examples (Pye and Sayce 2014):

- Community Futures Kent working with District Councils, Police Independent Advisory Group, leisure centres, National Trust, Kent Libraries and many more to create welcoming attitudes, Easyread information and greater access to premises via mystery shopping and whole-community planning
- Disability Wales co-developing with the Welsh Government a Framework for Action on Independent Living, committing to action across government to forge an inclusive and enabling society http://tinyurl.com/mcs34c7
- NDTi's Community Inclusion mentor programme which supports disabled and older people to engage in and contribute to their communities, and helps staff and organisations to understand how to build and support real inclusion http://tinyurl.com/kkmc7pw.

There is potential to embed co-production of people with mental health conditions, from different communities, with local authorities to build social participation into whole local plans (see Pye and Sayce (2014) for different structures to make this happen); and to enable more people with lived experience to take up elected leadership positions.

The Local Government Association has a long-standing Be A Councillor campaign which recognises that local government is only as vibrant, effective and relevant as the people elected to run it. The campaign works to increase the talent pool from which councillors are elected and ensure councils better represent their electorate.

In 2015 the LGA worked with the Government Equalities Office on a pilot programme to encourage more disabled people to consider becoming a councillor. Potential candidates were mentored by councillors and political experts http://tinyurl.com/a33czuv

But what can be done in an era of cost containment?

Increasingly there is a group of people with mental health challenges who are becoming ever more excluded, likely to live in poverty, without work, often in debt, with insecure housing, in unsafe neighbourhoods, with impacts on relationships, sometimes then incarcerated (see Chapter 7). Social movements and networks of (for instance) people living on benefits, or people from particular ethnic or faith or geographical communities, must have a voice. The Time to Change 300 voices project is one example. The major challenge is for work on social participation to be, itself, fully inclusive.

It could be argued that no progress is possible when neo-liberal governments pursue policies of austerity, leaving resources for everything from social care to Access to Work short and many user-led organisations decimated.

One response to this is to argue that policies that have moved the mental health and wider disability movements forward have secured gains even in tough times, for instance:

- In 2013 mental health organisations succeeded in lobbying for the Mental Health (Discrimination) Act, which stripped away outdated laws barring people with mental health conditions from being company directors, MPs or serving on juries. Times of cost constraint can be good times to get symbolically important legal changes – where they incur low costs but enable politicians to 'do something' for a particular constituency
- Under a conservative government in the 1990s, pursuing a smaller state, gains included the introduction of direct payments in 1996. Advocates were smart about 'going with the flow' of consumerism to get independent living measures by reframing them in terms of consumerist rhetoric without diluting their own ambitions
- Conversely, in 2007 a Labour Government committed to greater equality, brought in increased coercion in the form of community treatment orders.

This suggests that in any era it *may* be possible to make gains by framing demands to fit with prevailing priorities. It is also possible to shift resources from more to less restrictive approaches: witness the shift from psychiatric institutions to 'community care' that grew particularly strongly through the 1980s and 1990s.

A major priority is to build the case, and mobilise power bases and levers to move resources from ineffective approaches that breach human rights to support for people to take social and economic power. It is vital to press the public, private and voluntary sectors to use resources – whatever their level – far more effectively than at present.

CONCLUSION

People with lived experience have been voicing the horrors of the 'milksop society' and unfair coercion for well over 150 years. There have been some great achievements since then. The closure of (most of the) large institutions. Law that progressively outlawed discrimination in employment, education, transport and services – and required systemic change through positive public sector duties. The presence of more and more diverse voices in the public space talking openly about lived experience. The development of peer support and effective support for full participation, from education to standing for elected office.

Anti-stigma campaigns like Time to Change, See Me and Like Minds Like Mine have opened a door by starting a shift in attitudes and in experiences of discrimination. Next there is a need to go for the material changes beyond the door – to seize social and economic power. In the same period that attitudes have improved there has been 'no improvement in life outcomes such as employment, income, relationships and physical health – outcomes that matter to all humans', as Mary O'Hagan put it so starkly.

Some elements of anti-stigma work have failed to meet requirements of evidence: using damaging messages like 'it's an illness like any other'; achieving only short-term 'contact on equal terms'; diluting impact through sectional interests intent on increasing use of treatments and therapies rather than participation; or not mobilising power to secure change.

This is why we need a new overarching paradigm – participation rights – under which people can rally, however they view their madness or distress, across their 'super-diversity' of experience and identification. This book has argued that the participation rights approach best addresses all the drivers of stigma and discrimination that Link and Phelan outline. It engages with our common humanity, breaks out of identity politics, disrupts separation, builds on strengths and capabilities – and draws on different forms of power to generate social change. It extends power to include leadership, formal and networked groupings, co-production with decision-makers, targeted incentives, systemic use of legal rights. And it puts participation at the heart of mainstream policy and practice, setting a positive agenda rather than merely targeting negative discrimination. Participation also creates the conditions for ongoing, repeated contact on equal terms, which is known to significantly change attitudes and behaviour; and does so through ordinary life, rather than relying on specific 'interventions'. We also need priorities for action.

Whilst many governments have ratified the UNCRPD, arguably the Convention is so broad that governments can pick and choose actions to demonstrate progress. This is why it is so important for a social movement to set out the most significant demands and measure progress against them – as well as requiring accountability against the framework as a whole.

This books suggests a dual push on removing the most egregious and symbolic discrimination, by ending discriminatory mental health law; and pushing hard and progressively on participation rights, particularly in independent living, education and employment. This must be inclusive of people living in poverty and link to wider anti-poverty strategies.

To move forward there are many levers that can be pulled – from test cases to the power of contracting and consumerism. This requires clever targeting, effective framing; and mobilising generations of people with lived experience who did not live through the identity politics era of the 1980s and 1990s, who are networked and communicate in changing ways.

In the end it is the combined power of people with lived experience and the alliances they can muster that will impact on serious change. Combined power is not necessarily collective, not always organised through committees and systems of representation. In 2014 John Evans described how in the 1970s disabled people 'escaped' from Cheshire homes by sending xeroxed newsletters around to each other and dreaming of alternatives. Thus began the independent living movement that ultimately – after demonstrating what works, and lobbying decision-makers – transformed national social care policy.

Movements that are not 'organised' can be smart and communicate widely so they become self-reinforcing. They can set challenges to business and government – but also work with lawyers, journalists, allies in business and health services, who can spread ideas and practice; they can build power bases and make use of the tools of power. Movements can emerge – not one but several, loosely linked, from Justice for LB to employment campaigning groups. Creating one unified 'movement' is hard – as feminists and disability activists have found (Hopkins et al. 2007). Sharing ideas and goals is more feasible. The participation rights model could act as a strategic basis for diverse activism, drawing on best thinking about how to overthrow discrimination.

This is not simple, especially in times of great inequality, when people with lived experience are diverse and do not agree, when organisations and networks are ill-resourced. A priority for campaigning is a stronger set of user-led organisations as springboards, through which people can gain mutual support, generate culture and debate strategy. There may be opportunities in the UK's cross-party consensus that mental health is a policy priority – as long as the agenda is turned to participation rights.

Above all, it is the large numbers of people living with mental health challenges and allies, with diverse talents, positions and sources of influence, who can be catalysts for change. Debating the ideas to underpin social action is critical, to channel the available sources of power and to seize the participation rights that are the fundamental right of every human on the planet.

Reflective Exercises

What do you think would be the best levers to achieve significant reductions in coercion – compulsory detention, compulsory treatment, seclusion – and who could lead this work?

What do you think would be the best levers to use to secure better employment and pay for people living with mental health difficulties?

NOTE

1   The Helping Families in Mental Health Crisis Act, which amongst other provisions incentivises states to have out-patient commitment, i.e. compulsory community treatment

RESOURCES

Mandela, N. (1994). *Long Walk to Freedom*. London: Abacus.

- Contains invaluable learning about long- and short-term campaign strategy and determinants of social change

Campbell, J. (2008). *Fighting for a Slice or for a Bigger Cake?* Cambridge: Cambridge University Annual Disability Lecture.

- Links equality for disabled people to wider policy agendas, broader struggles and alliances

DRC (2007). *The Disability Agenda.* London: DRC.

- Proposes that central policy objectives – from enhancing skills to reducing child poverty – can only succeed if disability is put at the heart of the policy development

Pye, M. and Sayce, L. (2014) *Inclusive Communities: Guidance for DPOs.* London: Disability Rights UK.

- Proposes that DPOs put the social, economic and political rights of disabled people at the heart of local priority developments – for instance, engaging with health and well-being agendas (on social citizenship) and local enterprise partnerships (LEPs) (on economic citizenship).

Lakoff, G. (2004). *Don't Think of An Elephant: Know Your Values and Frame the Debate.* White River Junction, VT: Chelsea Green Publishing.

- A classic text on how to think about framing debates

References

Ackroyd, P. (1999). *Blake*. London: Vintage

Ackroyd, P. (2001). *London: The Biography*. London: Vintage

Alakeson, V. (2014). *Delivering Personal Health Budgets*. London: Policy Press

Amering, M. Mikus, M. and Steffen, S. (2012). Recovery in Austria: Mental Health Trialogue. *International Review of Psychiatry*. 24, pp. 11–18

Andrews, J., Briggs, A., Porter, R, Tucker, P. and Waddington, K. (1997). *The History of Bedlam*. Oxford: Routledge

Arboleda- Flórez, J. and Stuart, H. (2012). From Sin to Science: Fighting the Stigmatization of Mental Illnesses. *Canadian Journal of Psychiatry*. 57, pp. 457–463

Arnstein, S.R. (1969). A Ladder of Citizen Participation. *Journal of the American Institute of Planners*. 35, 4, pp. 216–224

Banks, J. Blundell, R. and Emmerson, C. (2015). Disability Benefit Receipt and Reform: Reconciling Trends in the United Kingdom. *Journal of Economic Perspectives*. 29, 2, pp. 173–190

Beeforth, M. Conlan, E. Field, V. Hoser, B. and Sayce, L. (1990). *Whose Service Is It Anyway? Users' Views on the Co-ordination of Care*. London: RDP

Beltran, R.O. Scanlan, J.N. Hancock, N. and Luckett, T. (2007). The Effect of First Year Mental Health Fieldwork on Attitudes of Occupational Therapy Students Towards People with Mental Illness. *Australian Occupational Therapy Journal*. 54, pp. 42–48

Beresford, P. Nettle, M. and Perring, R. (2010). *Towards a Social Model of Madness and Distress? Exploring What Service Users Say*. York: JRF

Bickenbach, J.E. (1999). Minority Rights or Universal Participation: The Politics of Disablement. In Jones, M. and Marks, L.A. (eds). *Disability, Divers-Ability and Legal Change*. Netherlands: Martinus Nijhoff, pp. 101–115

Bizub, A.L. and Davidson, L. (2011). Stigma-busting, Compeer, and the Psychology Student: a Pilot Study on the Impact of Contact with a Person Who has Mental Illness. *The Humanist Psychologist*. 39, pp. 312–323

Blakeley, T.A. Collings, S.C.D. and Atkinson, J. (2003). Unemployment and Suicide. Evidence for a Causal Association? *Journal of Epidemiology and Community Health*. 57, pp. 594–600

Bond, G.R. Drake, R.E. and Becker, D.R. (2008). An Update on Randomized Controlled Trials of Evidence-Based Supported Employment. *Psychiatric Rehabilitation*. 31, 4, pp. 280–290

Bowis, J. (1995). *Speech to Mind and Stonewall Conference on Lesbian and Gay Mental Health*. London

Bracken, P. and Thomas, P. (2005). *Post-Psychiatry: Mental Health in a Post-Modern World*. Oxford: OUP

Branfield, F. (2009). *Developing User Involvement in Social Work Education*. London: SCIE

Brindle, D. (2013). Mental Health Anti-stigma Campaign Fails to Shift Health Professionals' Attitudes. *Guardian*. 3 April

British Social Attitudes 30 (2013). London: Nat Cen Social Research

British Social Attitudes 32 (2015). London: Nat Cen Social Research

Buckmaster, L. and Thomas, M. (2009). *Social Inclusion and Social Citizenship –Towards a Truly Inclusive Society.* Research Paper no. 8, 2009–10. Canberra: Parliament of Australia

Bynoe, I. Oliver, M. and Barnes, C. (1991). *Equal Rights for Disabled People: The Case for a New Law.* London: Institute for Public Policy Research

Burns, T. (2013). *Our Necessary Shadow: The Nature and Meaning of Psychiatry.* London: Penguin Books

Burns, T. Catty, J. Becker, T. Drake, R.E. Fioritte, A. Knapp, M. Lauber, C. Rossler, W. Tomov, T. Van Bussbach, J. White, S. and Wiersma, D. (2007). Effectiveness of Supported Employment for People with Severe Mental Illness: A Randomised Control Trial. *The Lancet.* 370, 9593, pp. 1146–1152

Burns, T. Rugkasa, J. Molodynski, A. Dawson, J. Yeeles, K. Vazquez-Montez, M. Voysey, M. Sinclair, J. and Priebe, S. (2013). Community Treatment Orders for Patients with Psychosis (OCTET): A Randomised Controlled Trial. *The Lancet.* 381, 9878, pp. 1627–1633

Bywater, L. (2012). The Flexible Leader: An Adaptable Approach to Managing Your Team. At https://www.wjmassoc.com/insight/the-flexible-leader/

Caldwell, T.M. and Jorm, A.F. (2000). Mental Health Nurses' Beliefs about Interventions for Schizophrenia and Depression: A Comparison with Psychiatrists and the Public. *Australian and New Zealand Journal of Psychiatry.* 34, pp. 602–611

Caldwell, T.M. and Jorm, A.F. (2001). Mental Health Nurses' Beliefs about Likely Outcomes for People with Schizophrenia or Depression: A Comparison with the Public and Other Healthcare Professionals. *Australian and New Zealand Journal of Mental Health Nursing.* 10, pp. 42–54

Cameron, D. (2013). *Speech to Disability Confidence Conference.* London

Campbell, P. (2000). The Role of Users of Psychiatric Services in Service Development – Influence Not Power. *Psychiatric Bulletin.* 25, pp. 87–88

Campbell, P. (2006). *Movement in the 1980s.* 2 November. http://studymore.org.uk/mhhglo.htm#selfadvocacy

Campbell, J. (2008). *Fighting for a Slice or for a Bigger Cake?* Cambridge: Cambridge University Annual Disability Lecture

Care Quality Commission. (2011). *Count Me In 2010.* London: Care Quality Commission

Care Quality Commission (2013). *Monitoring the Mental Health Act 2011–12.* London: Care Quality Commission

Care Quality Commission (2015). *Monitoring the Mental Health Act 2013–14.* London: Care Quality Commission

Centre for Studies in Inclusive Education (2014). *Contrasting Responses to Diversity: School Placement Trends 2007–2013 for all Local Authorities in England.* London: CSIE

Chadwick, P. (2002). Understanding One Man's Schizophrenic Experience. *Nursing Times.* 98, 38, p. 32

Chakrabarti, S. (2014). *The State of Freedom in Britain.* Lecture. London: LSE. 14 June

Chamberlin, J. (1988). *On Our Own.* London: Mind

Chamberlin, J. (1993). *Psychiatric Disabilities and the ADA. An Advocate's Perspective.* Boston: National Empowerment Center

Chesler, P. (1972). *WOMEN AND MADNESS.* New York: Doubleday

Clark, T. with Heath, A. (2014). *Hard Times: The Divisive Toll of the Economic Slump.* New York and London: Yale University Press

Clement, S. Van Nieuwenhuizen, A. Kassam, A. Flach, C. Lazarus, A. de Castro, M. and Thornicroft, G. (2012). Filmed v. Live Social Contact Interventions to Reduce Stigma: Randomised Controlled Trial. *British Journal of Psychiatry.* 201, pp. 57–64

Cole-King, A. (2013). *Stigma Kills.* At https://bma.org.uk/news-views-analysis/live-and-learn/2013/september/the-day-i-found-out-that-stigma-can-kill. Downloaded August 2014

Cole-King, A. (2013a). *You Can Cope.* At http://www.collegeofmedicine.org.uk/u-can-cope-suicide-prevention-campaign. Downloaded August 2014

Cole-King, A. (2013b). *Feeling on the Edge.* At http://www.connectingwithpeople.org/sites/default/files/Feeling%20on%20the%20edge.pdf. Downloaded August 2014

Cook, G. (2014). *Promoting Contribution.* London: ippr

Corker, E. Hamilton, S. Henderson, C. Weeks, C. Pinfold, V. Rose, D. Williams, P. Flach, C. Gill, V. Lewis-Holmes, E. and Thornicroft, G. (2013). Experiences of Discrimination Among People Using Mental Health Services in England 2008–11. *The British Journal of Psychiatry.* 202, 55, pp. 58–63

Corrigan, P. (2005). *On the Stigma of Mental Illness.* Washington, DC: American Psychological Association.

Corrigan, P.W. Larson, J.E. and Rusch, N. (2009). Self-Stigma and the "Why Try" Effect: Impact on Life Goals and Evidence-Based Practices. *World Psychiatry.* 8, 2, pp. 75–81

Coward, R. (1989). *The Whole Truth. The Myth of Alternative Health.* London: Faber and Faber

Crawford, M. (2000). Homicide is Impossible to Predict. *Psychiatric Bulletin.* 24, p. 152

Crowe, T.P. Deane, F.P. Oades, L.G. Caputi, P. and Morland, K.G. (2006). Training Recovery Oriented Mental Health Teams. *Psychiatric Services.* 57, pp. 1497–1500

Crown Prosecution Service (2010). *Policy for Prosecuting Cases of Disability Hate Crime.* London: CPS

Crowther, N. (2013). A Tough but Fair Deal for Disabled People? Blog at https://makingrightsmakesense.wordpress.com/author/crowtherconsulting/page/2/

Crowther, N. (2014). Refreshing the Disability Rights Agenda – a Future Imagined. www.makingrightsmakesense.wordpress.com

Crowther, N. (2014a). Why Campaigning for the Right to Work and Employment Should be a Priority. www.makingrightsmakesense.wordpress.com

Crowther, N. and Sayce, L. (2013). *Taking Charge of Employment Support.* London: Disability Rights UK

Cumming, E. and Cumming, J. (1957). *Closed Ranks. An Experiment in Mental Health.* Cambridge, MA: Harvard University Press

Daone, L. and Scott, R. (2003). *Ready Willing and Disabled: Investigating Attitudes and Other Obstacles to Employing Disabled People.* London: Scope

Davidson, G. (2011). *Deciding Who Decides: the Assessment of Mental Capacity in Canada.* Belfast: Queen's University

Dearing, K.S. and Steadman, S. (2008). Challenging Stereotyping and Bias: A Voice Simulation Study. *Journal of Nursing Education.* 47. pp. 59–65

Deegan, P.E. (1994). Recovery: The Lived Experience of Rehabilitation. In Spaniol, L. and Koehler, M. (eds). *The Experience of Recovery.* Boston: Center for Psychiatric Rehabilitation, pp. 54–59

Demos (2013). *Disability in Austerity.* London: Demos with Scope

Dept. of Health (2013). *No Health Without Mental Health. Mental Health Dashboard.* London: Dept. of Health

Dept. of Health (2014). *Data revolution to transform mental health.* Press release. London: Dept. of Health

Disability Rights Commission (2002). *DRC Response to the Draft Mental Health Bill, England and Wales.* London: DRC

Disability Rights Commission (2002a). *Annual Review 2001–2.* London: DRC

Disability Rights Commission (2003). *Coming Together: Mental Health Service Users and Disability Rights.* London: DRC

Disability Rights Commission (2006). *Equal Treatment: Closing the Gap. A Formal Investigation into Physical Health Inequalities Experienced by People with Learning Disabilities and/or Mental Health Problems.* London: DRC

Disability Rights Commission (2007). *The Disability Agenda.* London: DRC

Disability Rights Commission (2007a). *Maintaining Standards Promoting Equality.* London: DRC

Disability Rights UK (2015). *Disability Rights Handbook.* London: DR UK

Disability Rights UK (2015). *Taking Charge: A Practical Guide to Living with a Disability or Health Condition.* London: DR UK

Downie, R.S. Fyfe, C. and Tanahill, A. (1990). *Health Promotion: Models and Values.* Oxford: OUP

DRTF (1999). *From Exclusion to Inclusion: A Report of the Disability Rights Task Force on Civil Rights for Disabled People.* London: Department for Education and Employment

DWP (2001). *Recruiting Benefit Claimants: Qualitative Research with Employers in ONE Pilot Areas.* Research Series Paper no 150, prepared by Bunt, K. Shury, J. and Vivian, D. London: DWP

DWP (2003). *Disabled for Life? Attitudes Towards, and Experiences of, Disability in Britain.* London: DWP

DWP (2014). *Family Resources Survey and Households Below Average Income Data, 2012/13.* London: DWP

DWP (2014). *Employment and Support Allowance: Outcomes of Work Capability Assessments, Great Britain*, quarterly official statistics bulletin March 2014. https://www.gov.uk/government/uploads/system/uploads/attachment_data/file/297936/esa-wca-outcomes-mar-14.pdf

English Heritage (2014). The Age of the Madhouse. http://www.english-heritage.org.uk/discover/people-and-places/disability-history/1660-1832/the-age-of-the-madhouse. Downloaded 23 November 2014

Equality and Human Rights Commission (2010). *How Fair is Britain? Triennial Review 2010.* London: EHRC

Equality and Human Rights Commission (2013). *Hidden in Plain Sight: Inquiry into Disability-related Harassment.* London: EHRC

Evans-Lacko, S. Malcolm, E. West, K. Rose, D. London, J. Rusch, N. Little, K. Henderson, C. and Thornicroft, G. (2013). Influence of Time to Change's Social Marketing Interventions on Stigma in England 2009–2011. *The British Journal of Psychiatry.* 202, 55, pp. 77–88

Evans-Lacko, S. Corker, E. Williams, P. Henderson, C. and Thornicroft, G. (2014). Effect of the Time to Change Anti-Stigma Campaign on Trends in Mental-Illness-Related Public Stigma Among the English Population in 2003–13: An Analysis of Survey Data. *The Lancet.* 1, pp. 121–128

Evans, S. (2007). *Disability, Skills and Work: Raising our Ambitions.* London: Social Market Foundation

Fanshawe, S. and Sriskandarajah, D. (2010). *You Can't Put Me In A Box: Super-Diversity and the End of Identity Politics in Britain.* London: ippr

Faulkner, A. and Kalathil, J. (2012). *The Freedom to Be, the Chance to Dream: Preserving User-Led Support in Mental Health.* London: Together

Fearn, A. and Wyllie, A. (2005). *Public Knowledge of and Attitudes to Mental Health and Mental Illness.* New Zealand: Ministry of Health

Fevre, R. Robinson, A. Jones, T. and Lewis, D. (2008). *Workplace Bullying and Harassment in Britain.* London: EHRC

Fletcher, A. and O'Brien, N. (2008). Disability Rights Commission: From Civil Rights to Social Rights. *Journal of Law and Society.* 35, 4, pp. 520–550

Forder, J. Jones, K. Glendinning, C. Caiels, J. Welch, E. Baxter, K, Davidson, J. Windle, K, Irvine, A. King, D. and Dolan, P. (2012). *Evaluation of the Personal Health Budget Pilot Programme.* London: Dept of Health

Foucault, M. (1967). *Madness and Civilisation: A History of Insanity in the Age of Unreason.* London: Tavistock Publications

Fredman, S. and Spencer, S. (2006). *Delivering Equality: Towards an Outcome Focused Equality Duty.* Oxford: Oxford University

Friedrich, B. Evans-Lacko, J. London, D. Rhydderch, C. Henderson, C. and Thornicroft, G. (2013). Anti-Stigma Training for Medical Students: the Education Not Discrimination Project. *The British Journal of Psychiatry.* 202, 55, pp. 89–94

Fuller Torrey, E. (2008). *The Insanity Defence: How America's Failure to Treat the Mentally Ill Endangers Its Citizens.* New York: W.W. Norton

Gable, K.N. Muhlstadt, K.L. and Celio, M.A. (2011). A Mental Health Elective to Improve Pharmacy Students' Perspectives on Mental Illness. *American Journal of Pharmaceutical Education.* 75, pp. 1–6

Gilman, C.P. (1892). The Yellow Wallpaper. *The New England Magazine.* January

Goffmann, E. (1963). *Stigma: Notes on the Management of Spoiled Identity.* New York: Simon and Schuster

Goldacre, B. (2012). *Bad Science.* London: Fourth Estate

Golding, P. and Middleton, S. (1982). *Images of Welfare: Press and Public Attitudes to Poverty.* Oxford: Martin Robertson

Goleman, D. McKee, A. and Boyatzis, R.E. (2003). *The New Leaders.* New York: Sphere Books

Gowar, C. (2014). *Inclusive Communities: A Research Report.* London: Disability Rights UK

Grausgruber, A. Meise, U. Katschnig, K. Schony, W. and Fleischhacker, W.W. (2006). Patterns of Social Distance Towards People Suffering from Schizophrenia in Austria: A Comparison Between the General Public, Relatives and Mental Health Staff. *Acta Psychiatrica Scandinavica.* 115. pp. 310–319

Grayling, A.C. (2014). What is Poverty? In Prospect and JRF. *Poverty in the UK: Can it be Eradicated?* pp. 6–7

Hamer, H. (2014). Insiders or Outsiders? Mental Health Service Users' Journeys Towards Full Citizenship. *International Journal of Mental Health Nursing.* 23, pp. 203–211

Hamilton, S. Corker, E. Weeks, C. Williams, P. Henderson, C. Pinfold, V. Rose, D. and Thornicroft, G. (2015, in submission). Factors Associated with Experienced Discrimination Among People Using Mental Health Services in England

Hansson, L. Jormfeldt, H. Svedberg, P. and Svensson, B. (2011). Mental Health Professionals' Attitudes Towards People with Mental Illness: Do They Differ from Attitudes Held by People with Mental Illness? *International Journal of Social Psychiatry.* 49. pp. 48–54

Hardest Hit (2012). *The Tipping Point.* London: Hardest Hit Press

Health Committee (2013). *Post-Legislative Scrutiny of the Mental Health Act 2007.* London: House of Commons

Health and Social Care Information Centre (2014). *Inpatients Formally Detained in Hospitals Under the Mental Health Act 1983 and Patients Subject to Supervised Community Treatment, England – 2013-2014.* London: HSCIC

Henderson, C. Corker, E. Hamilton, S. Williams, P. Pinfold, V. Rose, D. Webber, M. Evans-Lacko, S. and Thornicroft, G. (2014). Viewpoint Survey of Mental Health Service Users' Experiences of Discrimination in England 2008–2012. *Social Psychiatry and Psychiatry Epidemiology.* 49, pp. 1599–1608

Henderson, C. and Thornicroft, G. (2013). Evaluation of the Time to Change Programme in England 2008–11. *The British Journal of Psychiatry.* 202, pp. 45–48

Henderson, C. Williams, P. Little, K. and Thornicroft, G. (2013). Mental Health Problems in the Workplace: Changes in Employers' Knowledge, Attitudes and Practices in England 2006-2010. *The British Journal of Psychiatry.* 202, 55, pp. 70–76

Hewstone, M. (2003). Intergroup Contact: Panacea for Prejudice? *The Psychologist.* 16, 7, pp. 352–355

Hewstone, M. (2012). *Impact of Diversity on Inter-Group Relations.* Speech to University of Helsinki 11 May 2012

Hewiston, M. (2013). Interview with John Kirwan. *New Zealand Herald.* 16 March

Hogarth, T. Owen, D. Gambin, L. Hasluck, C. Lyonette, C. and Casey, B. (2009). *The Equality Impacts of the Current Recession. Equality and Human Rights Commission Research report 47.* London: EHRC

Holt-Lunstad, J. Smith, T.B. and Layton, J.B. (2010). Social Relationships and Mortality Risk: A Meta-Analytic Review. *PLOS Medicine.* 7, 7, pp. 1–19

Hopkins, D. McKie, L. Watson, L. and Hughes, B. (2007). The Problem of Emotion in Care: Contested Meanings from the Disabled People's Movement and the Feminist Movement. In Flam, H. and King, D. (eds). *Emotions and Social Movements.* Abingdon: Routledge, pp. 257–276

Hornstein, G.A. (2012). *Agnes's Jacket. A Psychologist's Search for the Meanings of Madness.* Herefordshire: PCCS Books

Iles, V. and Sutherland, K. (2001). *Organisational Change: A Review for Health Care Managers, Professionals and Researchers.* London: National Co-ordinating Centre for NHS Service Delivery and Organisation

Independent on Sunday (1993). *Breaking Out of the Asylums.* 19 December

Institute of Medicine (2006). *Improving the Quality of Health Care for Mental and Substance-Use Conditions.* Washington, DC: Institute of Medicine

Ipsos Mori (2013). *Generational Attitudes and Values.* London: Ipsos Mori

Jamison, K.R. (1995). *An Unquiet Mind. A Memoir of Moods and Madness.* New York: Alfred A. Knopf

Joint Committee on Human Rights (2010). *Implementation of the Right of Disabled People to Independent Living.* London: the Stationery Office

Julius Wilson, W. (1997). *When Work Disappears.* New York: Random House

Just Fair (2014). *Dignity and Opportunity for All: Securing the Rights of Disabled People in the Austerity Era.* London: Just Fair

Kalathil, J. (2007). *Themes from the Literature on Recovery from Mental Distress: A Short Summary.* London: Survivor Research

Kalathil, J. (2011). *Recovery and Resilience: African, African-Caribbean and South Asian's Women's Narratives of Recovering from Mental Distress.* London: Mental Health Foundation and Survivor Research

Kassam, A. Glozier, N. Leese, M. Loughran, J. and Thornicroft, G. (2011). A Controlled Trial of Mental Illness Related Stigma Training for Medical Students. *BMC Medical Education.* 11, p. 51

Kirwan, J. (2010). *All Blacks Don't Cry.* New Zealand: Penguin

Lacey, N. (2014). *The State of Freedom in Britain.* Lecture. London: LSE. 14 June

Langan, J. and Lindow, V. (2004). *Mental Health Service Users and their Involvement in Risk Assessment and Management.* York: JRF

Lapsley, H. Nikora, L.W. and Black, R.M. (2002). *Kia Mauri Tau! Narratives of Recovery from Disabling Mental Health Problems.* Wellington: Mental Health Commission

Lawn, S. Battersby, M. Polsm, R. Lawrence, J. Parry, T. and Urukalo, M. (2007). The Mental Health Expert Patient: Findings from a Pilot Study of a Generic Chronic Condition Self-Management Programme for People With Mental Illness. *International Journal of Psychiatry.* 53, pp. 63–74

Layard, R. Clark, D. Knapp, M. and Mayraz, G. (2007). *Cost-Benefit Analysis of Psychological Therapy.* CEP Discussion Paper no. 829. London: London School of Economics and Political Science

Leff, J. Trieman, N. and Gooch, C. (1996). Teams Assessment of Psychiatric Services Project 33: Prospective Follow-up Study of Long-stay Patients Discharged from Two Psychiatric Hospitals. *American Journal of Psychiatry.* 153, 10, pp. 1318–1324

Le Francois, B.A. Menzies, R. and Reaume, G. (eds) (2013). *Mad Matters: A Critical Reader in Canadian Mad Studies.* Toronto: Canadian Scholars' Press Inc.

LLDC (2011). *Inclusive Design Strategy.* London: London Legacy Development Corporation

Linden, M. and Kavanagh, R. (2012). Attitudes of Qualified vs. Student Mental Health Nurses Towards an Individual Diagnosed With Schizophrenia. *Journal of Advanced Nursing.* 68. pp. 1359–1368

Link, B. (2011). *Stigma: Concepts and Public Perceptions.* Paper to Stigma and Mental Illness Conference, Northeastern Ohio Universities Colleges of Medicine and Pharmacy

Link, B. Castille, D.M. and Stuber, J. (2008). Stigma and Coercion in the Context of Outpatient Treatment for People with Mental Illnesses. *Social Science & Medicine.* 67, pp. 409–419

Link, B.G. and Phelan, J.C. (2001). On the Nature and Consequences of Stigma. *Annual Review of Sociology.* 27, pp. 363–385

Local Government Association and Innovations in Dementia (2012). *Developing Dementia Friendly Communities: Learning and Guidance for Local Authorities.* London: LGA

Lockwood, G. Henderson, C. and Thornicroft, G. (2014). Mental Health Disability Discrimination: Law, Policy and Practice. *International Journal of Discrimination and the Law.* Published online 19 May 2014. DOI: 10.1177/1358229114534541

London Borough of Newham (2004). *Inclusive Education Strategy 2001–4.* London: LB Newham

Lyons, C. Hopley, P. and Horrocks, J. (2009). A Decade of Stigma and Discrimination in Mental Health: Plus CA Change, Plus C'est la Meme Chose (the More Things Change, the More they Stay the Same). *Journal of Psychiatric & Mental Health Nursing.* 16, pp. 501–507

Macintyre, A. (1999). *Dependent Rational Animals. Why Human Beings Need the Virtues.* London: Duckworth

Magliano, L. Read, J. Rega, S. Oliviero, N. Sagliocchi, A. Patalano, M. and D'Ambrosio, A. (2011). The Influence of Causal Explanations and Diagnostic Labelling on Medical Students' Views of Schizophrenia. *Academic Medicine.* 86, pp. 1155–1162

Malcolm v London Borough of Lewisham (2008). *UK House of Lords session 2007-8. UKHL 43*

Mancini, M.A. Hardiman, E.R. and Lawson, H.A. (2005). Making Sense of it all: Consumer Providers' Theories about Factors Facilitating and Impeding Recovery from Psychiatric Disabilities. *Psychiatric Rehabilitation Journal.* 29, pp. 48–55

Mandela, N. (1994). *The Long Walk to Freedom.* London: Abacus

Marwaha, S. and Johnson, S. (2004). Schizophrenia and Employment – a Review. *Social Psychiatry and Psychiatry Epidemiology.* 39, 5, pp. 337–349

Mason, M. (2011). *Sorry I Don't Have the Time: Poems About Modern Life.* London: Micheline Mason

Massie, B. (2006). *Employers Ill-Equipped To Take On Staff With Mental Health Problems.* Press Release 16 October. London: DRC

Massie, B. (2014). *Breaking the Link Between Poverty and Disability.* London: Labour Party

McGarty, C. Yzerbyt, V.Y. and Spears, R. (2002). Social, Cultural and Cognitive Factors in Stereotype Formation. In *Stereotypes as Explanations: The Formation of Meaningful Beliefs about Social Groups.* Cambridge: Cambridge University Press, pp. 1–15

McNamara, J. (1996). Out of Order. Madness is a Feminist and a Disability Issue, In Morris, J. (ed.). *Encounters with Strangers.* London: Women's Press

Mdac (2013). *Legal Capacity in Europe.* Budapest: Mental Disability Advocacy Center

Mental Health Foundation (2010). *The Lonely Society.* London: Mental Health Foundation

Metropolitan Asylums Board (1903). *Tooting Bec Asylum Under the Metropolitan Asylums Board.* Descriptive Notes written for the occasion of the inspection by the Board on the 13th June 1903

Mind (2007). *Policing in the 21st Century: Reconnecting Police and the People. Response from Mind.* London: Mind

Mind (2014). *Huge Rise in Sanctions for People with Disabilities.* 12 November

Ministry of Health (2005). *Public Knowledge of Mental Health and Mental Illness. Update of 1997 Benchmark Survey.* Wellington: Ministry of Health

Ministry of Health and Health Promotion Agency (2014). *Like Minds Like Mine National Plan 2014–19.* Wellington: Ministry of Health

Molyneux, J. and Irvine, J. (2004). Service User and Carer Involvement in Social Work Training: A Long and Winding Road? *Social Work Education.* 23, 3, pp. 293–308

Morris, J. (ed.) (1996). *Encounters with Strangers: Feminism and Disability.* London: Women's Press

Mowbray, C. Moxley, D. and Collins, M. (1998). Consumers as Mental Health Providers: First Person Accounts of Benefits and Limitations. *Journal of Behavioural Health Services and Research.* 25, pp. 397–411

Munson-Barkshire, A. (1981). The Production and Reproduction of Scandals in Chronic Sector Hospitals. Downloaded 23 November 2014 from http://www.sochealth.co.uk/resources/national-health-service/democracy-involvement-and-accountability-in-health/complaints-regulation-and-enquries/the-production-and-reproduction-of-scandals-in-chronic-sector-hospitals-1981/official-inquiry-reports-into-national-health-service-mental-hospitals/

Nash, K. (2014). *Secrets and Big News: Enabling People to Be Themselves at Work.* London: Kate Nash Associates

National Alliance for the Mentally Ill (1993). *History of NAMI.* Video. Arlington Virginia: NAMI

NDTI (2014). *The Cost Effectiveness of Employment Support for People with Disabilities.* Bath: NDTI

Nguyen, E. Chen, T.F. and O'Reilly, C.L. (2012). Evaluating the Impact of Direct and Indirect Contact on the Mental Health Stigma of Pharmacy Students. *Social Psychiatry and Psychiatric Epidemiology.* 47, pp. 1087–1098

Nizette, D. McAllister, M. Marks, P. and Elder, R. (2012). *Stories in Mental Health: Reflection, Inquiry, Action.* Melbourne: Elsevier

NSUN (2014). *Mental Healthwatch Handbook: Improving Mental Health with Your Community.* http://tinyurl.com/l3jy7n8

Offe, C. (2014). *Shaping Tastes: Attitude Campaigns and Persuasion as Tools of Public Policy.* Lecture to the London School of Economics, 5 June

Office for Disability Issues (2013). *Fulfilling Potential: Building a Deeper Understanding of Disability in the UK Today.* London: ODI

O'Hagan, M. (2010). *Two Accounts of Mental Distress.* www.maryohagan.com

O'Hagan, M. (2014). *Madness Made Me: A Memoir.* Wellington: Open Box

O'Hara, M. (2014). *Austerity Bites: A Journey to the Sharp End of Cuts in the UK.* London: Policy Press

Onken, S. (2012). *Honouring the Voyage, Reaching the Destination: Mental Health Recovery in Wellbeing.* Presentation to ASPAC Conference, Western Australia

ONS (2013). *Personal Well-Being Across the UK 2012–13.* London: ONS

O'Reilly, C.L. Bell, J.S. and Chen, T.F. (2010). Consumer-led Mental Health Education for Pharmacy Students. *American Journal of Pharmaceutical Education.* 74, pp. 1–8

Pazamanick, B., Scarpitti, F.R. and Dinitz, S. (1967). *Schizophrenics in the Community.* New York: Meredith

Perkins, R. (2001). The You'll Nevers. *Openmind.* 107, January–February

Perkins, R. (2009). *Realising Ambitions. An Independent Review to Government.* London: DWP

Perkins, R. (2012). UK Mental Health Policy Development: A Counter-argument Deriving from Users' Experiences. In Phillips, P. Sandford, T. and Johnston, C. (eds). *Working in Mental Health: Practice and Policy in a Changing Environment.* London: Routledge, pp. 14–24

Perkins, R. (2012a). *Surviving and Thriving: A Health, Work and Well-being Tool.* London: Disability Rights UK

Perkins, R. (2014). *Recovery, Peer Support and Personal Development.* Speech to Kensington and Chelsea Mind Conference *The Road to Recovery.* London

Perkins, R. and Rinaldi, M. (2002). Unemployment rates among patients with long-term mental health problems. *Psychiatric Bulletin.* 26, pp. 295–298

Perkins, R. and Slade, M. (2012). Recovery in England: Transforming Statutory Services? *International Review of Psychiatry.* 24, 1, pp. 29–39

Pescosolido, B.A. Martin, J.K. Long, J.S. Medina, T.R. Phelan, J.C. and Link, B.G. (2010). 'A Disease Like Any Other'? A Decade of Change in Public Reactions to Schizophrenia, Depression, and Alcohol Dependence. *American Journal of Psychiatry.* 157, pp. 1321–1330

Pettigrew, (1998). Inter-Group Contact Theory. *Psychology.* 49, pp. 65–85

Phelan, J. (2005). Geneticisation of Deviant Behaviour and Consequences for Stigma: The Case of Mental Illness. *Journal of Health and Social Behaviour.* 46, pp. 307–322

Pinfold, V. Thornicroft, G. Huxley, P. and Farmer, P. (2005). Active Ingredients in Anti-stigma Programmes in Mental Health. *International Review of Psychiatry.* 17, pp. 123–131

Porter, R. (ed.) (1991). *The Faber Book of Madness.* London: Faber

Powell, A. (1930). *The MAB and Its Work 1867–1930.* London: Metropolitan Asylums Board

Powell, E. (1961). *Speech to Annual Conference of the National Association of Mental Health.* 9 March 1961

Pye, M. and Sayce, L. (2014). *Inclusive Communities: A Guide for Local Authorities.* London: Disability Rights UK

Quarmby, K. (2011). *Scapegoat: Why We are Failing Disabled People.* London: Portobello

Radar (2009). *Lights Camera Action. Promoting Disability Equality in the Public Sector.* London: Radar

Radar (2010). *Doing Careers Differently.* London: Radar

Radar (2011). *Making Rights Real Now.* London: Radar

Rao, H. Mahadevappa, H. Pillay, P. Sessay, M. Abraham, A. and Luty, J. (2009). A Study of Stigmatized Attitudes Towards People with Mental Health Problems Among Health Professionals. *Journal of Psychiatric and Mental Health Nursing.* 16, pp. 279–284

Read, J. Haslam, N. Sayce, L. and Davies, E. (2006). Prejudice and Schizophrenia: A Review of the 'mental illness is an illness like any other' Approach. *Acta Scand.* 114, pp. 303–318

Reed, H. and Portes, J. (2014). *Cumulative Impact Assessment: A Research Report.* Landman Economics and the National Institute of Economic and Social Research (NIESR) for the Equality and Human Rights Commission. London: EHRC

Rehman, H. and Owen, D. (2014). *Mental Health Survey of Ethnic Minorities.* London: Ethnos Research and Consultancy

Repper, J. and Breeze, J. (2007). User and Carer Involvement in the Training and Education of Health Professionals: A Review of the Literature. *International Journal of Nursing Studies.* 44, 3, pp. 511–519

Repper, J. and Carter, T. (2011). *Using Personal Experience to Help others with Similar Difficulties: A Review of the Literature on Peer Support in Mental Health Services.* London: University of Nottingham and Together

Repper, J. and Perkins, R. (2003). *Social Inclusion and Recovery: A Model for Mental Health Practice.* London: Bailliere Tindall

Repper, J. and Perkins, R. (2013). *The Team Recovery Implementation Plan: A Framework for Creating Recovery-focused Services.* London: ImROC

Repper, J. and Watson, E. (2012). A Year of Peer Support in Nottingham: Lessons Learned. *Journal of Mental Health Training, Education and Practice.* 7, pp. 70–78

Richmond Mind (2013). *Caring with a Difference: A Study of the Diverse Needs and Aspirations of Families, Friends and Carers of People with Mental Distress in Richmond.* London: Richmond Mind

Rinaldi, M. Miller, L. and Perkins, R. (2010). Implementing the Individual Placement and Support (IPS) Approach for People with Mental Health Conditions in England. *International Review of Psychiatry.* 22, 2, pp. 163–172

Rinaldi, M. Montibeller, T. and Perkins, R. (2011). Increasing the Employment Rate for People with Long-Term Mental Health Problems. *The Psychiatrist.* 35, 9, pp. 339–343

Rinaldi, M. Perkins, R. Hardisty, J. Glyn, E. and Souza, T. (2006). Not Just Stacking Shelves. *A Life in the Day.* 10, 1, pp. 8–14

Roberts, A. (2008). A Crusade for Dignity. *The Guardian.* 3 September

Rogers, A. and Pilgrim, D. (2000). *A Sociology of Mental Health and Illness.* Oxford: Oxford University Press

Rose, D. (2014). The Mainstreaming of Recovery. *Journal of Mental Health.* 23, 5, e pp. 217–218

Rose, N. (1998). Governing Risky Individuals: the Role of Psychiatry in New Regimes of Control. *Psychiatry, Psychology and Law.* 5, 2, pp. 177–195

Rose, N. (2013). *Mental Illness: Five Hard Questions.* Lecture to University of Nottingham. 15 May

Roth, D. Antony, M.M. Kerr, K.L. and Downie, F. (2000). Attitudes Toward Mental Illness in Medical Students: Does Personal and Professional Experience with Mental Illness Make a Difference? *Medical Education.* 34, pp. 234–236

Royal College of Psychiatrists (2008). *Rethinking Risk to Others in Mental Health Services.* London: RCP

Royal College of Psychiatrists (2011). *The Equality Act and Adult Mental Health Services: Achieving Non-discriminatory Age-appropriate Services.* Occasional paper OP82. London: RCP

Rubenstein, M. (2014). *Sharp Fall in Employment Tribunal Claims.* 18 June blog

Rush, B. (2008). Mental Health Service User Involvement in Nurse Education: A Catalyst for Transformative Learning. *Journal of Mental Health.* 17, pp. 531–542

Sachs, A. (2007). cited in Disability Rights Commission (2007). Legal Achievements 2000–2007. *Legal Bulletin.* 12. London: DRC

Sadow, D. and Ryder, M. (2008). Reducing Stigmatizing Attitudes Held by Future Health Professionals: The Person is the Message. *Psychological Services.* 5, pp. 362–372

Sadow, D. Ryder, M. and Webster, D. (2002). Is Education of Health Professionals Encouraging Stigma Towards the Mentally Ill? *Journal of Mental Health.* 11, pp. 657–665

Sainsbury Centre for Mental Health (2002). *Breaking the Circle of Fear. A Review of the Relationship Between Mental Health Services and African and Caribbean Communities.* London: Sainsbury Centre for Mental Health

Sainsbury Centre for Mental Health (2008). *Implementing Recovery: A New Framework for Organisational Change.* London: SCMH

Sartorius, N. (2000). Breaking the Vicious Cycle. *Mental Health and Learning Disabilities Care.* 4, 3, pp. 80–82

Sartorius, N. (2014). *Postulates of Anti-stigma Work Re-examined.* Lecture to the University of Western Australia, Perth

Sayce, L. (1998). Stigma, Discrimination and Social Exclusion: What's in a Word? *Journal of Mental Health.* 7, 4, pp. 331–343.

Sayce, L. (2000). *From Psychiatric Patient to Citizen: Overcoming Discrimination and Social Exclusion*. Basingstoke: Macmillan

Sayce, L. (2003). Beyond Good Intentions: Making Anti-Discrimination Strategies Work. *Disability and Society*. 18, 5, pp. 625–642

Sayce, L. (2008). Equality and Rights: Overcoming Social Exclusion and Discrimination. In Stickley, T. and Bassett, T. (eds). *Learning about Mental Health Practice*. London: Wiley, pp. 271–290

Sayce, L. (2009). Rights, Risk and Anti-discrimination Work. In Adams, R. Dominelli, L. and Payne, M. (eds) *Practising Social Work in a Complex World*. Basingstoke: Palgrave Macmillan pp. 99–113

Sayce, L. (2010). *Doing Seniority Differently: A Study of High Fliers Living with Ill-health, Injury or Disability*. London: Radar

Sayce, L. (2011). *Getting In, Staying In and Getting On: Disability Employment Support Fit for the Future. An Independent Review*. London: DWP

Sayce, L. and Boardman, A.P. (2008). Disability Rights: Recent Developments of the Disability Discrimination Act. *Advances in Psychiatric Treatment*. 14, pp. 265–275

Sayce, L. and Owen, J. (2006). Bridging the Gap: Results of the DRC's Formal Investigation into Health Inequalities. *Mental Health Practice*. 10, 2, pp. 16–18

Schmueker, K. (2014). *A UK Without Poverty*. York: JRF

SCIE (2013). *Co-production in Social Care: What it is and How to do it*. London: Social Care Institute for Excellence

Scull, A. (1993). *The Most Solitary of Afflictions: Madness and Society in Britain, 1700–1900*. New York: Yale University Press

Self, W. (2013). Psychiatrists: The Drug Pushers. *The Guardian*. 3 August

SENDPO (2014). *Confident Commissioning: Building Relationships Between Local Authorities and Disabled People's User Led Organisations*. South East Network of Disabled People's Organisations

Series, L. (2013). Legal Capacity and the UN Convention on the Rights of Persons with Disabilities. *Mind Legal Newsletter*. 12, pp. 6–7

Shakespeare, T. (2014). *Disability Rights and Wrongs Revisited*. London: Routledge

Showalter, E. (1987). *The Female Malady*. Harmondsworth: Penguin

Simmons, S. (1995). *The History of Tooting Bec Hospital*. Unpublished paper held at London Metropolitan Archives

Sin, Chi Hoong, Hedges, A. Cook, C. Mguni, N. and Comber, N. (2009). *Disabled People's Experiences of Targeted Violence and Hostility*. London: OPM

Slade, M. (2009). *Personal Recovery and Mental Illness. A Guide for Mental Health Professionals*. Cambridge: Cambridge University Press

Slade, M. Amering, M. and Oades, L. (2008). Recovery: An International Perspective. *Epidemiologia e Psichiatria Sociale*. 17, pp. 128–137

Social Exclusion Unit (2004). *Mental Health and Social Exclusion*. London: ODPM

Spagnolo, A.B. Murphy, A.A. and Librera, L.A. (2008). Reducing Stigma by Meeting and Learning from People with Mental Illness. *Psychiatric Rehabilitation Journal*. 31, pp. 186–193

Speaker's Conference (2010). *Speaker's Conference on Parliamentary Representation*. London: House of Commons

Sriram, T.G. and Jabbarpour, Y.M. (2005). Are Mental Health Professionals Immune to Stigmatizing Beliefs? *Psychiatric Services*. 56, pp. 610

Staniland, L. (2011). *Public Perceptions of Disabled People. Evidence from the British Social Attitudes Survey 2009*. London: Office for Disability Issues

Stickley, T. Rush, B. Shaw, R. Smith, A. Collier, R. Cook, J. and Roberts, S. (2009). Participation in Nurse Education: The PINE Project. *Journal of Mental Health Training, Education and Practice*. 4, pp. 11–18

Stickley, T. Stacey, G. Pollock, K. Smith, A. Betinis, J. and Fairbank, S. (2010). The Practice Assessment of Student Nurses by People Who Use Mental Health Services. *Nurse Education Today.* 30, pp. 20–25

Strathclyde Centre for Disability Research and Glasgow Media Unit (2011). *Bad News for Disabled People: How the Newspapers are Reporting Disability.* Glasgow: Glasgow Media Unit

SW Thames Regional Health Authority (1974). *Inquiry into the Circumstances Leading to the Death of Mr. D. Carey at Tooting Bec Hospital.* London: SW Thames Regional Health Authority

Szmukler, G. (2010). *How Mental Health Law Discriminates Unfairly Against People with Mental Illness.* Lecture. London: Barnards' Inn Hall. 15 November

Tait, L. and Lester, H. (2005). Encouraging User Involvement in Mental Health Services. *Advances in Psychiatric Treatment.* 5, pp. 168–175

Takala, T. (2009). Gender, Disability and Personal Identity: Moral and Political Problems in Community Thinking. In Kristiansen, K, Vehmas, S. and Shakespeare, T. (eds). *Arguing About Disability: Philosophical Perspectives.* London: Routledge, pp. 124–134

Taylor, P. and Gunn, J. (1999). Homicides by People with Mental Illness: Myth and Reality. *The British Journal of Psychiatry.* 174, pp. 9–14

Tee, S. Lathlean, J. Herbert, L. Coldham, T. East, B. and Johnson, T. (2007). User Participation in Mental Health Nurse Decision-making. *Journal of Advanced Nursing.* 60, pp. 135–145

Thachuk, A.K. (2011). Stigma and the Politics of Biomedical Models of Mental Illness. *International Journal of Feminist Approaches to Bio-Ethics.* 4, 1, pp. 140–163

Thomas, C. (2004). Developing the Social Relational in the Social Model of Disability: A Theoretical Agenda. In Barnes, C. and Mercer, G. (eds). *Implementing the Social Model of Disability.* Leeds: The Disability Press

Thornicroft, G. (2006). *Shunned: Discrimination Against People with Mental Illness.* Oxford: OUP

Thornicroft, A. Goulden, R. Shefer, G. Rhydderch, D. Rose, D. Williams, P. Thornicroft, G. and Henderson, C. (2013). Newspaper Coverage of Mental Illness in England 2008–2011. *The British Journal of Psychiatry.* 202, 55, pp. 64–69

TNS BMRB (2015). *Attitudes To Mental Illness 2014 Research Report.* London: Time to Change

Trussell Trust (2014). *Food Bank Statistics.* http://www.trusselltrust.org/stats

Tuke, S. (1813). *Description of the Retreat.* York: The Retreat

UKCES (2013). *Scaling the Young Employment Challenge.* London: UKCES

UKCES (2014). *Growth Through People.* London: UKCES

UN High Commissioner on Human Rights (2014). *Statement on Article 14 of the Convention on the Rights of Persons with Disabilities.* Geneva: UNCHR

Vaidee, M. (2012). The UK 'Expert Patient Program' and Self-care in Chronic Disease Management: An Analysis. *European Geriatric Medicine.* 3, pp. 201–205

Van den Ven, L. Post, M. de Witte, L. and van den Heuvel, W. (2005). It Takes Two to Tango: The Integration of People with Disabilities Into Society. *Disability and Society.* 20, 3, pp. 311–329

Van Oorschot, W. (2006). Making the Difference in Social Europe: Deservingness Perceptions Among Citizens of European Welfare States. *Journal of European Social Policy.* February, 16, pp. 23–42

Wahl, O. (1995). *Media Madness. Public Images of Mental Illness.* New Jersey: Rutgers University Press

Wahl, O.F. (1999). Mental Health Consumers' Experience of Stigma. *Schizophrenia Bulletin.* 25, pp. 467–478

Walker, A. (2014). *In Conversation at Sydney Opera House.* May 2014

Walker, G. and Bryant, W. (2013). Peer Support in Adult Mental Health Services: A Metasynthesis of Qualitative Findings. *Psychiatric Rehabilitation Journal.* 36, pp. 28–34

Warner, R. (2009). Recovery from Schizophrenia and the Recovery Model. *Current Opinion in Psychiatry.* 22, pp. 374–380

Watson, E. Hudson, M. and Sayce, L. (2014). *A Literature Review of The Attitudes and Behaviours Held by Mental Health Staff Toward Those They Serve and Interventions Which May Alter These.* London: Time to Change

Wax, R. (2012). *What's So Funny About Mental Illness?* Blog June 2012. Downloaded August 2014.

Wax, R. (2013). Sadness and Depression: Not the Same Thing. Blog 12 August 2013. Downloaded December 2014 from www.rubywax.net/blog/sadness-and-depression-not-the-same-thing

Whitley, R. Gingerich, S. Lutz, W.J. and Mueser, K.T. (2009). Implementing the Illness Management and Recovery Program in Community Mental Health Settings: Facilitators and Barriers. *Psychiatric Services.* 60, pp. 202–209

Wilkinson, R. (2009). The Spirit Level: Why More Equal Societies Almost Always Do Better (with K. Pickett). London: Allen Lane

Williams, R. (2014). Poverty: A Christian Perspective. In Prospect and JRF. *Poverty in the UK: Can it be Eradicated?* pp. 8–9

Work Foundation (2015). *Fluctuating Conditions, Fluctuating Support: Improving Organisational Resilience to Fluctuating Conditions in the Workforce.* London: Work Foundation

Wyllie, A. and Lauder, J. (2012). *Impacts of National Media Campaign to Counter Stigma and Discrimination Associated with Mental Illness.* New Zealand: Ministry of Health

Index